The Industrial Revolution in World History

Now in its fifth edition, this book explores the ways in which the industrial revolution reshaped world history, covering the international factors that helped launch the industrial revolution, its global spread and its impact from the end of the eighteenth century to the present day.

The single most important development in human history over the past three centuries, the industrial revolution continues to shape the contemporary world. Revised and brought into the present, this fifth edition of Peter N. Stearns' *The Industrial Revolution in World History* extends his global analysis of the industrial revolution. Looking beyond the West, the book considers India, the Middle East and China and now includes more on key Latin American economies and Africa as well as the heightened tensions, since 2008, about the economic aspects of globalization and the decline of manufacturing in the West. This edition also features a new chapter on key historiographical debates, updated suggestions for further reading and boxed debate features that encourage the reader to consider diversity and different viewpoints in their own analysis, and pays increased attention to the environmental impacts.

Illustrating the contemporary relevance of the industrial revolution's history, this is essential reading for students of world history and economics, as well as for those seeking to know more about the global implications of what is arguably the defining socioeconomic event of modern times.

Peter N. Stearns is University Professor and Provost Emeritus at George Mason University, USA.

The Industrial Revolution in World History

FIFTH EDITION

Peter N. Stearns

NEW YORK AND LONDON

Fifth edition published 2021
by Routledge
52 Vanderbilt Avenue, New York, NY 10017

and by Routledge
2 Park Square, Milton Park, Abingdon, Oxon, OX14 4RN

Routledge is an imprint of the Taylor & Francis Group, an informa business

First edition published by Westview Press 1993
Fifth edition published by Routledge 2021

Library of Congress Cataloging-in-Publication Data
A catalog record has been requested for this book

ISBN: 978-0-367-50515-8 (hbk)
ISBN: 978-0-367-50514-1 (pbk)
ISBN: 978-1-003-05018-6 (ebk)

Typeset in Sabon
by codeMantra

Contents

Illustrations

Figures

Maps

Illustrations

Photographs

Debates

Acknowledgments

Alexis Frambes was extremely helpful in the preparation of this fifth edition. I should also acknowledge previous assistance from Laura Bell and Pearl Harris Scott. Thanks as well to Eve Setch and Zoe Thomson at Routledge for their encouragement. I am very grateful as well to the many world history students at George Mason whose work and interests have contributed to my work on this aspect of the global experience.

1 Introduction

Defining the Industrial Revolution

Assessing the industrial revolution is a historical challenge, but it also has a strikingly contemporary ring. In 2019 a number of economists, concerned about sluggish economic growth rates in the United States and elsewhere, urged the development of a new "science of progress" that would identify factors that promote economic dynamism. In practice, they were urging that the components that launched the industrial revolution be more clearly identified and updated: industrial history, in other words, may be crucial to dynamic policy today.

Many people would worry about this connection, urging that we use industrial history to help identify and explain menacing problems like environmental change or even some of the limitations of contemporary family life. Here too, however, they are saying—correctly—that an array of contemporary concerns cannot be properly evaluated without a grasp of the earlier industrial transformation. Industrial history is, in part, a framework for understanding the world around us today. Indeed—and we will take this up in the final chapter—assessments of the nature of modern life, its pros and cons, rest heavily on an understanding of what the industrial revolution has done and is doing to the human condition.

***

The industrial revolution was the most important single development in human history over the past three centuries. It is not, however, a historical episode alone. It continues to shape the contemporary world. Even the oldest industrial societies are still adapting to its impact, for example, in dealing with changes in the roles of women. Newer industrial giants, such as China, repeat elements of the original process but extend its range in new directions.

The phenomenon began about two and a half centuries ago. It has changed the world. Focused on new methods and organizations for producing goods, industrialization has altered where people live, how they play, how they define political issues—even, many historians would argue, how they have sex.

The industrial revolution was a global process from the first. It resulted from changes that had been occurring in global economic relations, and then it redefined those relations still further—and continues to do so.

This book explores what the industrial revolution was and how it recast world history—even beyond the particular societies in which it developed the deepest roots. Industrialization was the most fundamental force in world history in both the nineteenth and the twentieth centuries, and it continues powerfully to shape the twenty-first. Outright industrial revolutions occurred in three waves. The first happened in western Europe and the new United States beginning with developments in Britain in the 1770s. A second wave spread over of Russia and Japan, some other parts of eastern and southern Europe, plus Canada and Australia from the 1880s onward. The most recent unfolding began in the 1960s in the Pacific Rim (including China by the 1970s) and, two decades later, in Turkey and India, and in Brazil and other parts of Latin America. Each major wave of industrialization quickly spilled over into other societies that were not industrialized outright, altering basic social and economic relationships. Because industrialization was a global phenomenon from the first, it helps focus key comparisons: between specific revolutionary processes, such as the German and the Japanese, and between societies advancing in industrial growth and those where the process is at least delayed.

The industrial revolution involves fundamental change, but it is an odd kind of revolution. Indeed, some historians take issue with the term itself. This is a transformation that spins out, in any given society, for several decades. In its early stages it may have little measurable impact on overall production rates, which are still determined by more traditional methods of work. Yet the use of new machinery and redefinitions of how labor is organized quickly create a sense of major change, even among groups not directly involved. Fear of threats to established habits and awe at the profusion of goods that industrialization produces intermingle. Characteristic early attempts to protest the new system show that the magnitude of change strikes home—and the failure of these efforts, forcing redefinition of protest itself, demonstrates how unstoppable this economic machine becomes. In this sense, and in the broader sense of altering the whole context of life, this is revolution indeed. Ultimately, industrialization's role in changing the framework of world history is its most important face.

DEBATE #1: *WAS THIS A REAL REVOLUTION?*

There are four related reasons to fuss a bit over use of the word "revolution" to describe the process of industrialization that first began in Great Britain. This is not the most important debate industrialization inspires, but it reflects some of the complexities involved.

Point 1: the word revolution is overused in modern culture. We are recurrently told about revolutions in skin care or sports equipment. Have historians of industry, eager to highlight the importance of their subject, fallen victim to verbal hyperbole?

Then there is the fact that people involved in what we call the industrial revolution did not quickly adopt the term. In the great French political revolution of 1789, participants began talking about revolution almost immediately. As early as July, 1789, right when things were heating up, the popular press in France was talking explicitly about the revolution that was taking shape. But in Britain it was a full century before the term "industrial revolution" was introduced. To be sure, French observers by the 1830s (accustomed to revolutions) were talking about a *révolution industrielle* to describe what they saw in Britain and, often, hoped could occur in their own country. Still, there was a revealing lag. Why was it harder for participants to see the revolutionary qualities of industrialization than to apply the term to political upheaval?

And historians themselves have muddied the picture in several important ways. First, as we will discuss further in debate #2, it is increasingly claimed that major manufacturing changes preceded the industrial revolution in Europe, and later in Japan, by raising production levels and intensifying work habits well before "revolutionary" technology like the steam engine. A related complication: it was once assumed that modern consumerism was the result of industrialization, but now it turns out that in Western societies it was the other way around, at least in terms of an initial consumer push. So was the "revolution" just extending existing trends? And if so, was it revolutionary?

Most important, many historians, working on the British and other early cases, have painstakingly demonstrated that measurable changes were in many ways surprisingly slow—which is one reason that even scholars who adopt the word revolution admit that it takes several decades. The economic historian N.F.R. Crafts, for example, working on the exemplary British case, has substantially revised downward any notion of rapid early growth in gross domestic product, and even in industrial production more explicitly. He sees British manufacturing only growing about 1.5 percent per year in the four decades after 1760, and less than 3 percent annually in the three decades after 1800. Similar findings have been advanced for France, where it is also acknowledged that the industrial revolution took shape unusually slowly. Obviously, major technological change initially impacted only a small part of

(*Continued*)

overall manufacturing, and even less of the total economy—hence the modest growth.

Given these facts—which are generally accepted now for the early instances—can one nevertheless make the claim that the term "revolution" fits? The term continues to be widely used, and while partly this is a matter of habit, the fact is that argument can still be mounted. Overnight revolution, clearly not, but massive transformation, almost certainly yes. But how can the hesitations be batted away? Some suggestions would include: think of cumulative impact over time; think of some rapid, dramatic effects at least in a few industrial sectors (including effects, through exports, on economies elsewhere); think of the sheer range of human conditions that would quickly be drawn in, beyond the manufacturing economy itself. What is the best argument that, despite some caveats, the idea of revolution still fits?

For Further Reading: Peter Temin, "Two Views of the British Industrial Revolution," *Journal of Economic History* 57 (1977); David Greasley and Les Oxley, "Endogenous Growth or 'Big Bang': Two Views of the First Industrial Revolution," *Journal of Economic History* 57 (1977); C.K. Harley and N.F.R. Crafts, "Cotton Textiles and Industrial Output Growth during the Industrial Revolution," *Economic History Review* 48 (1995). And of course, the rest of this book.

From the beginning, industrialization has been a set of human changes, and historians' understanding of this human side has informed some of the most exciting research findings of recent decades. Researchers note that among the big factors and large processes there were individual faces, some excited, some in pain. Early developers in factory industry had to depart from their parents' habits, an approach that often required considerable personal sacrifice and generated familial strain. For example:

- In northern France in the early 1840s, Louis Motte-Bossut set up a large mechanical wool-spinning factory. His parents had run a much smaller, more traditional textile operation, manufacturing with only a simple sort of machinery; they prided themselves on being able to watch over every detail of their operation and directly supervise a small labor force. Motte-Bossut, in contrast, aspired to make France the factory equal of England—during a visit there he had illegally taken away the plans for state-of-the-art factory equipment. His large factory quickly became one of the leaders in the region, but his parents would not set foot in it, judging its scale and its riskiness to be genuinely immoral.

- In Germany, Alfred Krupp was born in 1812 into a successful merchant family in the city of Essen. His father, however, a poor businessman, had decimated the family fortune; Friedrich Krupp had twice set up steel-manufacturing plants with swindling partners, the outcome being his failure and public disgrace. Alfred was sent to work in a factory at age thirteen, while his sister labored as a governess. In 1826 Alfred began his own firm on the basis of his meager inheritance, manufacturing scissors and hand tools. No technical genius, but bent on avoiding his father's mistakes, Krupp applied a single-minded devotion to his firm's success. As a result, he built one of the giant metallurgical firms during the crucible decades of German industrialization.
- Chung Ju Yung was a South Korean villager who in the 1940s, at age sixteen, walked 150 miles to Seoul to take a job as a day laborer. He soon moved into modest business activity and began to help build South Korea's industrial revolution. By the 1980s, when Chung was in his sixties, his firm, Hyundai, had 135,000 employees and forty-two overseas offices, engaging in activities ranging from automobile manufacture to the construction of huge petroleum supertankers.

The entrepreneurs who masterminded part of the industrialization process came from varied backgrounds. Rags-to-riches stories were not unknown, but the most consistent thread involved the ability to recognize the potential of new technology and to break through some of the economic habits that had dominated the previous generation. This ability was as characteristic of factory owners from business families, like Motte-Bossut, as of manufacturers from peasant or worker origins.

Factory owners formed only part of industrialization's human story, of course. Workers also shaped the industrial revolution, and they, too, faced change, often involuntarily, in making their contribution. Children formed one category. They had always worked, in most social groups. They assisted their parents on the farm and in the household and provided some of the menial labor for craft manufacturing, often under strict employer control. They continued to work in the early factories but in a much less personal atmosphere, amid the dangers of powered machinery and the new demands for physical exertion or unrelenting pace. Government hearings held in Great Britain a few decades after the industrial revolution began there pinpointed what was probably the most shocking exploitation of child labor: Children had moved from providing supplemental labor to being beasts of burden. For the growing cotton factories in Lancashire—greedy for workers and particularly interested in the "small and nimble fingers" of children to help tend the machines at low cost—gangs of children were recruited from the urban poorhouses. Many came from families displaced from rural manual manufacturing by the expansion of the very factories they now served. As factory hands, they were housed in miserable dormitories and often beaten to spur production. Shifts of children worked day and night, alternating with time in the dormitory. As an 1836 report suggested, "It is a common tradition in Lancashire that the beds never get cold." Not surprisingly, some children committed suicide, having been driven to physical and emotional despair.

Women were another category. Persis Edwards came to the new textile factories of New Hampshire in the 1830s from a farm background. Like most of the new factory hands, she expected to work only a few years, saving most of her wages to send back to her rural family or to accumulate a nest egg for her marriage. In 1839 she wrote to a cousin that she liked her job "very well—enjoy myself much better than I expected." However, she complained (doubtless judging by the standards of labor she had grown up with) that the work made her feel "very much confined, could wish to have my liberty a bit more." Another female relative commented in a letter a bit more bleakly, noting that factory women had lower status than their peers who taught school or made dresses in an artisanal shop; her personal reaction was equivocal: "I was so sick of it at first. I wished a factory had never been thought of but the longer I stay the better I like [it]."

By 1907, during the first phase of Japanese industrialization, 62 percent of the factory labor force was female, mostly drawn from distant agricultural villages. As in Europe at an earlier time, a growing population plus the decline of rural manufacturing jobs made peasant families eager to send some of their number to the cities, regardless of the stress involved in adjusting to new settings and new work. Factory recruiters contracted with fathers or brothers in Japanese peasant families, giving them a fee for the commitment of a daughter or sister to what was a system of near-slavery. Factory women worked twelve hours a day, received food and dormitory housing, and had to buy most of their goods in the company store. They were granted only a small amount of spending money, because the factory directors had found that any financial latitude prompted the women to run away. Most of the women probably hoped to return to their native village to marry a farmer, but more often they stayed in the cities, marrying a worker or falling into prostitution. An English social worker visiting Tokyo commented on the lives of these industrial women: "Female factory workers not only lived in a desert of thought but also their physical environment [was] a kind of desert as well."

The human meaning of the industrial revolution obviously varied in all sorts of ways. Industrialization that occurred early, like Britain's, brought the strains of sheer novelty, as techniques were explored that had no precedent. Later industrializers could copy, but they faced the competition of existing industrial nations, which imposed stresses as well. Industrialization in the context of Japanese culture had an impact different from that in France, with a distinctive mix of opportunities and problems in each case. Comparison is essential, along with the core components. At least as important is the fact that the industrial revolution varied with the type of group and type of individual involved. Factory owners could see industrialization in terms of progress and opportunity, though they might, depending on personality, have anxieties and worries as well. Newly recruited or compelled workers had less margin in their adjustments to the industrial economy, and they were readier to think in terms of deterioration and disorientation—though, as the New England factory women suggested, adjustments were possible, and real benefits were discernible. Finally, a third group, initially the largest, saw industrialization developing around them—in Britain in 1800, in Japan in 1900—and had to decide how it would alter their lives even as they remained in the countryside or labored in traditional artisanal shops or commercial businesses.

This book deals with the unfolding of the industrial revolution in its various major settings around the world and with its international impact outside leading centers. It also, at various points, suggests some of the debates the industrial revolution inspires, some purely historical though challenging, some still important in contemporary life. Key topics are the processes industrialization involved, the causes that promoted it, and the ways in which it transformed a range of international relationships. The discussion will not, however, lose sight of the human dimension: The industrial revolution meant change—a more decisive set of changes than most people had ever experienced historically. It meant opportunity, excitement, stress, and degradation, and these diverse features formed an essential part of the conversion from an agriculturally based to an industrially based society.

Technology and Work Organization

The industrial revolution constituted one of those rare occasions in world history when the human species altered its framework of existence. Indeed, the only previous development comparable in terms of sheer magnitude was the Neolithic revolution—the conversion from hunting and gathering to agriculture as the basic form of production for survival. Both the industrial revolution and the Neolithic revolution brought fundamental changes in how people worked, where they lived (settled communities rather than nomadic bands, then cities instead of rural communities and farms), what potential economic surplus was available, and how many people could be supported around the world. These changes inevitably had ramifications reaching into almost every aspect of human experience—into the habits of thought and the relations between men and women as well as into systems of production and exchange. The full story of the industrial revolution is precisely the examination of these multiple impacts.

The essence of the industrial revolution, however, was fairly simple. Stripped to its bare bones, the industrial revolution consisted of the application of new sources of power to the production process, achieved with the transmission equipment necessary to apply this power to manufacturing. And it consisted of an increased scale in human organization that facilitated specialization and coordination at levels preindustrial groupings had rarely contemplated and that often increased the intensity of work quite apart from technology.

The industrial revolution progressively replaced humans and animals as the power sources of production with motors powered by fossil fuels (supplemented by waterpower and, very recently, by nuclear power). The key invention in Europe's industrial revolution was the steam engine, which harnessed the energy potential of coal. Later industrial revolutions also used electric and internal combustion motors (developed by the 1870s) and petroleum as well as coal. Before the industrial revolution, almost all production in manufacturing and agriculture relied on equipment powered by people or draft animals, with some small assistance from waterwheels. Except for waterwheels, used mainly to mill grain, almost all tools were designed for manual use. Animals often pulled plows for farming, but planting and harvesting were done by hand, by workers aided by simple tools like sickles. Looms for weaving cloth were powered by foot pedals, and the fibers were strung by hand. The industrial revolution progressively introduced steam or other power to the production process and steadily increased the proportion of the process accomplished by equipment without direct human guidance. Power looms thus not only replaced foot pedals but also crossed threads automatically after a worker initially attached them to the frame. Machine tending involved making sure the thread supply remained constant and dealing with snapped threads or other breakdowns; the cloth itself did not have to be touched by hand until it was gathered. Dramatic new sources of power—vastly more potent than what people and animals could provide, and transmitted to the product by semiautomatic machinery—were the technological core of the industrial revolution.

The organizational facet of the industrial revolution was initially symbolized by the factory, but the organizational principles spread beyond the factory itself. The industrial revolution brought together groups of people in the production process. Most production operations before the late eighteenth century centered on the household, with collaboration and specialization among ten or fewer people. Even though many early industrial factories were small, they promoted the grouping of greater numbers of people for the production process. They also increased the amount of specialization; tasks were subdivided, so the total production was increased even aside from the new technology. In contrast, most work gangs before the industrial revolution—even the large ones like the slaves in the mines and agricultural plantations of the Americas—had been relatively unspecialized. Finally, industrial-style organization involved more conscious management of workers toward a faster as well as a more fully coordinated work pace. Here, too, was a contrast with the more relaxed work styles characteristic of much preindustrial labor, including a good bit of slave labor. Thus, redefined work discipline and specialization, along with growth in the size of the work unit, defined the organizational core of the industrial revolution. Labor systems that could not match these organizational characteristics, including slavery and household production, declined or even disappeared during the industrialization process.

The two central features of industrialization—revolutions in technology and in the organization of work—yielded one clear result: a great increase in the total output of goods and in individual worker output. Per capita productivity went up, in some cases massively. A spinning worker in 1820 France or Britain using steam-driven spindles instead of a manual spinning wheel could produce literally a hundred times the thread of a preindustrial counterpart. This productivity gain was unusual in weaving—early mechanical looms simply doubled output, but this alone had huge impacts. Increased output could and often would be used in various ways: to increase inequality in the standard of living, to support higher tax revenues, to provide for rapidly growing populations, or to change and possibly improve material conditions for the masses. These varied results and the balance among them form vital topics to explore in dealing with the impact of industrialization on individuals and societies.

The risk in analyzing the industrial revolution is oversimplification, because its essential features seem simple. Exploring the history of industrialization involves multiple tasks: tracing why certain parts of the world were open to new technologies and new organizational forms; analyzing why different industrial societies established somewhat different policies (for example, varying the role of government in triggering and guiding the industrialization process); and understanding the host of different human reactions that emerged, even in a single industrial society, as people adjusted to innovations like steam-driven machines and factories. The full history of the industrial revolution, in other words, involves variety and complexity. Nevertheless, even as we probe these richer human meanings, the barebones definition must not be forgotten; in any industrialization process, the technological and organizational substratum inevitably looms large.

Issues in Interpretation

The industrial revolution raises all sorts of interpretive issues, including what caused it in the first place. We will encounter key issues in virtually every section of this book. A few issues apply even to the basic definition, since historians continue to discuss how to come to terms with this watershed in the human experience.

The industrial revolution involved certain general processes. Participants in industrialization had to deal with work systems, with the rise of new kinds of stores, with new habits of time. These changes involved hosts of individual events: a manufacturer deciding on his factory rules, a peddler realizing that the growing quantity of goods required a village shop instead of itinerant hawking, a manufacturing worker learning to listen for the clock-based factory whistle. These events, multiplied by the hundreds of thousands of individuals involved, constituted the new work processes, the rise of new kinds of commerce, the sense of a new urgency in work time.

The essence of the industrial revolution does not, however, flow from very many clearly labeled seminal events, such as the inauguration of a new president or the signing of a major treaty. Event-based history proceeded as industrialization took hold: Britain fought the armies of Napoleon, Japan installed a new constitution, Russia was battered by a 1905 revolution. The industrial revolution was involved in these events and had some obvious events of its own: James Watt's invention of the steam engine, the passage of new child labor laws, the establishment in Japan of a ministry of industry. But fitting industrial history and event-based history together is not easy, and most students of industrialization deal with a distinctive set of historical markers.

The industrial revolution does not even have a tidy beginning or end—unlike political revolutions. For example, Great Britain started opening steam-powered factories in the 1780s. The change quickly swept through a few important industries—cotton spinning was almost entirely mechanized within a decade—but the economy as a whole changed far more slowly. By 1850 there were still as many craft workers as factory workers and as many rural people as urban. Industrialization had changed the work lives as well as the prospects and outlook of the nonfactory majority, but it had not yet revolutionized them. And although productivity had exploded in a few sectors, overall per capita output grew only gradually (about 2 percent per year) because so much of the population still worked in traditional settings.

Industrialization, in fact, frequently gained momentum several decades after the first serious introductions of new equipment and factories. Some societies, as we will see, experimented with a few factories and had no subsequent industrial revolution at all. But even many regions that did industrialize in some manufacturing sectors saw a greater wave of change forty or fifty years after their initial engagement. What is sometimes called a "second industrial revolution" in western Europe, late in the nineteenth century, generated another set of fundamental changes, and similar redefinitions occurred elsewhere. Thus both Japan and Russia redefined and accelerated their industrialization processes in the 1920s and 1930s, a half century after their serious involvement began. Industrial revolutions, clearly, are long and evolving.

Complexities of this sort have certainly dented an earlier schematic image of the industrial revolution. In the 1950s economic historian W. W. Rostow sought to create something of a model of industrial revolution, abstracted from particular historical developments but fitting all industrial revolutions—from Britain's first effort through Japan's more recent drive to possible revolutions in the future (he wrote before the Pacific Rim's surge into the fray). Rostow emphasized a few "takeoff" decades in which the initial introduction of new technology spurred particularly rapid change in the relevant sectors. More recent work on industrialization points instead to the variety of changes that occurred even as the first factories were introduced: Some craft sectors grew, some industrial sectors remained atypical and small, and no precise pattern of industrial dynamism existed from one region to the next. Many societies saw an intensification of production before a full "revolution" took hold. Furthermore, preliminary phases did not lead, lockstep, to some standardized maturation. Whereas Germany moved quickly to a focus on relatively large factories in heavy industry (though this move accompanied maintenance of a substantial artisanal sector), France achieved impressive manufacturing growth rates through a different blend, combining some factories with pressures to speed up craft operations in industries such as furniture making. But if industrial revolutions are uneven, slow, and particular, with no one case quite like the next, there is no need to discard the term *revolution*. After all, many effects of political revolutions also unfold slowly, and they never change conditions as much or as rapidly as proponents imagined. Industrial revolutions spring from previous changes—this is an obvious aspect of causation and helps explain why some societies have industrial revolutions and others, despite considerable effort, do not. Industrial revolutions take time, and they involve different parts of the labor force in quite different degrees of change. They do, however, produce some fundamental shifts, building from the increasing introduction of new technologies and new organizational forms even if (as in the French case most obviously) the introduction is not only gradual but somewhat idiosyncratic.

The revolutionary quality of industrialization becomes still more obvious in the world context. British and even French industrialization proceeded, as we shall see, from earlier patterns of economic and social change. The introduction of steam-driven equipment denoted a real shift, but one occurring within an already dynamic context. Industrial revolutions later on, based in large part on imitation of earlier ones elsewhere, developed revolutionary characteristics more quickly. Russia began to form a factory labor force within the same generation as it abolished rural serfdom and began to spread literacy; Japan produced a new entrepreneurial class only a generation after abolishing feudalism;

South Korea launched its industrialization only a generation after the economic and political oppression of Japanese occupation. The massive social and political transformations involved in cases like these took place with bewildering speed, and the industrial revolution played a central role in them.

In sum, the variety and unevenness of industrial development make the concept of industrial revolution undeniably slippery. No initial definition can substitute for the exploration of actual cases, and no orderly schema fully captures reality. Nevertheless, the phenomenon does involve revolutionary levels of change, so that societies that have generated a real industrial revolution differ from those contemporary ones that have introduced some mechanized manufacturing but not a full revolution. The debates about the concept properly remind us of its complexity but need not distract us from the fundamental—indeed, revolutionary—alterations the process generates over time. The huge differences between the Britain of 1880 and that of 1780, the United States of 1900 and that of 1820, or the Japan of 1960 and that of 1880 took shape gradually and unevenly—but they unquestionably occurred. Indeed, the first use of the term *industrial revolution*, by a British observer in the 1880s, belatedly reflected the powerful alterations in the basic structures of that society and implicitly anticipated comparable sea changes in other societies in which the force of new technology and new organizational principles took root.

The Range of the Industrial Revolution

The sheer potency of the industrial revolution raises several other definitional issues, though they can be more quickly handled. First, if an industrial revolution begins (though often in societies already changing rapidly) with the widespread adoption of new equipment and the factory form in several key industries, when does it end? This issue is closely attached to the warnings against oversimplification. Because many industrial forms spread gradually, the process does not have a neat termination point. French peasants, for example, began widespread use of tractors only after World War II. They had previously adopted new kinds of hand tools and some new processing equipment; they had certainly increased their production for the market; and they had used mechanical transportation like trains and steamships. But their substantial commitment to mechanization in the production process came surprisingly late (though it was quite enthusiastic when it finally arrived). Could France be regarded as industrialized before its vital peasant sector was fully engaged? Clearly, the unevenness of industrialization means that fundamental changes may continue for well over a century after the process identifiably began. Furthermore, the industrial revolution generated recurrent change even in the sectors it first affected. Many British cotton workers, faced in the 1890s with new U.S.-devised machines that allowed a single worker to tend eight to sixteen mechanical looms rather than the two to four of early industrialization, judged that their work lives were changing in a far more radical fashion than those of their predecessors. They were probably wrong, but they had an arguable case. Industrial societies accept, whether they like it or not, a commitment to recurrent cycles of technical and organizational innovation—that is, periodic renewal of a sense of unsettled upheaval.

The most revolutionary period of the industrialization process ends, however, when most workers and managers (whether in factories or smaller workshops) use some powered equipment and operate according to some of the principles of industrial organization. At this point, the larger society has gained an ability to apply industrial procedures to most branches of the economy, and although it may not have done so fully (as with the somewhat laggard French peasants), virtually every major group has faced some serious adjustment to the impact of the industrial revolution. Historically, this point has been reached seventy to one hundred years after serious technological innovation first began. Thus, for example, it is legitimate to peg the end of the U.S. industrial revolution at about 1920, when factory production overwhelmingly dominated other forms in manufacturing and when half the population lived in cities. Vast economic changes were to occur after 1920, extending the transformations the industrial revolution had wrought, but the industrial context was set.

The definition of the industrial revolution, thus, includes a massive set of changes that begin when radical innovations in technologies and organizational forms are extensively introduced in key manufacturing sectors and that end, in the truly revolutionary phase, when these innovations are widely, though not necessarily universally, established in the economy at large. Subsequent changes, often quite unsettling, are virtually ensured, but they arise within the contours of an industrial society.

But what, then, is an industrial society? This is a second definitional issue in expanding the idea of industrial revolution beyond its most basic elements. What kinds of social alterations followed from new machines, factories, stores, and offices? The industrial revolution was a systems change: New technology and organization boosted production and propelled manufacturing over agriculture as the industrial society's greatest source of wealth and employment. To handle factory and related jobs, and because industrial machines began to take over some of the production previously performed in the countryside, cities grew rapidly. By 1850 half of Britain's population lived in cities, the first such urban achievement in human history—for even the most effective agricultural societies had never been able to free more than 25 percent of a population from the rural economy.

A systems change of this sort inevitably, though again gradually, affected every aspect of human and social life. Personal habits changed as people learned a new sense of time and discipline. The status of old people changed. The industrial revolution in Europe and the United States gave the elderly some new functions, such as babysitting for their working adult children, but it diminished their status: jobs became associated with high energy and the ability to learn new techniques, and the elderly were culturally downgraded because they seemed to lack these qualities. The industrial revolution changed the nature of war, too, as was obvious from the U.S. Civil War (1861–1865) onward: industrial war meant more rapid and massive troop movements, devastating weaponry, and greatly increased death and maiming in battle.

Because of the power of the industrial revolution, virtually everything was altered, including art, politics, relationships between parents and children, and diplomatic relations, to name just a few areas of change. By the 1850s the industrial revolution was beginning to encompass the whole of history, particularly in societies that were directly industrializing, but also to some extent around the world. Change was not complete; otherwise, we could have expected to see in the 1990s each industrial society virtually identical to the next, which was not the case. Continuities from preindustrial cultural and political patterns plus different experiences in the industrial revolution process itself maintained important differences. Nevertheless, in a real sense the history of the industrial revolution is the history of the modern world; no factors even remotely rival industrialization's influence on explaining what has gone on in the world—and what still goes on as adjustments to the alteration of basic human systems continue. Even sweeping shifts in human loyalties, such as the rise of nationalism, though they follow from new ideologies, can be traced directly to the disruption of local ties and the intensive contacts among different parts of the world that industrialization fostered: people became nationalistic to provide themselves identities that might replace meanings the industrial revolution destroyed.

Yet a focus on the industrialization phenomenon itself must be somewhat selective. To gain a sense of what it involved in terms of new stresses and new opportunities, we need not march through every subsequent war in which new ships, cannons, and industrially produced propaganda were put into operation. The emphasis must be on the most direct human and institutional impact and on some general patterns in areas such as combat or human aging. We can put this understanding into play in dealing with the specifics of the world's military history or of social welfare developments. Highlighting the kinds of changes that most directly, almost inexorably, resulted from new technology and new organization of production during the century or so in which major societies were intensively engaged in the industrial revolution provides the guidelines for the most meaningful analysis.

Chronology and Geography

Two mistakes in dealing with the industrial revolution are particularly common, though understandable. First, the phenomenon is too often pinned to a single time period—the late eighteenth and early nineteenth centuries—as though because it began at that point it somehow ended then as well. In fact, the industrial revolution has surged forward in several chronological phases—the first, when it began and spread directly only within the West; the second (late nineteenth to early twentieth centuries), when it matured and began to exceed Western boundaries; and the third (post–World War II), when it became effectively global. Our lives today are being shaped by this ongoing third phase. And in each phase, industrial timetables cut across more conventional historical divisions, such as the French Revolution or World War I. Industrial history has its own chronology, and it must be seen as an ongoing process.

The second common error involves geography. Because industrialization began in the West, its treatment is often limited to Western history. But in fact the industrial revolution arose in a global context, had quick global consequences, and has now become a global phenomenon. Only the world-history scale can capture it correctly.

Thus, as early as the 1820s, Latin American economies, newly free from Spanish control, began to suffer from the competition of British machine-made goods; both local production and merchant activity declined, with many people thrown out of more traditional manufacturing work. In the 1830s the economic pressures of industrialization pried China open, when industrializing Western nations insisted on access to Chinese goods and markets and had the industrially generated military might to drive home their demands. Yet the industrial revolution occurred in individual societies and must be understood in this context as well. Even in Western history, British industrialization, because it came first, is sometimes sketched as if it preempted the field. Yet it is obvious that British patterns could not be entirely typical of the process elsewhere, even in other European nations. The industrial revolution must be seen as a basic development that occurred in many different places, which means that particular national or regional patterns of industrialization must be compared, even though some key elements are shared.

Furthermore, industrialization both united and divided the world, and this tension also continues. Industrial technologies and expanding manufacturing output quickly brought all major areas closer together almost literally. This is the reason that China found its traditional desire to regulate foreign commerce impossible by the 1830s and that Africa, its rivers newly penetrable by steamboats, opened perforce to new levels of international trade. The shrinking of the world through industrial forms of transportation and communication has intensified with every passing decade. Yet the industrial revolution created new divisions, separating countries engaged in the process from those that for many reasons, including the pressures placed on them by the industrial states, were unable to join the parade. The split between "have" and "have-not" regions was and is primarily a split between industrial and (at least as yet) nonindustrial regions, and it is a novel and nasty kind of division. The cast of characters is not constant. Japan—definitely a have-not nation extensively bullied by the industrial West in the 1870s and 1880s—obviously managed to grab a seat at the industrial feast. Nevertheless, the overall tension that industrialization generated in the world at large, simultaneously drawing regions into closer contact and creating new and agonizing differences among them, continues to describe much of the framework of world history. Both aspects, the shared systems and the stark divisions, must be captured when the industrial revolution is understood as it should be—as a world process.

The international framework also clarifies why the industrial revolution must be seen as a process over a long stretch of time, indeed as a process that is still occurring. An economist put it this way:

> During the first two hundred years of industrialization, from the late eighteenth to the late twentieth centuries, societies with about 20 percent of the world's population industrialized directly. Currently, particularly with the transformations occurring in China, India, Brazil, and elsewhere, another 40 percent of the world's peoples seem to be coming on board, for better or worse. The dynamism of the industrial phenomenon continues.

Like all major shifts, the industrial revolution has brought with it advantages and disadvantages. For example, industrialization has improved human health by dramatically reducing infant mortality rates around the world. Yet it has worsened the quality of our natural environment, and continues to do so, contributing, for example, to higher rates of cancer.

Understanding these diverse results is essential for dealing with recent world history and for gaining insight into ourselves. For a final compelling aspect of the industrial revolution centers on the unresolved and contested issues this massive upheaval still generates. To be sure, as we will see, some lively old debates have died down a bit; we no longer worry as much as historians once did about British workers' standards of living in the early nineteenth century because we know they had some atypical features compared with several other industrial revolutions and even more because we know the conditions improved in the long run. Industrialization's impact on the quality of life more generally, however, is still very much in debate. Almost surely, satisfaction with work declined for many people—even to the present day. Did other gains compensate?

Some debates hinge on shifts in our own social standards. Fifty years ago, laws that regulated women's work hours seemed to be pure humanitarian gain. Now we realize that the laws made women less employable because they reduced flexibility and that the laws resulted from a blend of humanitarianism and selfish male interests. Even laws that gradually removed children from most work situations look different today, as we see higher rates of child depression and even suicide associated with maladjustments to schooling; maybe factory work was not so bad for some.

Many debates focus on the global aspect of industrialization. Why did a few countries respond to Western industrialization with industrial revolutions of their own, whereas most did not, at least until recently? Why are some countries today much farther away from industrialization than others? These are tough questions to handle without a value judgment that there must be something wrong with the countries that continue to struggle. But properly approached, and viewed with a realization that right from the start industrialization imposed on certain regions new hardships that would be difficult to overcome, the resulting discussions are legitimate—and unavoidable.

And what about globalization, the most recent framework for the ongoing industrial revolution? Does it pull more countries toward industrial success, or does it bleed some countries to the profit of others? (Or both?) Will a few factories that pay low wages and often harm the local environment lead to fuller industrialization in the future—giving workers new skills, even though offering low pay—or will they merely perpetuate unequal status in the global economy? Why have debates about economic globalization taken a nastier turn during the past decade?

Historians and social scientists know a lot about what happens with industrialization and what continues to happen with the process even today. But there are still some tough calls, and this book is designed to encourage intelligent debate as well as to provide up-to-date information about what we do know.

Ultimately, the big question is this, and it's really hard to answer: Given all its changes and problems, and all the shifts that have occurred in the ways people evaluate their lives, has the industrial revolution, on balance, been a good thing, or should we focus less on celebrating its undeniable new technological mastery and more on trying to undo or remedy some of its key effects?

Part 1

The First Phase, 1760–1880

Western Primacy, Global Contexts, and Global Results

2 Britain's Revolution

New Processes and Economic Transformation

This chapter centers on the question of how Britain first definitively began to pull away from the economic patterns that were characteristic of highly commercial agricultural societies. The transformation of key production sectors proved crucial.

The Background Before the eighteenth century the most advanced economies in the world featured a combination of craft manufacturing (its most skilled components based in cities) and a large labor force committed to agriculture. This was true in Europe and India, and also largely in China, another powerhouse, though there were some bigger urban shops in the silk industry. Most production, both manufacturing and agricultural, was based on manual household labor, with larger village groups combining for certain operations like harvesting and road building. The use of slave crews for the commercial production of key agricultural goods like sugar and tobacco had spread, particularly in the Americas, with no major changes in technology. Several societies had developed sophisticated craft skills for the production of luxury cloth, metal goods, and other items. China, Japan, India, the Middle East (including North Africa), and western Europe stood at the forefront in terms of artisanal technology and the vital capacity to produce iron and iron products. Africa had a well-established ironworking tradition, and metallurgy and armaments manufacturing were advancing in Russia by 1700.

Western European technology had gained ground from the fifteenth century onward. Western production of guns, based on earlier ironworking skills developed initially for the production of great church bells, provided a crucial military edge, particularly in naval conflicts. Western metallurgy generally led the world by the sixteenth century. During the seventeenth century, growing dominance in world trade spurred the growth of textile production in many parts of western Europe, and here, too, technological refinements occurred that made the West effectively an international leader. Western biases concerning the rest of the world began to take on a technological cast, with scorn for the many peoples slow to imitate Western developments. A Western missionary in the seventeenth century described how, in his opinion, the Chinese could not be persuaded

> to make use of new instruments and leave their old ones without an especial order from the Emperor to that effect. They are more fond of the most defective piece of antiquity than of the most perfect of the modern, differing much in that from us who are in love with nothing but what is new.

Even with all of these developments, however, Western technology was not consistently superior even by 1700, and it remained firmly anchored in the basic traditions of agricultural societies, particularly in terms of reliance on human and animal power. Agriculture itself had scarcely changed in method since the fourteenth century. Manufacturing, despite some important new techniques, continued to entail combining skill with hand tools and was usually carried out in very small shops. The most important Western response to new manufacturing opportunities involved a great expansion of rural (domestic) production, particularly in textiles but also in small metal goods. Domestic manufacturing workers used simple equipment, which they usually bought themselves, and relied on labor from the household. Many combined their efforts with farming, and in general their skill levels were modest. The system worked well because it required little capital; rural householders invested a bit in a spinning wheel or a hand loom, and urban-based capitalists purchased the necessary raw materials and, usually, arranged for sale of the product. Output expanded because of the sheer growth of worker numbers, not because of technical advancement; indeed, the low wages paid generated little incentive for technical change.

Western Europe in 1700 was an advanced agricultural society, with an unusually large commercial sector and a great deal of manually operated manufacturing. The region was developing a certain fascination with machines but most decidedly was not industrialized. Recent comparative work has emphasized that several other countries, headed by China, maintained similar economic levels.

DEBATE #2 *WHEN DID WESTERN EUROPE BECOME "SPECIAL" IN RELEVANT WAYS? OR, HOW FAR BACK MUST WE GO TO CAPTURE THE ROOTS OF THE INDUSTRIAL REVOLUTION?*

Explaining any major historical development is likely to involve questions about chronological perspective: how deep in time do some of the causes lie? In the case of the industrial revolution, which became such a huge departure from traditional patterns, it is certainly tempting to speculate that some underlying factors must have been lying in wait for quite a while. On the other hand, as we will see, most of the standard explanations of industrialization focus on developments in the eighteenth century itself. Is this approach too limited?

Discussions of deep-seated causes have been encouraged by a growing twenty-first-century need, among some scholars, to highlight Western distinctiveness, at a time when several Asian societies have been outstripping Western growth rates. No one contests the fact that the industrial revolution did begin in the West, but there may now be an added temptation to call attention to deep-seated Western features in response to the Asian challenge.

At least three possibilities warrant attention, not in offering a full causation package but in contributing some unexpectedly early ingredients.

An early onset of Western individualism is one candidate. There is no doubt that Western society was becoming more individualistic than most by the eighteenth century. But what if this characteristic took hold earlier? Several studies argue that Western Christianity formed a seedbed for individualism, perhaps back as far as the Middle Ages. One recent offering calls attention to Christian efforts to prevent incest by insisting that, in most cases, close kin should not intermarry. This contrast with kin-based family arrangements elsewhere, the argument goes, forced more attention to individual development, ultimately producing the kind of individual motivation that would prove vital for economic innovation. While the study does not make a direct connection with industrialization, it strongly suggests a link by insisting that the family rules of Western Christianity lie at the base of what the authors called contemporary WEIRD societies—Western, Educated, Industrialized, Rich, and Democratic. To which one admiring scholar-reader added, "They're looking at what created the modern Western world."

This line of argument of course raises key questions. Was the West distinctively individualistic before the eighteenth century, as a matter of fact? And even if so, how does the characteristic lead into the kind of industrial innovation that would show up decisively only in the eighteenth century? (If individualism is all that great, why not earlier results?)

Studies of clocks and a clock-based sense of time have also generated arguments about an early Western advantage. Mechanical clocks were first developed in western Europe in the thirteenth and fourteenth centuries—other societies used other timing devices—and they were steadily improved. There is no question that the

(*Continued*)

West led the world in clockmaking literally until the twentieth century. From this, two arguments have emerged that potentially connect with the industrial revolution—despite the fact that this came about much later. First, one powerful study urges that other societies, and particularly China, simply could not keep up with the West because there is was inadequate freedom for technical innovation and scientific inquiry. Clocks, in other words, were the first sign of the Western advantage that would ultimately spread more broadly. Second, as use of clocks spread, more and more people in the West gained a new sense of time, and the importance of using time wisely, that would be directly relevant to the kind of efficiency that would feed into the industrial revolution (perhaps in combination with Western individualism).

Here too there are questions of fact. Granted a Western lead in clocks—this is clearly true—does this mean that China and other societies were technologically laggard more generally? How good were the clocks, before the nineteenth century, and how many people had regular access to them? And how much does a sense of clock time have to do with industrialization anyway? What kinds of connections make sense?

A third early-onset argument does not go back quite so far, but it too argues that the roots of the industrial revolution took shape well before the eighteenth century. Here the emphasis rests on what is called the "industrious revolution" that began to develop from about 1600 onward. Proponents argue that a growing demand for goods began to motivate more people to produce more for sale on the market, rather than just for household needs, and that this in turn encouraged harder work, at the expense of traditional leisure time. In the long run, this would set up conditions in which major technological innovation made sense, but the more subtle changes associated with the industrious revolution were a vital preliminary. Indeed some go so far as to argue that these more general changes, including the effort to press for harder work, were actually more important than the later technology breakthroughs, and this argument has been applied to modern Japan as well.

Debate here has focused again part on simple facts: some historians argue that there is little sign that people were actually working longer and harder before the factory system set in, though there is some acknowledgment that new levels of consumer demand emerged earlier than once thought. Beyond this, do the features of the industrious revolution really help explain the more dramatic departures associated with the industrial revolution? Again, how far back do we have to go?

All of this obviously invites juxtaposition with the more commonly discussed causes of the industrialization. In a global age, it also invites thinking about how much the industrial revolution had to do with Western-ness, given the obvious fact that many other parts of the world figured out how to join the process—not immediately, to be sure, but fairly quickly. And can you think of any other early Western markers that deserve attention?

For Further Reading: On individualism claims, Jonathan Schulz, Duman Bahrami-Rad, Jonathan Beauchamp, Joseph Heinrich, "The Church, Individualism, Kinship and Global Psychological Variation," *Science* 366 (Nov., 2019); on the debate over time, David Landes, *Revolution in Time: Clocks and the Making of the Modern World* (Cambridge, MA, 1983); Robert Finley, "China, the West, and World History in Joseph Needham's 'Science and Civilisation in China'," *Journal of World History* 11 (2000). On the industrious revolution, Jan de Vries, *The Industrious Revolution* (New York, 2008); Gregory Clark and Y. van der Werf, "Work in Progress? The Industrious Revolution," *Journal of Economic History* 587 (1998).

A Changing Context Three changes began to combine during the eighteenth century to accelerate manufacturing and ultimately generate the world's first industrial revolution. They affected much of western Europe, but particularly Britain, where the revolution first took shape.

1 New agricultural methods and products came into use in the late 1700s. Peasants in many parts of Europe, including Ireland, France, and Prussia, began to grow potatoes, a New World crop long regarded with suspicion. Potatoes offered several advantages over the grains Europeans had traditionally relied upon as staple food. Higher caloric value could be produced from smaller and sometimes less fertile plots of land, and for many decades potatoes were less subject to periodic diseases than were grains. Increasing adoption of the potato supported the beginnings of rapid population growth in Europe by the 1730s. Britain's population, for example, doubled between 1750 and 1800, and that of France rose by 50 percent. The potato also freed a percentage of rural labor for work in other areas, again because of its caloric yield from small plots. At roughly the same time, farmers in Holland began to develop new drainage systems by which swampland could be converted to agricultural use. They also introduced nitrogen-fixing crops that enabled them to keep fields in use every year rather than resting them every third year to regain fertility. With less fallow land and more land in use

overall, food production expanded, which contributed to population growth and to the release of new workers for other potential work activities.

Although agricultural improvements took shape in various places, they received enthusiastic support in Britain, where aristocratic landlords were particularly interested in new and more rewarding production for market sales. Draining marshes added cultivable land in eastern England. Innovators like "Turnip" Townshend spread the word about using nitrogen-fixing crops to increase production by eliminating fallow land. As in other parts of Europe, increased food supplies spurred British population growth and reduced the percentage of the labor force required for agriculture.

2 The early eighteenth century provided the context in which the pattern often called protoindustrialization (or an "industrious revolution") began to intensify in several areas. Domestic manufacturing systems spread further as more workers became available. Population growth and new consumer interests created new markets, particularly for textiles. Many rural workers began to farm only part time, taking orders for thread and cloth from urban merchants at other times. This capitalist system increased production. Though the workers involved used traditional methods based on manual labor and cooperation of the family in a household operation, they began to see themselves as different from peasants—more interested in urban fashions, for example, which created additional markets.

3 Another set of changes provided a context for new technologies. Massive strides in European science, in an already active commercial economy, encouraged attention to new devices in the manufacturing field. A host of scientific societies took shape that combined researchers with merchants and manufacturers and led to excited discussions about down-to-earth technological possibilities. Advances in chemistry helped trigger the discovery of new techniques for manufacturing and glazing pottery in eighteenth-century England. New scientific knowledge about the behavior of gases set a context for considering the possibility of harnessing steam to provide a moving force to replace unreliable water and wind as power sources. The first steam engine was invented by a French refugee in Holland in the late 1600s; several Dutch scientists discussed the prospect of propelling a boat by steam. Around 1700 the engine was improved in England by Thomas Newcomen, who applied it to drainage pumps for coal mines. A steam truck was invented in France in the 1760s, though it was never put to use. In the same decade, James Watt, a Glasgow craftsman who produced scientific instruments, perfected the steam engine, allowing it to be applied to industrial use. In a poem written in 1789, the English scientist Erasmus Darwin (grandfather of the evolution-theory biologist Charles) ecstatically praised the engine's possibilities:

Soon shall they arm, unconquer'd steam! afar
Drag the slow barge, or drive the rapid carp;
Or on wide-waving wings expanded bear
The flying chariot through the fields of air.
—Fair crews triumphant, leaning from above,
Shall wave their handkerchiefs as they move;
Or warrior bands alarm the gaping crowd,
And armies shrink beneath the shadowy cloud.

Along with changes in agricultural production and a stream of new inventions and attendant intellectual enthusiasm came additional shifts in England's domestic manufacturing system, initially beneath the surface. The nation was already a leader in world trade. It had a growing population by the 1730s, and the public was expressing interest in more fashionable clothing—an early manifestation of new consumer tastes. This setting prompted a handful of domestic producers to think about expanding their operations, in a gradual shift that proved to be the forerunner of a new organization of manufacturing labor. For example, the Halifax area in Yorkshire in the late seventeenth century was a significant center for the production of wool cloth by local artisans in the countryside who often combined their manufacturing with farming. Output from each worker was low, though the profits could provide some useful supplementary income. Even substantial farmers put their hand to the loom from time to time or used family members for textile production. In the 1690s a few workers began buying more wool than they could handle themselves; they hired others to work the wool at home for them and, without abandoning their own labor at first, were on the route to becoming manufacturers. By the next generation, these same manufacturing families, a minority of the wool workers in the region overall, were beginning to separate themselves socially from their employed labor. They were no longer willing to share a beer; they were thinking of their workers as a class apart. One of them wrote in 1736, during a trade depression, "I have turned off [laid off] a great many of my makers and keep turning off more weekly." His "makers," clearly, had become disposable subordinates in the process of production, and a traditional manufacturing system was beginning to yield to a more structured hierarchy.

DEBATE #3: *POPULATION AND INDUSTRIALIZATION: IS THERE AN OPTIMAL BALANCE?*

The fact that British and then West European industrialization occurred amid massive population growth is undeniable. But in many societies, population density and growth seem to retard industrial development, by consuming resources that might otherwise be

(*Continued*)

devoted to investment and by increasing poverty and so limiting demand for manufactured goods. At an extreme, overpopulation can even lead to food deprivation, damaging the capacity of the labor force. Many development economists have pointed to population trends in parts of the Middle East, Latin America and now in Africa as a problem for the industrial future. Chinese authorities, in moving toward population control after 1978 through government-mandated limits on births per family, clearly assumed that too much growth inhibited industrial potential, and the results seem to have proved them right. Chinese industrialization has surged as the population began to stabilize. Industrial growth in Latin America also accelerated after the 1970s when population growth began to slow.

So was European population growth a "good thing" for industry, in contrast to these other cases? Population pressure helped force workers off the land, compelling them to take often low-paying and unpleasant factory jobs that many might otherwise have tried to avoid. Unexpectedly large families even motivated businessmen in some cases, goading them to invest in industrial growth to help provide income and managerial jobs for their offspring. What made the European case distinctive?

Here are some possibilities to discuss. (1) European density was lower than that of some Asian societies when the industrial process began (and the same would obviously be true in the new United States); this may have provided unusual flexibility. (2) Even as industrial growth advanced Europe sent literally millions of immigrants abroad to relieve pressure. (3) The population surge may not in fact have contributed to European industrialization, as the other key causes of Western industrial progress simply compensated. (4) And by the same token, societies that have been slower to industrialize, amid population growth, may have been held back by other factors.

The conundrum of population and industry has of course a contemporary twist. Many industrial societies now are seeing a stabilization of population or even a decline—Japan is the most obvious case in point. What will this do to the industrial future? Is it possible to come up with a historically informed optimum relationship between population and industrial trends?

For Further Reading: E.A. Wrigley, *Poverty, Progress and Population* (Cambridge, 2004); Haiwen Zhou, "Population Growth and Industrialization," *Economic Inquiry, Western Economic Association International* 47 (2009), 249–265.

Adding New Technology By the 1730s several of the strands of change—population growth, protoindustrialization, scientific enthusiasm—were beginning to combine in England. Protoindustrialization meant that although the total number of agricultural workers grew, even as aristocratic landlords consolidated their holdings and sponsored more efficient methods, the percentage of a rapidly growing population employed in agriculture declined. Market opportunities for manufacturing production rose, however, despite frequent slumps, through population growth, expanding international trade, and the growing appetite for consumer goods like fashionable clothing. As more and more workers and small businesses began expanding their operations by hiring wage workers, the profile of a new manufacturing middle class began gradually to emerge.

Finally, new technology began to be developed for the sector that most obviously invited it: the domestic production system. In 1733 an English artisan, John Kay, invented the flying shuttle, a new kind of loom for weaving cloth that automatically moved thread horizontally through a frame when activated by a foot pedal. This machine was nothing fancy, and no new power source was involved, but one worker with a child as assistant could now do the work of two adults. Inventions for automatically winding fiber to make thread followed in the 1760s. New opportunities and the evolving attitudes of the growing manufacturing class, plus the excitement surrounding technological change and the resultant encouragement to invention, were pushing the traditional production system well beyond its former bounds.

By the 1760s, then, several key ingredients of the industrial revolution had been assembled in England, after several decades of protoindustrial changes within the domestic manufacturing system. New entrepreneurs were ready to manipulate workers in novel ways. Inventions increased the number of industrial processes handled automatically. The manufacturing sector and its labor force were growing steadily. Then came a usable steam engine, which by the 1770s could be hooked up to some of the semiautomatic inventions already devised for manual textile workers. Because steam power was concentrated and could not be transmitted over long distances, workers had to be assembled near the engines to do their work; small factories had to replace household production sites. This final change, too, was developing rapidly in certain key sectors by the 1770s. Britain's industrial revolution was under way.

Britain Becomes the Workshop of the World

The initial explicit stages of the world's first industrial revolution—as opposed to the previous preparatory decades—involved a number of elements. Rapid innovation transformed several sectors of industry, with new technology and organization at the core of change. Without this innovation, the industrial revolution could not have been identified. At the same time, many branches of the economy were affected only slightly, and thus some overall measurements of industrialization remained modest. Within the innovative sectors, intense misery pervaded the experience of many of the human beings involved; the industrial revolution was built on the backs of exploited labor. It is vital to note as well that early industrialization in even a few manufacturing sectors threw thousands of rural producers (many of them women) out of work, because factory products were so much cheaper; this is an aspect of industrial change that would become quite familiar—it persists today—and also further explains the British ability to form a new, urban labor force. Finally, as the revolution caught on, it inevitably brought in its wake further change in both technology and business practices. Most of these developments occurred during decades when Britain nearly monopolized the new processes, winning a growing world role on the strength of its industrial advantage (see Map 2.1).

A Revolution in Cotton The cotton industry commanded the central role in Britain's early industrialization. Compared with other fibers, cotton had characteristics that made it relatively easy to mechanize; it broke less often than wool and, particularly, linen. Further, cotton was a new product line in Europe, more open to innovation. It had been widely used in India, and an Asian market for cotton cloth already existed. In England, however, its novelty facilitated the introduction of new machines, though the raw fiber had to be imported. Workers were displaced indirectly by the rise of cotton because traditional linen production declined. However, the lack of a large established labor force in cotton obviated the need to prompt many traditional workers to change their ways directly, which limited resistance. At the same time, cotton had great appeal as a product: it could be brightly colored for a population increasingly eager to make a statement through clothing, and it was easily washed, so it appealed to people who were developing more stringent notions of personal cleanliness. Cotton was in demand, and this demand invited new techniques to produce the cloth in quantity. Finally, in the 1730s the British government took a further step to promote the industry: it slapped high tariffs on imports from India, hoping, correctly, that local production would step in.

By the 1730s a series of inventions began to shift cotton manufacturing increasingly toward a factory system. The accuracy of the flying shuttle, designed originally to improve hand weaving, was refined enough over another thirty years to make possible the application of nonhuman power. Edmund Cartwright patented a power loom in 1785. His description of his procedures revealed the new kind of thinking being applied to technical issues: "It struck me that as plain weaving can only be three movements which were to follow one another in succession, there

Map 2.1 The Beginning of the Industrial Revolution: Great Britain, c. 1750–1820.

would be little difficulty in producing them and repeating them." Indeed, mechanization involved isolating parts of the production process that could be accomplished through highly standardized, accurate motion and then applying to such motion equipment that could be linked to power sources. Weaving turned out to be among the more complicated activities to mechanize, and Cartwright's loom had to undergo substantial improvements before it could be widely used, by around 1800.

More impressive developments occurred in the preparatory phases of making cotton. In about 1764 James Hargreaves invented a spinning jenny device, which mechanically drew out and twisted the fibers into threads—though this advance, too, was initially applied to handwork, not to a new power source. Carding and combing machines, which ready the fiber prior to spinning, were developed at about the same time. Then, in 1769, Richard Arkwright developed the first water-powered spinning machine. It twisted and wound threads by means of flyers and bobbins operating continuously. These first machines were useful for making only the cheapest kind of thread, but other devices invented by 1780 began to make possible the spinning of finer cotton yarns. These could be powered by steam engines as well as waterwheels. The basic principles of mechanized thread production have not changed to this day, though machines grew progressively larger, and a given worker can now tend a far greater number of spindles. Other inventions pertinent to the industrialization of cotton cloth production included new bleaching and dying procedures (in the 1770s and 1780s) and roller printers for cloth designs, which replaced laborious block printing by hand—another new method that increased production a hundredfold while reducing workers' skill requirements.

Cotton production by the 1790s was advancing with extraordinary rapidity. New machines required a factory organization, for the power could not be transmitted widely. Workers had to be removed from household production and clustered around the new machines; cotton spinning was entirely concentrated in factories by this time. Because mechanical weaving lagged, this initial industrialization spurred a massive expansion of domestic looms. The thread produced was distributed from huge warehouses in the new factory centers such as Manchester. Power weaving came into general use in the Manchester area only after 1806. Its full conquest of the cotton industry began after 1815—to the immense distress of the hundreds of thousands of workers who had been drawn into the surrounding countryside to do the weaving: the rise of factories meant a further *deindustrialization* of many rural areas and small towns. At the other end of the scale, there were massive fortunes to be made in the industry. Robert Owen, a store assistant, began his Manchester factory in 1789 by borrowing £100, and by 1809 he was in a position to buy out his partners in his New Lanark Mills for £84,000 in cash—this in a country where only about 4 percent of the population earned more than £200 per year.

Sales of manufactured cotton goods soared, for with the new machines output increased and prices plummeted. Exports were essential, and by 1800 approximately four pieces of cotton cloth were sold abroad for every three disposed of at home. As late as 1840 cotton continued to provide about half the entire value of British exports. Continental Europe was a major market, but it consumed only about a third of Britain's export production in this field. Latin America was seized by British cotton exports after Spanish rule was cast off early in the nineteenth century. By 1820 the impoverished region was buying a quarter as much cotton cloth from Britain as was Europe, and by 1840 the figure had risen to a full half. India and Southeast Asia were deindustrialized by a combination of British factory competition and colonial policy as foreign machine products beat out domestic hand labor; cotton imports from Britain rose by 1,500 percent between 1820 and 1840. Africa was another major market. Of the major nations, only China held out—until its economy was forced open in the early 1840s.

Other Sectors Until about 1840, Britain's industrial revolution centered substantially on changes in the cotton industry, its massive results being expanded production and world outreach, but other developments were vital as well. Mechanization of wool spinning and weaving was well under way by 1800, impeded only by the higher cost and greater fragility of wool fiber. New machines and procedures were introduced into beer brewing; the big factories established include the great Guinness brewery in Dublin. Pottery manufacturing concentrated important developments in industrial chemistry during the late eighteenth century, and new methods reduced the work required in processes such as glazing and cutting. Several of these innovations created major health hazards for the workers involved. New grinding methods, for example, "hath proved very destructive to mankind, occasioned by the dust suckled into the body which … fixes so closely upon the lungs that nothing can remove it." But productivity per worker increased immensely, to the benefit of new pottery magnates such as Josiah Wedgwood. In the 1830s new printing presses were developed that could be powered by steam engines, and thus production in such fields as daily newspapers greatly expanded. A few commercial bakeries also introduced important new methods.

The most striking mechanical strides outside the growing textile sectors occurred in metallurgy and mining. During the eighteenth century, British manufacturers learned to produce coke from coal (by heating and concentrating it in special ovens) and to use coke instead of wood-derived charcoal for smelting iron ore. Coke production, in turn, depended on advances in furnace design and steam blasting (introduced by John Wilkinson in 1776). As coke supplies grew, furnace design for smelting and refining iron was also reconsidered, resulting in larger furnaces and higher output per worker. Henry Cort's reverberatory furnace for refining iron (developed in 1784) saved fuel but above all increased productivity by 1,500 percent. Steam-powered machines for rolling metal, which replaced manual hammering, soon followed. The iron industry began to expand rapidly. Britain had produced 25,000 tons of unrefined iron (called "pig iron") in 1720; by 1796 the figure was 125,000 and by 1804 was 250,000.

The growth of the iron industry had several further consequences. Coal mining surged to provide the fuel for iron smelting and for steam engines generally. Major advances in work methods at the coal face did not develop, though there were important improvements in timbering mine pits to allow deeper shafts. Transportation from the coal face did demand attention. Wooden and metal rails were laid down to facilitate carts of coal being pulled by horses or people; soon after 1800, experiments with steam-driven engines to pull the carts began. At the same time, the number of miners increased rapidly because this vital industry remained extremely labor-intensive.

At the other end of iron production, machine building expanded steadily. Inventions of new equipment, from spinning machines to the steam engine, did not always translate readily into production methods beyond the prototypes. Twelve years passed, for example, between Watt's construction of a working model engine (1765) and usable cylinders that could be widely manufactured. Before 1800, machine building was scattered in small shops and was performed with hand methods. Even after this date the industry long demanded highly skilled workers laboring with relatively little sophisticated equipment of their own. But attention in France and the new United States to the manufacturing of guns led to the development of precise patterns for designing machine parts, so that these parts could be interchangeably used on a given machine. Several machines were designed to bore and turn the machine pieces, and their industrial use gradually spread in Britain (and the United States and western Europe) during the early decades of the nineteenth century. The same systems were deployed to allow factory production of clocks and watches, where Europe and the United States would lead the world for over a century.

Headed by advancements in the cotton industry, Britain's early industrial revolution featured dramatic new methods that subsequently generated improved productivity and more standardized products in a host of industries. Heavy industry—mining and metallurgy—gained ground rapidly, though the importance of the labor force and the total product long lagged behind textiles. Vast numbers of new workers were drawn into factories and mines. Some were relatively unskilled, for many of the new processes required only modest training compared with older methods; but some, as in machine building, applied extensive skills to new products. Developments were not uniform. Many production branches, as in the manufacturing of brass and other small metal goods, were scarcely touched, though they often expanded because of growing demand. Nor was progress steady. Great lags often intervened, as in mechanical weaving, between the initial devices and their widespread applicability. Britain's industrialization was a revolution, but it neither occurred overnight nor was it tidily packaged.

The revolutionary quality, however, showed through in a host of ways. Urban growth was one of these. Cities of various sorts exploded in Britain in the late 1700s and early 1800s, the result of burgeoning banking operations, growing port activities, and so on. The biggest expansion, however, occurred in the factory centers as factories were built near energy sources and a large labor force accumulated there to facilitate factory operations. Manchester, Britain's cotton capital, grew from a modest town of 25,000 in 1772 to a metropolis of 367,232 by 1851. Leeds, Birmingham, and Sheffield—centers of textiles or metalwork—grew by 40 percent between 1821 and 1831 alone. Britain's industrialization revolutionized where many people lived by drawing work increasingly into the big-city context (and of course by making agriculture more efficient, thus less labor-intensive). During this period the majority of British families changed their residence and much of their framework of daily life as they shifted from reliance on agriculture to involvement with industry.

Industrialization Exacts a Price

The industrial revolution, even in its early phases, prompted major changes in business scale. Many operations started small; because initial textile machinery, in particular, was not costly, many small-scale innovations could draw on a wide array of available business talent. But there was obvious challenge. Traditional textile equipment for a domestic manufacturing operation cost a fraction of what was required to set up an early factory. By the 1780s British textile mills were valued at £3,000–£4,000, many times the £25 cost of a good hand loom. The first multistoried factory powered by steam, established in 1788, was valued at £13,000; its steam engine alone, large for the time at thirty horsepower, cost £1,500. Plants for metallurgy and mining operations were more expensive still.

Businesses did not immediately have to adopt radically new methods of capital formation and management systems, but the pressure to innovate was quite real. Many firms were established as partnerships because necessary capital was unavailable otherwise. Many factories, launched under the eye of an ever-present owner, had to generate a small bureaucracy when it became clear that directing the labor force, providing the necessary technical expertise, arranging for the purchase of raw materials, and selling the goods simply escaped the capacity of any individual. Borrowing arrangements became steadily more elaborate, although abundant capital kept interest rates fairly low in early British industry.

Family firms had to branch out to hire outsiders to participate in more specialized management structures. And although massive profits were possible—Robert Owen's achievement was replicated in a host of cases as a new class of wealthy factory owners began to emerge in the 1820s—the possibility of failure was ever present. Sales recessions were frequent, particularly in industries like cotton that depended on exports. Poor harvests reduced income at home and cut deeply into industrial sales. Significant economic crises occurred at least once a decade; a particularly severe recession followed the end of the Napoleonic Wars in 1815. Workers suffered most in these catastrophes as unemployment soared, but many manufacturers collapsed financially as well.

Conditions of Work The early industrial revolution in Britain was built on the backs of cheap, mercilessly driven labor. In rural areas, the standard of living fell for many workers, who were pressed both by population growth and by competition from machine-made goods that quickly cut into branches of domestic manufacturing. Many rural women, for example, lost their manufacturing income when spinning was mechanized. With less land available for small farmers, less supplementary employment, and competitive pressure on agricultural wages, stark misery spread in many agricultural districts. Although hand weavers enjoyed some real prosperity before 1800, when thread production soared but mechanized weaving had yet to take hold, their pay began to plummet thereafter. By 1811, wages were down one-third from their 1800 levels, and by 1832, when hand weaving in cotton was dying out in Britain, they had fallen by a full 60 percent. Industrialization was not entirely to blame for this collapse—population pressure and displacement of small farmers by aristocratic landlords played a role—but there can be no doubt of the massive hardships involved. Further, although the worst misery was centered in areas remote from the factories, the widespread deterioration also cut into the standard of living of industrial workers, who faced growing competition for jobs.

In the factories proper, however, wages in some sectors held up somewhat better, for new workers had to be drawn in. Mining wages, for example, seemingly improved during Britain's early industrial revolution. Skilled workers, needed to set up and maintain the new machines, also did well, often winning long-term contracts and other benefits. On the other hand, many employers—desperate for workers, but desperate also to keep costs down to protect their expensive investments and allay their fears of business failure—looked for labor shortcuts. This search was the inspiration for hiring orphans who were shipped in droves from London and other large towns to the factory centers in return for employer provision of food and barracks housing. Extensive use of child and female labor was not in itself novel—families had always depended on work by all members to survive—but use of children and young women specifically because of the low wages they could be pressed to accept reflected the pressures of early industrial life and unquestionably constrained the nascent working class in the factories. To be sure, factory-produced goods such as clothing and utensils fell in price, but there were drawbacks, too. Urban housing often was costlier than its preindustrial rural counterpart, and food costs fluctuated. Historians of Britain's industrial revolution have debated the standard-of-living question for many decades without definitively agreeing about whether conditions grew worse or better. Certainly there was variety, and factory workers were not the worst-paid group in the British population. Certainly also, however, particularly before about 1819, there was widespread suffering in the factory cities, where few workers were able to afford much above a bare subsistence even as more of their employers grew fat from the fruits of the new industry.

Other pressures added to the burdens on the new factory workers. No regular provision for illness or old age cushioned industrial life, and factory workers, unlike many small farmers, had no plot of land to fall back on for at least a modest food supply if their strength began to fail. The frequent economic slumps often caused unemployment rates to soar as high as 60 percent for several months or even a year, even for skilled workers, and food prices often went up in these periods. Not surprisingly, many workers, even those capable of improving their earnings, found industrial life extremely unpredictable, even nerve-wracking, and in the worst slumps, death rates rose in the factory centers. Furthermore, and again even for workers whose pay might have increased modestly, the industrial revolution cut into leisure time. The labor force was prodded to work harder than its preindustrial counterpart, and work hours inched up as employers sought to maximize use of the expensive machinery. Some textile factories drove their workers sixteen hours a day, Saturdays included. Traditional festival days, when rural workers had taken time off, came under attack as the new factories fined workers for unauthorized absences. Finally, factory jobs exposed many workers to new physical dangers, such as dust from textile fibers, accidents in the coal mines, and maimings by the fast-moving—usually unprotected—machinery.

The early industrial revolution depended on the jobs that growing numbers of workers needed in order simply to survive. Necessity, not attraction, lay at the root of the formation of Britain's new factory labor force. Relatively low pay—declining pay in some circumstances—helped subsidize the investment in new machinery and supported the gains that motivated successful entrepreneurs; increased work time contributed to growing output along with the machines themselves. And although the misery was worst in the early decades of industrialization (real wages and urban health conditions began to improve in the 1820s or at least in the 1830s) and although debate continues about exactly how bad things were, there is no doubt that desperately hard work and scant reward were characteristic of the early industrialization process in Britain.

Not surprisingly, the working conditions of early manufacturing generated serious protest among many British workers, though labor organization was illegal and poverty limited the resources available for protracted struggle. Many workers struck or rioted against cuts in pay or high food costs. Beyond these specific efforts, a number of factory hands articulated a larger sense of the exploitation to which they were, in their judgment, subject, and about the gap that had opened between them and the factory masters. A Manchester cotton spinner in 1818 condemned his employers for their

> ostentatious display of elegant mansions, equipages, liveries, parks, hunters and hounds ... They are literally petty monarchs, absolute and despotic, in their own particular districts; and to support all this, their whole time is occupied in contriving how to get the greatest quantity of work turned off with the least expense.

The spinner also excoriated the "terrible machines" that had so worsened the quality of work as compared with preindustrial life.

Some risings raised sweeping claims. In a series of riots between 1810 and 1820, manual workers attacked and destroyed the textile equipment that threatened their jobs, or at least their accustomed wages. These Luddite workers claimed inspiration from a mythical leader, Ned Ludd, whose office was supposedly in Sherwood Forest, and they pointed to a world of work in which skills would be valued, workers treated as equal producers rather than factory "hands," and machines outlawed. Their efforts failed, as did more ambitious unionization attempts in textiles and mining during the 1820s and early 1830s. But the resentment of the new working class that the factories had assembled could scarcely be denied. The industrial revolution created a new division between the directors of manufacturing—factory owners and managers—and the workers they sought to control. To many observers, this was one of the essential and deeply troubling features of the wider industrial revolution. A middle-class traveler to Manchester in 1842, W. Cooke Taylor, put it this way in a published travel account:

> As a stranger passes through the masses of human beings which have accumulated round the mills and print works ... he cannot contemplate these "crowded hives" without feelings of anxiety and apprehensions almost amounting to dismay. The population, like the system to which it belongs, is NEW; but it is hourly increasing in breadth and strength. It is an aggregate of masses, our conceptions of which clothe themselves in terms that express something portentous and fearful ... as of the slow rising and gradual swelling of an ocean which must, at some future and not distant time, bear all the elements of society aloft upon its bosom, and float them

> Heaven knows whither. There are mighty energies slumbering in these masses ... The manufacturing population is not new in its formation alone; it is new in its habits of thought and action, which have been formed by the circumstances of its condition, with little instruction, and less guidance, from external sources.

Change Generates Change: After 1820

By the 1820s, then, Britain's industrial revolution had introduced new technologies in cotton and other textiles, in pottery and metallurgy, and in aspects of coal mining. It had generated an unparalleled export surge that brought Britain's achievement home to peoples almost around the world. It had destroyed several traditional manufacturing sectors at home and abroad. It had introduced factory organization to many branches of production and had prompted massive growth in British cities. It had created a dynamic new business class and an even more novel, as well as more numerous, working class. Even in a society already heavily commercial, with an important manufacturing sector, it had fundamentally altered the framework of social and economic life.

And the revolution would not stop. Innovations were not constant, but they continued occurring. Existing machines became more refined; the number of spindles on a cotton-spinning machine, for example, increased periodically, and each increase greatly heightened production per worker. The number of workers in major industries grew inexorably. So did the average size of factories and firms, their growth permitting greater specialization of labor and more bureaucratic management. These developments brought innovation in business practices and labor conditions beyond what the initial industrial revolution had required.

One measure of the persistent change was output. It is true that, as we have seen, historians properly caution about exaggerated growth claims, the fact is that huge surges took place in key industries. Already in 1830, Britain was producing about 24 million tons of coal, four-fifths of the world's total; by 1870 the figure was 110 million, still half of all the coal mined around the world. British pig iron production was 700,000 tons in 1830; thirty years later it had more than quintupled, to almost 4 million tons. Raw cotton imports rose sixfold in the twenty years after 1830. In the same period, the average productivity per worker doubled. All this meant steadily rising exports. By 1870, British exports exceeded those of France, Germany, and Italy combined, and they were three times the level of exports from the United States. Rising output boosted industrial profits, which provided additional capital for still further changes and began to permit some definite (if modest) improvements in the standard of living of most workers, even as income inequality continued to increase.

The early industrial revolution in Britain involved more than expansion from an earlier base. It also meant radical new directions. A new breakthrough in metallurgy in 1856 brought changes greater in many ways than those previously created by the use of coke and coal. Henry Bessemer (along with inventors in other countries) worked on the problem of removing chemical impurities, in particular carbon, from pig iron. The conventional procedure demanded extremely labor-intensive operations, as highly skilled workers called "puddlers" stirred molten ore to remove the carbon. After repeated experimentation, Bessemer found that a redesigned furnace could accomplish the same results automatically; a blast of compressed air passing through the molten iron could extract the carbon. Not only were labor costs reduced, but the Bessemer converter made possible the construction of much larger blast furnaces, another huge productivity gain. Finally, the same procedures enabled industry to use the controlled reintroduction of carbon to make steel, a much tougher metal than iron that was previously extremely expensive to manufacture. An industry already transformed was transformed anew, in a pattern that would be repeated often as the industrial revolution proceeded.

The most dramatic extension of industrialization in Britain after the initial decades occurred in the field of transportation. As output grew, pressure on transportation facilities inevitably increased. Goods had to be carried to market, raw materials to the places of manufacture. Improved roads and, especially, the spate of canal building helped, but inventors—aware from prior industrial experience that concerted experiments could produce dramatic results—looked for more genuine innovation. Initiatives with rail transport had already begun in the coal mines; the first steam engine for hauling coal out of the mines on tracks was introduced in 1804. Some of the wagons were pulled on rails by horses, but locomotives were also developed under the guidance of George Stephenson. In 1821 a group of inventors and entrepreneurs chartered a railway line between Darlington, a mining center, and the port of Stockton. The first full-scale locomotive was unveiled in 1825, but its frequent breakdowns almost resulted in the cancellation of further experiments. An improved model featuring a larger boiler that could produce greater heat was tested in 1827 and put to regular use just a few months later. With this success established, a more ambitious rail line was opened in 1829 between the cotton port of Liverpool and the great factory center in Manchester. A contest was set up for locomotive design, and one model attained a speed of 28 miles per hour—an achievement marred, however, by a breakdown before the test was completed. More reliable models operated at about 16 miles per hour, a speed that was sufficient for launching a spate of railway building in Britain, and soon elsewhere.

Developed at about the same time were steam-driven ships (the first transatlantic steamship lines opened in 1838). These, combined with the railroads, plus faster communication via the newly invented telegraph, truly revolutionized the conveyance of goods, people, and information. More bulk could be transported over longer distances at greater speed than ever before. This result of industrialization also generated additional change. Labor recruitment could reach out more widely. Coal and iron (and soon steel) production had to expand simply to meet the demand generated by railroad construction and operation. The industrial revolution was beginning to feed itself, sprouting new branches to deal with the opportunities presented by prior developments. This acceleration inevitably attracted foreign attention to the wonders of Britain's achievement. A growing number of countries judged the power of Britain's transformation not only in economic but also in military terms, and this dual interest was yet another spur to the ongoing momentum of the revolution. Here was another reason that Britain's revolution would soon spread to other parts of Western society.

3 New Causes

Why Did the Industrial Revolution Happen, and Why Did It Happen in Eighteenth-Century Britain?

Explaining the industrial revolution is a challenge to historians and other history-users. New kinds of debates have surfaced recently, particularly through attempts to take a more global approach. Identifying the factors that caused the industrial revolution is vital not simply as a historical exercise but as the basis for understanding the complexity of the hurdles awaiting societies that tried to establish an industrial revolution even after Britain showed the way. The variety of developments that combined to create the first industrial revolution had somehow to be replicated, though not necessarily in identical fashion. This same daunting variety helps explain why a number of regions have not managed to launch full-scale industrialization to this day. Complex causes persist as a factor in world affairs.

Not surprisingly, historians have offered different emphases, including the "industrious revolution" argument that calls attention to previous, though largely non-technological, shifts in manufacturing. Occasionally, industrialization is presented as flowing simply from a few dramatic inventions and from some new thinking about the economy, notably Adam Smith's market-oriented theories issued in 1776 that stressed the importance of vigorous economic competition free from government controls as a means of generating innovation and growing prosperity. Inventions were involved, of course—but why did they occur? And why did Britain produce more inventions than other countries (followed, in the formative decades of industrialization, by France and the United States)? New economic theories helped produce some policies favorable to industrialization, but these did not cause the process; they came too late, and they affected too few people. (Indeed, one key step in Britain's industrialization, the imposition of tariffs on cottons from India, occurred before free market logic began to gain ground.) Any explanation of the industrial revolution must account for new behaviors on the part of literally thousands of people: the entrepreneurs who gradually moved toward a factory system, the workers who staffed the factories, the investors who provided the capital, the consumers who eagerly accepted the machine-made products. A number of powerful factors had to combine to generate a change as substantial as even the early phases of industrialization.

Key Ingredients For the industrial revolution to occur, considerable investment funds were required—the new machines were expensive, far costlier than any manufacturing equipment previously devised, even in the very small factories that characterized much early industry. Also needed was access to raw materials, including textile fibers, but particularly coal and iron, the sinews of the industrial revolution but very expensive to transport over long distances. Government interest in supporting economic innovation was a factor, and various kinds of specific government policies helped. Of major importance was an available labor force that did not have more acceptable employment options, for although some workers might be attracted to the industrial *life* because of high pay for their particular skills, the excitement of innovation, and greater independence from traditional family and community controls, most workers entered factories because they had little choice. Finally, industrialization, particularly in its first manifestation in Britain, required an aggressive, risk-taking entrepreneurial spirit that would drive businesses to venture into innovation. All these ingredients must be considered in connection with the causes of the industrial revolution.

A list of this type helps guide the assessment of causation, and it may sort out why some societies could respond to industrialization more quickly than others—but it does not explain why it happened. Take raw materials, for example. A large seam of coal ran from Britain through Belgium and northern France to the Ruhr Valley in Germany, and the most intense early industrialization developed along this coal seam. Iron ore deposits also existed in western Europe, in some cases close to the coal sources. Without these raw materials—and especially coal as the energy source for smelting metal and powering the steam engine—early industrialization would have been impossible. Western Europe also had abundant wool and, through already established colonial trade, initial access to cotton (grown in the southern colonies of British North America and in parts of Asia). On the whole, however, raw materials form preconditions for industrialization, not active causes; several other societies were in as good a position as Europe when it came to resources, and we will see a few cases where industrialization occurred without a particularly good resources base. Furthermore, obviously, coal had been present a long time, but something else had to happen to make it more desirable.

Other factors, more plausible as active causes, turn out to have their own complexities. Recent work has emphasized the military purchases in Britain's industrialization. The growing navy required guns but also other metal products like chains and pulleys. Yet other European countries were expanding their militaries, without the quick connection to industrialization. So were the British purchases an active cause, or simply an ingredient dependent on other, more basic factors?

Here's another dilemma. The scientific revolution occurred in western Europe just a century or so before industrialization began in Britain. A few discoveries, like some that came out of studying the behavior of gases, proved directly relevant, as in Watt's work on the steam engine. But historians have shown pretty clearly that the new scientific activity did not on the whole link to early industrial technology; the marriage would occur only toward the mid-nineteenth century, when industrialization was already well under way. More general effects of modern science may still apply, as we will see, but specific links fall short.

Similar difficulties affect linkage between Europe's growing commercialization and early industrialization. It is certainly true that many Europeans had become familiar with production for the market, and that consumer interest in buying goods was unquestionably rising by the early eighteenth century. Like science, all this formed part of a favorable context. But direct connections are hard to prove. It turns out that China, an older commercial society, was as well positioned as Europe in this area, in terms of living standards and experience with a market economy. Furthermore, the European banks that had grown with greater trade rarely lent money to industrial activities, seeing them as too risky, and few established merchants participated. Early industrialists were more likely to emerge from craft backgrounds, though there were some exceptional landowners and traders involved.

Europe's growing role in world trade forms a more direct backdrop than commercialization in general. From the late fifteenth century onward, western European countries, ultimately headed by France, the Netherlands, and Britain, had won a growing role in international commerce. European ships and merchant companies dominated a great deal of international trade, even in some cases in which exchanges did not directly involve Europe at all. Increasingly, a hierarchy emerged in the international economy, in which Europeans acquired minerals and agricultural goods from other areas (including their colonies in the Americas, India, and elsewhere) and in return sold manufactured products, including fine furniture, cloth, clocks, and metal goods such as guns. Because Europeans could price their goods to include the cost of processing, they were in general able to profit from the exchange. Not all parts of the world actively engaged in trade with western Europe at this point, but parts of eastern Europe (which sent grain, furs, and timber supplies), the Americas (precious metals, sugar, and tobacco), and India and Southeast Asia (spices, tea, and gold) added steadily to western Europe's wealth. The active slave trade that Europeans ran between Africa and the Americas was another source of profit.

Europe's role in preindustrial world trade set up the industrial revolution in several ways. Growing amounts of commercial experience developed through the trading companies, and new technologies relating to shipbuilding and warfare received impetus. Governments were encouraged to pay attention to the importance of fostering trade, though this attention at times led to heavy-handed efforts at control. Trade leadership helped stimulate a taste for new products. We have seen that growing interest in cotton cloth originated first from trade with India, particularly in Britain, and then the tariffs imposed in the 1730s were explicitly designed to encourage local manufacturing. At the same time, Britain used its holdings in India and particularly the southern colonies in North America to provide raw cotton for its new textile branch. Trade also provided capital through the growing wealth of many business and landowning groups.

Most directly, experience in global competition pushed manufacturing innovation directly. It helped European entrepreneurs realize that a focus on exporting manufactured goods elsewhere was a source of profit. And it directly encouraged innovation to counter traditional Asian superiority in production. Again the cotton trade provides an explicit example. European trading companies began handling printed cotton cloth from India as early as the sixteenth century. They could make money selling these colorful goods not only in Europe but in other markets. However, by the late seventeenth century some European businessmen began to wonder if the goods could not be made in their own countries, with even more profit possible. The deterrent was the experience and low cost of Indian artisans. But if machines could be devised to do the printing more efficiently, this competitive barrier could be overcome. From Switzerland to Britain, from the late seventeenth century onward, Europeans began experimenting with new technologies, and by the mid-eighteenth century were ready to supply the market with factory-made goods. Here was a concrete case in which Europe's industrial revolution, which was to have such dramatic effects on the wider world, stemmed in great part from Europe's changing position in the wider world, and a particular desire to catch up or surpass Asian manufacturing competitors.

DEBATE #4: *WHY ARE THE CAUSES OF THE INDUSTRIAL REVOLUTION STILL IN DISPUTE?*

Scholars have been trying to figure out why the industrial revolution occurred for at least a century and a half, and there is still no definitive agreement on what caused it. Why is this so, and what does the inconclusiveness say about relevant historical understanding?

Explaining such a big development as industrialization is simply difficult, because there are so many potential factors involved. This is, after all, not lab science, where experiments can be repeated to narrow down the analysis. We have already seen the figuring out the relationship between population and the causes of industrialization is a complicated task.

(*Continued*)

This does not mean, however, that no progress has been made. Early explanations of initial industrialization often focused on the role of governments and formal economic ideas, and these approaches are now downplayed. In particular, the rise of laissez-faire economics, associated particularly with the work of Adam Smith, is no longer regarded as a major factor. Smith wrote his great work, *Wealth of Nations,* in 1776, but the shape of the British industrial revolution was already beginning to emerge. The idea of fostering competition and reducing traditional economic regulations may have furthered industrial growth, but it almost certainly did not launch it. Similarly, the role of eighteenth-century governments, in building new roads and canals and helping to set up a better banking system, while not irrelevant, no longer seems front and center.

But uncertainties and disagreements persist, arguably for three reasons. First, despite the fact that industrialization has been studied for a long time, new facts and greater precision continue to emerge. One of the great recent efforts to explain the British industrial lead, focused on rising labor costs and relatively inexpensive coal—thus explaining why it was both desirable and possible to focus on new fossil fuel technologies—simply offers better data than ever before, based on more exhaustive research.

Second, and somewhat contradictorily, several of the factors often discussed in industrialization are very hard to pin down, which does not mean they are irrelevant. How can the nature and role of "entrepreneurial spirit," be captured precisely? How relevant were the undeniable changes in Western culture associated with the Scientific Revolution and Enlightenment? We know that actual scientists did not contribute a lot to early technologies, but the growing emphasis on new knowledge and secular progress may well have set the stage for many of the developments that launched the industrial process. Should the cultural factor be downplayed simply because it cannot be quantified?

Third: the comparative framework has greatly changed over time, both because of new knowledge about societies outside western Europe and because of the undeniable fact that, beginning with Japan but now extending to many other cases, "nonwestern" societies have proved perfectly capable of mounting industrial revolutions of their own.

Thus one of the really productive recent debates about industrialization, focused on the "great divergence" from more traditional economies, has simply asked the question: why Europe, and not China? (Some similar discussions have involved India.) A strong argument can be made that China, with its rich technological tradition, had just as favorable a government, just as resourceful businessmen as Europe did (though details here are still disputed). What, then, was different about the West? Possibly culture, but one conclusion focuses more prosaically on the importance of colonies—which Asian societies did not have—as sources of cheap raw materials and earnings that could be plowed into new investment. It is also true that European businessmen had long been aware of their disadvantage in international competition and were possibly particularly eager—compared, for example, to their Chinese counterparts—to figure out how to catch up and perhaps move beyond.

(A sidebar: should analysis focus mainly on the British experience, which was undeniably first, or the fact that within just a few decades many other Western societies joined in? Is it more important to try to explain the lead case or the fact that a larger society soon differentiated itself from the rest of the world?)

So there are at least three approaches still to choose from, though some can be combined: a focus on precise factors, like rising labor and timber costs and accessibility of coal, applicable particularly to Britain; a larger exploration of prior cultural changes and business spirit; and the new challenge of figuring out why the West turned out to differ from other dynamic economies. There is no question that debate continues.

Does the fact that definitive explanation is still elusive mean that the discussion is not worthwhile? Big issues in history, like this one, are ambiguous, and this may actually be an advantage of gaining experience in historical analysis—since many other problems are ambiguous as well. Further, beyond the fact that there has been progress in the explanation process, discussing the options, even amid uncertainty, gives us a better understanding of what industrialization was all about, well beyond simply listing production growth or the series of new inventions. And there is always that chance that looking at this aspect of the past may give us useful clues about what kinds of factors to emphasize today, in seeking to stimulate responsible economic growth.

So, ultimately, there are two questions to work on here. First, what seems to be the best package of factors aimed at explaining why industrialization occurred? Second, how useful—or discouraging—is the ongoing process of debate itself?

For Further Reading: Robert Allen, *The British Industrial Revolution in Global Perspective* (Cambridge, 2009); Kenneth Pomeranz, *The Great Divergence: China, Europe and the Making of the Modern World Economy* (Princeton, NJ, 2000); Jack Goldstone, *Why Europe? The Rise of the West in World History* (New York, 2008); Peter N. Stearns, *Debating the Industrial Revolution* (London, 2015).

Three Approaches: British/Western, Comparative and Global

Several approaches currently vie for attention in explaining the industrial revolution, though they overlap to some extent.

The first explanation is highly focused, in looking at particular features of the European or British situation by the eighteenth century. One recent study by Robert Allen, for example, simply asserts that Britain industrialized because its wage costs were rising but it had unusually cheap coal: technological innovation resulted directly from this very simple economic calculus. Businessmen turned to coal-driven machines to cut labor costs. Then, once Britain's industrial success became clear, by the early nineteenth century, other Western countries had to follow suit because of competitive example.

Most scholars would still add to this intriguingly barebones approach, pointing out, for example, that it is still vital to explain why Western countries were so quick to follow Britain's lead but other regions were not. They might add in the changing culture, throughout the West, that followed from the scientific revolution and solidified during the Enlightenment. They could point the fact that European governments in general were eager to encourage economic growth as part of military competition, and thus willing to improve infrastructure (initially, roads and canals) and banking facilities, while backing merchant activities as well. The surge of new consumerism that flowed through western Europe in the seventeenth and eighteenth centuries created new eagerness for goods like cheap but fashionable clothing and tableware, producing new stimulus for manufacturing.

This line of argument would emphasize important special factors in the British situation but would add in as well some components that were more widely shared through western Europe, from politics to popular culture, that would explain the rapid capacity to follow British example.

A second approach, and the most recent, involves a more challenging comparative context. It urges that Europe, even including Britain, was not very different from other leading manufacturing centers like China and India; therefore, a causation scheme that relies heavily on some overall European distinctiveness is off the mark. This view again follows from historians' growing realization that China and India benefited hugely from the world economy of the sixteenth and seventeenth centuries, earning large profits from the South American silver that European merchants used to pay for the Asian exports. Just like Europe, in broad outline, China had a strong merchant sector, widely sought manufactured exports, and much available labor. So why did Europe industrialize first? Colonies provide part of the answer, in supplying cheap raw materials (including the silver from Spanish holdings), new capital, and some additional spur to export manufacturing for colonial markets.

There was also the sheer accident that British coal mines, unlike the Chinese mines, flooded easily and so encouraged the invention and use of the early steam engine to pump out water. It turned out, of course, that the engine had wider applicability as well. Beyond this specific comparative calculation, recent work has reemphasized the importance of the changes in European culture. If the scientific revolution is not applicable directly, it did encourage a new faith in the progress of knowledge and technology that provided prestige for inventors and businesspeople and thus a unique context in which industrialization could take root. China, it turns out, despite a host of favorable ingredients, did not offer this precise mixture, and then a set of additional impediments would long hamper its ability even to respond to Europe's industrial example. So: colonies, some specific issues around coal, and cultural context may turn out to hold the key.

The third pattern of explanation plays down a specifically European focus—which can so easily exaggerate distinctive Western qualities—in favor of emphasizing shifting global relationships and outright European exploitation of its commercial and military position. From world trade, including the slave trade, Europe gained new levels of capital essential for taking risks on new inventions. From world trade, supplemented by the increasingly commercial domestic manufacturing, Europeans developed a growing middle class (from which most of the new industrialists would emerge) and a taste for pleasurable goods that would feed the expanding consumer markets. From world trade, Europeans learned about the appeal of cotton cloth (from India) and porcelains (from China), which spurred the efforts to generate factory substitutes back home. From world trade, Europeans learned the profits to be made in selling processed goods globally, while seeking cheap raw materials in return. And if this imbalance could be enhanced by special measures, like the British tariffs imposed to discourage Indian cotton production in favor of Britain's nascent industry, so much the better. The industrial revolution, in this model, emerged from the disproportionate advantages Europe was already gaining in the world's markets, and of course it would extend the international imbalances even further in the nineteenth century. The emphasis is on the global context of the industrial revolution and also on the special, exploitative position Europe had already achieved in this context, which explains both industrialization and the West's long (though not permanent) leadership in the whole process.

All three approaches have analytical merit. They can, of course, be combined to some degree. But a certain amount of choice, particularly between seeing the industrial revolution as a global economic result from the outset and viewing it as the product of some special Western or British mixture, is essential. The debate, in other words, stimulates a more precise assessment of historical factors, but it ultimately requires some reasoned prioritization.

Trigger: Why the Eighteenth Century?

All the factors pushing for the industrial revolution accelerated by the eighteenth century. The results of new science began to impact a wider culture; the Enlightenment, as an intellectual movement, brought new interest to technical progress and more discussion of the most effective economic policies; the growth of consumer expectations encouraged new markets; and Europe's world trade position improved steadily, particularly with new moves into India. The rapid expansion of domestic manufacturing gave some workers new spending money and growing urban contacts, which promoted new kinds of purchases and prepared an industrial labor force. Growing global trade helped build up domestic capital and provided further evidence of wider markets for manufactured goods.

Capping these developments and arguably providing a final push were the effects of the population explosion, coming after several decades, in the seventeenth century, of demographic stagnation. Food was crucial. The lack of major agricultural changes in Europe between the late Middle Ages and the 1690s was ironic, given Europe's commercial advance. By the 1690s, this anomaly had begun to yield, the result being an agricultural basis for further economic change, via population growth. After long hesitations because the goods were not mentioned in the Bible, western Europeans began to grow calorie-rich New World crops, headed of course by the potato. Again, larger world history fed industrialization. Further, with the Dutch leading, new methods of draining and fertilizing expanded the available land and fertility. With more food came more people.

Rapid population growth resulted from new food supplies and other developments such as a temporary lull in major plagues. There was also a pause in the most devastating kinds of warfare between 1715 and 1792. Increased population pushed workers to seek new (even unpleasant) kinds of jobs, provided growing markets for inexpensive manufactured goods, and prodded even some prosperous families to seek economic innovation. An eastern French family, the Schlumbergers, was a case in point. In the 1760s the head of the family ran an artisan shop, producing cloth but displaying no particular business dynamism. He had twelve children; that all of them lived to adulthood was somewhat unusual but illustrative of the impact of population growth in a single-family context. Simply in order to provide for his brood in the accustomed respectable middle-class fashion, Schlumberger had to expand his textile operations, hiring domestic manufacturing workers and then tentatively introducing some powered equipment. His children, building on their father's example, became dynamic industrialists in the early nineteenth century, creating large textile and machine-building factories and sponsoring the first local rail line. Population upheaval promoted economic dynamism in a number of ways and at various levels of the initial industrialization process in western Europe.

Britain as a Special Case

Finally, why was Britain—which was among the several areas of western Europe in which relevant changes had been taking shape—in the vanguard? Within the larger west European context, there were several special features in Britain. Population growth was extremely rapid in the eighteenth century, and this helped free available labor from agriculture. British landlords successfully pried land away from smallholding farmers through the government's Enclosure Acts. These required farmers to enclose their fields, usually by planting hedges, but the expense overwhelmed many small farmers, who had to sell out to the landlords. British agriculture became dominated by large estates, and although these employed many workers, they did not absorb a growing population as readily as peasant-dominated agriculture proved able to do elsewhere, and this created a labor force desperate for new options. The enclosed estates, in turn, increased agricultural market production, providing food for growing cities.

British artisans were also unusual. Most urban artisans in western Europe belonged to guilds, which tried to protect members' working conditions by limiting new technology and preventing any employer from creating undue inequality or threatening wage rates by hiring too many workers. Guilds were ideal for a relatively stable economy (and, usually, high-quality products), but they definitely inhibited both rapid labor mobility and changing techniques. Britain had once boasted a guild system, but it had virtually disappeared by the eighteenth century. The result was twofold: employers had unusual freedom to bring new workers into established branches of production, and they were at liberty to tinker with new methods—perhaps the most important single source of Britain's lead in inventions.

Britain's extensive international trade provided capital and markets and also supplies of vital materials such as cotton. The British aristocracy was more favorable to commerce than its counterparts on the European continent; some British landlords directly participated in setting up new mines and manufacturing, and tolerance for commercial development was high. The British government favored economic change. The tariff regulations in the eighteenth century, such as the barriers to the importation of cotton cloth from India, spurred new industries. Other laws that discouraged the export of new machinery or designs impeded rapid imitation elsewhere of British gains. Laws made the formation of new companies relatively easy and officially banned combinations of workers—what we would call unions—and this ban, in turn, constrained protest. During the eighteenth century a number of local governments began to build better roads, and then a wave of canal building developed at the end of the century. The new infrastructure facilitated the movement of both raw materials and finished goods. At the same time, the British government did not attempt to regulate

manufacturing extensively. Other European governments, though often eager to promote economic growth, tended to control manufacturing with regulations about product quality, techniques, and some working conditions. The British state was less interventionist. This was not always an advantage, as we shall see in other industrialization cases, but it may have served well in setting a favorable framework for the first industrial revolution.

Simple luck in terms of natural resources also aided Britain, which is where the point about low energy costs comes in. There were excellent holdings in coal and iron, which were often located quite close together. The island nation had not only coastal waterways but good navigable rivers, which further facilitated the transport of the two materials that were so vital to early industrialization but were extremely heavy and costly to move over land. Britain was also running low on timber supplies by the early eighteenth century—in part because its growing navy consumed so much wood—and had to search for alternative fuels, notably coal. This necessity, in turn, spurred industrial development, from the adaptation of the initial steam engine for mine pumping to the use of coal for smelting iron (see Illustration 3.1).

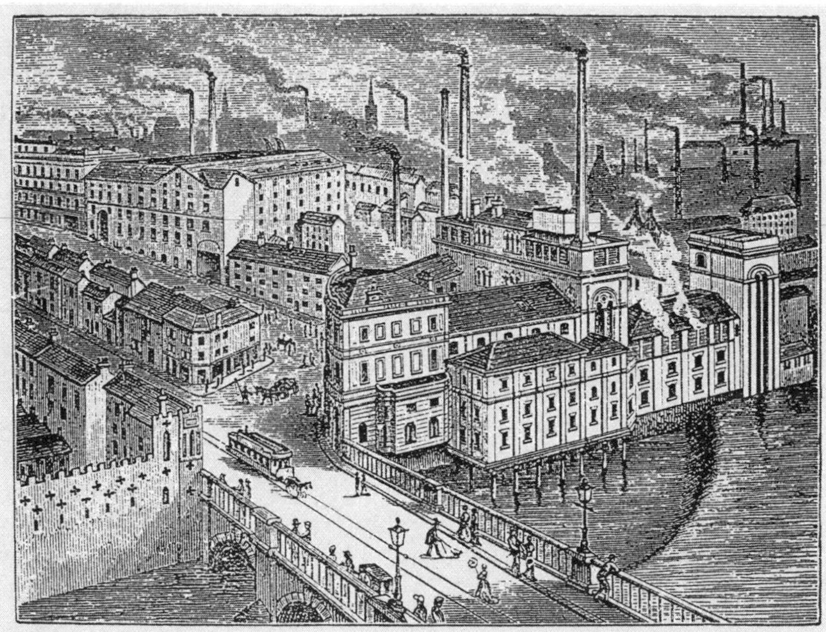

Illustration 3.1 In the 1800s, England's industries expanded and improved, causing towns such as Sheffield, located in northern England, to grow in population and importance. Sheffield factories produced high-quality steel, silver-plated items, and other metal goods (Granger Historical Picture Archive / Alamy Stock Photo).

Finally, Britain apparently provided a favorable setting for producing individuals inclined to taking risks in business. Good market opportunities and an extensive preindustrial manufacturing system formed part of this framework. New ideas about science and material progress spread more rapidly in Britain than in most other European countries. A relatively small government meant limited chances for success by seeking bureaucratic jobs. But historians have also debated other possible components encouraging a risk-taking, entrepreneurial spirit. For example, while Britain tolerated a number of Protestant religious minorities such as the Quakers and Methodists, this indulgence was incomplete: Protestants who were not members of the established Anglican Church could not attend universities or gain government employment. This ambivalence encouraged members of these minorities, eager to demonstrate God's favor, to seek opportunities in business. Certainly the Protestant minorities produced a disproportionate number of early manufacturers, who were stimulated by a belief that disciplined work, frugality, and economic drive were pleasing in the sight of God, and who were eager to get ahead where the chances lay—through entrepreneurial initiative.

In sum, Britain concentrated many of the changes developing generally in western Europe and added an array of special factors ranging from flukes of nature to new forms of callous manipulation of agricultural labor. Quite possibly the more general shifts taking place throughout Europe would have generated an industrial revolution elsewhere by the early nineteenth century; the uniqueness of the British combination should not be exaggerated. Nevertheless, the fact was that Britain came first and that its leadership can be explained.

For at least a half century the nation's effective monopoly on the industrial revolution was scarcely challenged. British industry enabled the country to hold up against the much larger population of France during the wars of the French Revolution and the Napoleonic era. By the 1830s Britain's industrial lead was so obvious, and its related need and ability to export cheap machine-made manufactured goods were so great, that the government changed its basic tariff policy. Britain became a pioneer in free trade, allowing imports of food and raw materials that helped keep prices (and wages) down while relying on manufacturing exports to balance the trade exchange and even to show a tidy national profit.

Britain was indeed pouring manufactured goods into the markets of the world. Machine-made textiles cut into customary production not only in Latin America and India but also in Germany. British iron products undersold traditional charcoal-smelted metal in France. Here, obviously, was a rude challenge. But here also was an opportunity. Britain's success in industrialization added another ingredient to the changes taking place in western Europe. Continental businesses and governments began to wake up to the possibility of copying British machine design and factory organization, realizing they must stir themselves lest they be engulfed in a British industrial tide. The industrial revolution began to spread.

For after Britain took the industrial lead, the whole question of causation takes on a different cast. The British model, and British success (including military success against Napoleon's forces), became causes in their own right for other Western societies ready and able to recognize the message. Still, however, the analytical challenge is not over, for while some societies imitated quickly, suggesting that they had conditions very similar to those spurring industrialization in Britain, other societies did not or could not follow up so readily. They were defined by different economic, political, and cultural factors, and in many cases were already being exploited by European commerce in ways that delayed a robust response. In fact, the next industrial revolutions extended the phenomenon in the West alone; only later would some other societies follow suit (though often with impressive results), in a process that remains globally uneven to the present day.

4 The Industrial Revolution in Western Society

"I am here in the centre of the most advanced industry of Europe and of the Universe." So wrote the young French textile entrepreneur Motte-Bossut during a visit to England in 1842. He was not exaggerating. A few years later, in 1851, when Britain celebrated its industrial might in the Great Exhibition at the Crystal Palace, it had no peer in any of the principal phases of mechanical production. Several European countries were superior in textile design, and the United States led in a few minor categories such as machine stitching and it was gaining ground the factory production of clocks and watches. But the British lead in textiles, metallurgy, mining, and machine building seemed insurmountable.

Britain's industrial superiority inevitably affected the next phase of industrialization. A list of causes of all the industrial revolutions launched between 1820 and 1870 has to include both the powerful example of Britain and the international activities of British businesses. The countries that first imitated Britain did so not only because they shared many of the same features that had produced the British surge, but also because they were geographically close (or in the case of the United States, historically and culturally close) to the industrial island. French textile factories surged in the north, which abutted the English Channel, and in Alsace, where the leading industrialists were Protestant and shared some contacts with Britain.

The industrial rise of Britain spurred West European and U.S. businesses. There were profits to be made and industries to defend lest British exports overwhelm the entire manufacturing base. Foreign governments had to take an interest as well. British economic might during the Napoleonic Wars demonstrated the relevance of industrialization to power politics. Gains in metallurgy and machine building had direct links to armaments. The obvious potential of the railroad motivated government officials interested in better transportation for troops or political officials, who otherwise would have preferred to stay away from the upheavals of economic change—a factor for several German states. Britain's success, in sum, was an active cause of the subsequent round of industrialization in societies having many of the same commercial, scientific, and social features that had spurred the British. Foreigners began to flock to Britain to learn, and British entrepreneurs and workers began to set up operations abroad.

There were three principal stages in the wider Western effort to copy Britain's mechanical advances. Before 1789, other European governments sent a few observers to learn about British technology. The French in 1764 dispatched a scientist to study British metallurgy, and on his return he used the new methods to develop one of France's great iron manufacturing firms, the de Wendel Company. The French government also paid a British metallurgist to set up a cannon foundry. Various German and Swiss states sent students also, and some of them brought back new textile equipment. Such transfers of technology were unusual, however, partly because British law forbade the export of new technology and the emigration of skilled workers.

Then the French Revolution exploded in 1789, and its turmoil and the ensuing European war interrupted major developments for over two decades. Yet the revolution also introduced important new legislation that (though the drafters largely did not so intend) helped pave the way for industrialization in western Europe. In France, and also neighboring territories such as Belgium and western Germany, the abolition of the guilds removed restrictions on the movement of labor and technical innovation. Western Europe became more like Britain in this way. Internal trade barriers were removed in countries such as France, and commercial law was regularized. Other laws prohibited combinations of workers—these, too, emulated the British lead and inhibited labor protest against change. Although those who launched the French Revolution did not intend to promote industrialization (and the ensuing disorder actually delayed it), the new laws and a general enhancement of the power of the middle classes, along with Britain's display of industrial success during the battles with Napoleon, completed the causation of western Europe's economic transformation.

When war ended in 1815, Europeans intensified their study of British patterns, seeking to circumvent British laws prohibiting technology transfer. In this third phase, a number of new industrial revolutions soon took shape. In 1819 the Prussian government sent a locksmith to study British machine building, and he returned to form a major plant in Berlin. The French and Dutch governments bribed British entrepreneurs to set up modern metallurgical factories directly; as a result the French steel industry took shape under James Jackson, and it was a Jackson grandson who in 1861 set up the first Bessemer converter in France. Belgian businessmen smuggled British machinery out of the country in rowboats, and in a few cases literally kidnapped skilled British workers. Francis Cabot Lowell, an American, visited Britain in 1810–1812, and two years later established the first power looms in the United States and the first major textile plant that combined mechanical spinning and weaving. French and Swiss metallurgists visited frequently. Alfred Krupp, a German, made his study trip in 1838, by which time Germans and others were also studying British railroads and mining engineering. The Belgian government directly hired George Stephenson to set up railroads in Belgium, and all the European states, plus the United States, imported British locomotives.

European and U.S. businesses also hired British workers. By 1830 there were at least 15,000 British workers in France, serving mainly as skilled technical personnel in textile and metallurgical plants. Employers offered huge bonuses and wages, sometimes double the local rate, to induce the vital British workers to emigrate. The results were not always happy, for some of the British workers involved were inferior types. A Swiss engineer complained:

> Not only do they cost a damned lot of money, but they are often drunkards. English workers who are both efficient and well behaved can earn a very good living at home ... British workers seldom fulfill the sanguine expectations of their foreign employers because they are handling materials to which they are not accustomed and because they are working with different people than they would be at home.

Needless to say, most European industrialists trained a local labor force as quickly as possible. Nevertheless, the British ingredient was often central to the process. French metallurgists, for example, found that it took at least a decade to teach French workers some of the necessary skills, mainly because their rural background did not generate the requisite motivation. British workers, accustomed to industry, were also attuned to the idea of innovating in return for making more money, an outlook that did not immediately arise elsewhere.

Also important was the direct emigration of British industrialists. Samuel Slater, an apprentice in one of the Arkwright textile plants, moved to the United States in 1789 under the sponsorship of a Rhode Island merchant; he soon established the first textile factory in the new nation. The first Swiss cotton factory was set up by two Britons; and another Englishman, along with a few imported British skilled workers who taught mechanical weaving, revolutionized Dutch cotton production after 1830.

No English family did more for European industrialization than the Cockerill clan in Belgium. William Cockerill brought modern textile machinery to France in the 1790s. In 1810 Napoleon made him a citizen, a status that allowed him to continue operations. A Cockerill machine-building plant in Liège, Belgium, employed 2,000 workers by 1812. By the 1830s the Cockerill operation included the largest integrated metallurgical and machine factory in the world, its owner boasting, "I have all the new inventions over at Liège ten days after they come out of England." Mining, shipbuilding, and railroad development fanned the Cockerill empire, which also expanded into Germany. A Belgian observer noted that the Cockerills saw "a mission to extend manufactures everywhere and to fill the whole world with machinery." Profit possibilities and a genuine missionary zeal made a heady combination.

The British role in stimulating wider industrialization was particularly crucial into the 1840s. Individual Britons continued to contribute thereafter, but by this point the industrial revolution was firmly anchored in

Belgium, France, the United States, and Germany, and was developing deep native roots. British industrial adventurers began to work farther afield, in Russia and Austria, for example, where full industrial revolutions were yet to emerge.

Even before the 1840s the British role should not be exaggerated, for it obviously combined with the emergence of new business interests in western Europe and the United States and with shifts in government policy. Furthermore, imitation was never precise. Each subsequent industrial revolution had its own flavor, sharing many features with the British process because of the nature of industrialization as well as emulation, but also responding to local constraints and opportunities. The difference in sheer timing was a factor as well. The British industrial lead forced some later industrial revolutions to develop different emphases. Textiles, for example, played a less prominent role in German industrialization, partly because British imports had made major inroads before the German process gathered momentum. This was one reason Germany's industrial revolution stressed heavy industry from the first. In addition, the possibility of imitating Britain meant that many west Europeans and Americans required less time for experimentation; they could begin with more sophisticated and productive machinery from the start. One result was that the next round of industrial revolutions did not impose quite so much new misery on the labor force as had occurred in early British industrialization. French and German industrial workers were not well paid, and wages had been traditionally lower in these countries in any event, but the intense deprivation of the British industrial slums and the reliance on virtual slave gangs of children were largely avoided.

In addition to coal-rich Belgium's rapid transformation, three follow-up industrial revolutions in Western society were particularly important. France, Germany, and the United States joined the industrial parade between 1820 and 1840, and each displayed distinctive features in the process. In combination, their industrial revolutions essentially completed the

Figure 4.1 Annual Production of Pig Iron, 1870.
Source: Adapted from Encyclopedia Britannica, 1951, vol. XII, p. 673.

industrialization of the Western world by the 1870s, increasing the worldwide impact of the industrial revolution while cutting into Britain's preeminence. By then all three countries, Germany and the United States in particular, were also spearheading further transformations of the industrial economy that extended the process of technological and especially organizational changes well beyond those of Britain's first stages. (See Figure 4.1)

France: An Eclectic Course

France, western Europe's richest and most populous country in the eighteenth century, faced several drawbacks in attempting to imitate the British achievement. Recurrent revolutions into the 1870s were not helpful to the business climate and perhaps even encouraged several French governments to be somewhat more protective of traditional economic groups than were their counterparts elsewhere. Certainly the French were fiercely protectionist in their tariffs against foreign (notably British) goods, which favored inefficient, old-fashioned textile and metallurgy firms that would otherwise have perished. But most countries seeking to emulate the British had a long protectionist phase to help safeguard their manufacturing, so the French tactic probably was not decisive. Far more important were deficiencies in natural resources. The French simply did not have the large coal reserves of Britain, Germany, or the United States. By 1848 they were, in fact, exploiting a higher percentage of their reserves than any other country, but they could not keep up. To do so they needed to import coal, a necessity that resulted in higher costs, particularly in metallurgy. France's ability to compete in heavy industry was further weakened after its war loss to Germany in 1871, when it surrendered most of its iron-rich province of Lorraine. Finally, French population growth, though substantial, was lower than that of most other Western nations, so there was less spur for workers to flock into factory centers. French factory cities grew, but far less than their counterparts elsewhere, and difficulties in recruiting labor—workers were able to indulge a preference to remain in the countryside—played a substantial role.

Because of these limitations, French industrialization was less impressive than that of several other countries, and the nation's relative economic strength declined as a result. There was a real industrial revolution nevertheless. About 20 percent of all manufacturing workers were employed in factory industry or coal mines by 1850. Cotton and wool production was substantially mechanized, and several new metallurgical centers featured large factories and advanced techniques. The French introduced a number of important inventions, including a mechanical loom for fine cloth, the Jacquard loom, that helped spread mechanization in textiles and ultimately helped inspire twentieth-century advances in circuit-board technology. French output began to expand rapidly. Coal production rose thirteenfold between 1820 and 1870, and iron production sextupled. The pace of French industrialization increased after 1842, when the national government agreed on a railroad system and sponsored its rapid development. Unlike in Britain, where most railway initiatives lay in private hands and the government provided only its right of eminent domain to aid in property acquisition, the French government built the rail systems directly, then turned over most of the lines to private companies on ninety-nine-year leases; the companies provided the rolling stock. France's national system was completed in the 1860s, and an active program of local development went forward thereafter, boosting French heavy industry in particular and making a major contribution to the transportation needed for industrialization more generally.

The French industrialization process featured some relative lags and a greater degree of government involvement than the British model. It also emphasized concurrent transformation of craft production. France had a well-established craft tradition, with export markets in such goods as fine furniture and silk cloth. Because of some limits on industrialization in other areas and as a means of circumventing British competition, many French manufacturers worked to expand craft output without totally revolutionizing the technology. Furniture makers, for example, began to standardize design and production, so workers could be trained more quickly and their output increased. They still worked in small shops with largely manual techniques, but they were almost mass-producing tables, cabinets, and other items that could be sold to middle-class households not only in France but abroad. The workers involved keenly sensed and resented the changes, lamenting a faster pace of work and a decline in creative artistry.

Through the rise of factory industry and the emphasis on substantial transformations within the craft system, France increased its annual per capita economic growth almost as rapidly as Britain in its industrial revolution period. Indeed, France pioneered in one of the obvious outcomes of the industrial revolution: a major innovation in distribution systems. More goods to sell and a growing urban market meant traditional small shops no longer sufficed. The first department store, aimed at high-volume sales particularly in clothing, opened in Paris in the 1830s.

Germany: Heavy Industry and Big Business

German industrialization got under way later than the French version. The absence of tariff protection for textiles hampered early development and certainly fostered a tremendous sense of industrial inferiority. Germany was also divided into separate states and industrialized only after a customs union created a larger national market in the 1830s. Full abolition of the guilds and serfdom also came late in Germany; these institutional features reduced labor mobility into the 1840s. Finally, unlike France and the United States, Germany contributed almost no new inventions to the early industrialization process and remained highly dependent on foreign technologies into the 1870s. Simply locating adequately trained skilled workers was a problem; one manufacturer complained in the 1830s that it was impossible to find a single German worker capable of making a machine screw.

Nevertheless, coal-mining output began to expand rapidly by the 1830s, almost doubling in that decade alone. Between the 1840s and 1870, German coal production expanded sevenfold, as deep mines were sunk, particularly in the rich Ruhr Valley coal basin. A few coke furnaces in metallurgy were installed early, but before 1850 only 10 percent of all iron was coke-smelted. In the 1850s, however, iron production expanded at a rate of 14 percent per year. By then the German states were also actively expanding their railroad network; most of the lines were built and operated by the state governments involved. In the 1870s Germany benefited from the acquisition of Alsace and Lorraine, which had strong concentrations of industrialized textiles and of metallurgy, respectively. Development of new smelting processes facilitated fuller use of phosphorus-rich Lorraine ore, another boost for Germany's ascendant heavy industry. By 1913 Lorraine alone was producing 47 percent of all the iron ore mined in Europe, most of which benefited Germany.

From the 1850s onward, German industrialization displayed several distinctive features. Sheer speed was one important point. So, too, was the unusual concentration of heavy industry, which followed from Germany's excellent resources in coal and iron and from the fact that Germany's industrialization was the first to take shape almost exclusively *after* the introduction of railroads, with their huge demand for coal and metal. In addition, the German government was extensively involved in supporting industrialization; an example was its state-based railroad policy. Because Germany had a smaller preindustrial middle class and less capital than Britain or France, government operations helped make up the difference. State backing for investment banks, for example, promoted the accumulation of investment funds.

Germany also quickly became a center for business combination. Many small firms continued to operate in crafts and retailing, so the picture should not be overdrawn. But Germany's stress on capital-intensive heavy industry, plus state backing, provided favorable conditions for experimenting with new kinds of big companies and cartels. By the 1870s gigantic firms like Krupp dominated much of German metallurgy and mining, with branches extending from the mines through the smelting and refining of metal to the production of armaments and ships. Huge capital demands in these industries encouraged German investment banks to facilitate big business to help ensure profits. Newer industrial sectors, such as chemicals and electrical equipment, were quickly dominated by two or three large firms, in part because of the backing of the investment banks. Two companies, the Allgemeine Elektrizitaets Gesellschaft and Siemens, controlled over 90 percent of the German electrical industry and developed extensive branches abroad. Not only did firms of this size accumulate massive capital, they were also in a position to set prices somewhat independently of market forces. Combinations of big business units also occurred in Germany. Several steel cartels formed that allocated market quotas for certain products in order to ensure that prices held up; a coal cartel set production limits for each member for the same purpose. By the late nineteenth century there were 300 cartels in Germany, many with extensive market control and political influence. Germany was not alone in the rise of big business, but it emphasized such arrangements more than Britain or France did.

The United States: Dynamism of a New Nation

Along with Germany's rise, U.S. industrialization formed the great new economic success story in world history between 1850 and 1900. U.S. industrial growth began in the 1820s with the importation of technological systems from Britain. Although U.S. inventors contributed significantly to the industrialization process through such achievements as the mechanical gin for removing seeds from cotton fiber and major strides in devising systems of interchangeable parts, the United States remained dependent on European technological advances throughout the nineteenth century—British and French at first, then German and Swedish in industries like chemicals. U.S. businesses were quick to imitate. Construction of locomotives began just a year after the first British model reached the United States. Only local lines were laid before 1830, but 3,000 miles of track were set out in the following decade, mainly in the Northeast, and major interregional lines were launched by the 1840s. As usual, the new infrastructure generated increased demand in heavy industry and facilitated other industrial operations. Extensive canal building also contributed to the burgeoning process.

Textile factories, which used water as well as steam power, formed the core of initial U.S. factory industry, and factory towns spread across New England. But there were also advances in machine building, printing, and other manufacturing sectors. The invention of the sewing machine in the 1840s initiated a transformation in clothing manufacture from handwork to faster-paced mechanized output, not only in New England but in midwestern factory centers like Cincinnati (by 1840 the nation's third-largest industrial city).

In its first stage U.S. industrialization increased the number of manufactured goods in circulation and encouraged the further development of market specialization in other areas such as agriculture, even as the bulk of the nation's economy remained nonindustrial. The process was also marked by relatively favorable labor conditions. Workers were in short supply, and recruitment required paying relatively high wages. Many women were drawn from farms into the factories in expectation of working a few years and then returning home with a nest egg. Skilled male workers were also relatively well treated. Unlike their counterparts in Europe, male workers also had the vote, which fostered their sense of connection to the larger society. Worsening conditions in the 1830s provoked a number of labor strikes; then, in the 1840s, growing numbers of immigrants, Irish in particular, fed the urban labor force, and standards of living deteriorated in many factory centers.

It is important not to take American industrialization for granted—this was after all the first industrial revolution to occur outside a West European context. The nation did have unusually close ties with Britain, which facilitated imitation, and it had an abundance of relevant natural resources. Also, a relatively small population (when the industrial revolution began) might have encouraged an interest in labor-saving technology—although historians have recently played down this factor. Rather, in keeping with some of the larger debates over causation, historians have shifted their emphasis to an American culture that surpassed even Europe's interest in science and technology, creating a favorable context for rapid change.

Without question, once the process began, in the United States as elsewhere, it continued to generate further transformations. The second stage of U.S. industrialization took off with the expansion of war industries during the Civil War. U.S. arms manufacturers extended their operations, beginning a tradition of arms sales abroad when the domestic market shrank after 1865. Development of intercontinental rail links spurred industrial growth on another front. Though backed by large government land grants, railroad companies were in private hands that pioneered a number of aspects of U.S. big business: huge capital investments, a large labor force, and attempts to ensure regional monopolies over service. As early as the 1850s American railroads began to devise appropriate forms of organization for a large company, commissioning engineers to plot out management structures and information flows and soon beginning to implement regional time zones to reduce confusion in this area. It was in this context in the 1870s that Andrew Carnegie introduced the Bessemer process into steel manufacturing on a large scale, lowering prices substantially in the bargain. Expansion of mining fed the growing use of steam engines in manufacturing and transport. The manufacturing labor force expanded rapidly as well through the growing recruitment of immigrant workers from southern and eastern Europe and, for a time on the West Coast, from Asia. Average factory size increased; by 1900 over 1,000 U.S. factories employed between 500 and 1,000 workers, and 450 more employed more than 1,000. Not only heavy industry but also textiles experienced this growth in factory size.

U.S. industrialization obviously displayed much the same surge toward big business that characterized Germany in these decades. Investment banks helped coordinate the growth of multifaceted companies. As in Germany, the sheer speed of the American industrial explosion altered the world's economic context with dizzying rapidity. Indeed, it was through industrial expansion, along with agricultural exports, that the United States began to make an independent mark in world history by the 1870s. Several U.S. companies began establishing branches abroad. Two U.S. firms, in sewing machines and agricultural equipment, were the largest industrial enterprises in Russia by 1900. More than in Germany, much U.S. public opinion remained committed to a rhetoric of free enterprise even as big business grew

(a)

(b)

Illustration 4.1 These lithographs are from an unusual series called *The Progress of Cotton*, published in the early nineteenth century, which shows all the steps in the processing of cotton from field to finished product (Everett Collection Inc / Alamy Stock Photo).

(c)

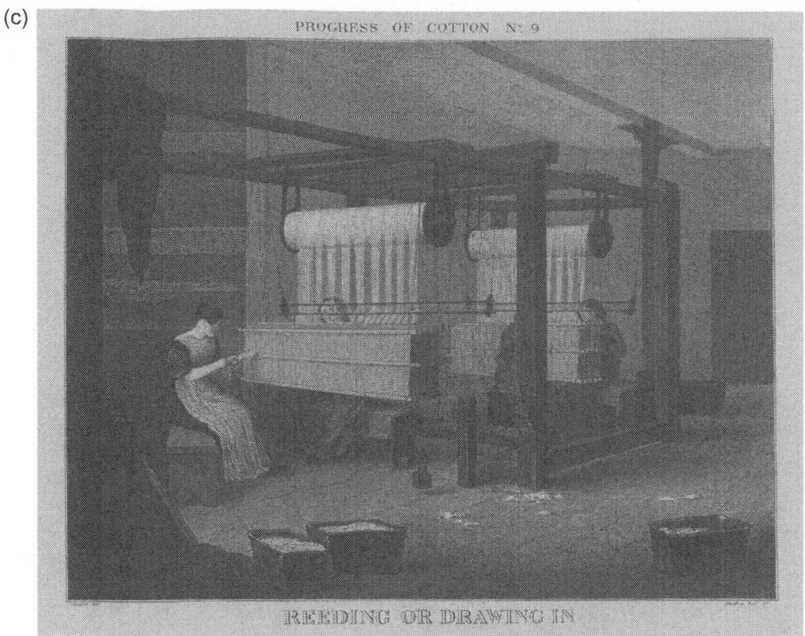

Illustration 4.1 (Continued).

and the government actively contributed to industrial expansion not only through grants of land but also through high protective tariffs.

The industrial revolution in the United States had three other distinctive features. First, what amounted to an industrialization of agriculture occurred along with the transformation of manufacturing. The vast lands of the westward expanding nation encouraged the development of new equipment, from horse-drawn harvesting machinery to tractors, which were in growing use by the end of the nineteenth century. Agricultural output expanded rapidly, providing the nation with vital export commodities by the 1870s. Farmers often warred with big business (over railroad rates, for example), but there was less disjuncture between the rural and urban economies in the United States than in France and Germany. The United States also avoided the outright shrinkage of the agricultural sector that came to characterize Britain, which traded industrial exports for dependence on food imports.

The United States also relied unusually heavily on foreign capital. The nation was rich in resources but lacked the funds to develop them as rapidly as industrialization required. Huge investments from Europe, in particular Great Britain, fueled U.S. industry throughout the nineteenth century, and the nation remained in international debt until World War I.

U.S. industrialization contributed important organizational innovations in addition to the growth of big business. Because of the importation of immigrant workers regarded by many U.S. industrialists as racially inferior to Anglo-Saxon stock, U.S. factory managers devoted great thought to the conscious control of their labor force. They developed factory police forces to quell strikes and by the late nineteenth century were experimenting with engineering research, called "time-and-motion studies," designed to calculate the movements of workers so that they could be systematized and sped up. Time-and-motion engineers set pay rates on the basis of optimal worker efficiency and subdivided tasks so that more and more workers performed in a routine, almost machinelike, fashion. European factories quickly introduced some of the same thinking, but the initiative in new organizational techniques came disproportionately from the United States. Ironically, the world's first large political democracy was a pioneer in rigid workplace hierarchies, building on the implications of the factory system to create greater management control.

The Industrial West by the 1880s

The spread of rapid industrial revolutions to Belgium, France, Germany, and the United States effectively converted the bulk of Western society into an industrial economy by the 1870s. Industrial revolutions were also under way in Scandinavia, northern Italy, and the Netherlands. A few regions, of course, were largely unaffected: southern Italy and much of Spain, for example, as well as regional pockets within industrial nations. Ireland, under British rule, industrialized little; it served as a cheap source of labor and agricultural goods. The American South was largely nonindustrial, even after slavery was finally abolished; it, too, served as a dependent economy, providing cotton and other raw materials to and buying manufactured goods from the North.

Nevertheless, the expansion of industrialization altered the economic balance both among Western nations and between the West and the rest of the world. Britain's huge industrial lead progressively dwindled as the German and U.S. share of the industrial pie expanded. The British found it difficult to accommodate to some of the forms that the industrial economy began to take by the 1870s. Britain provided less technical training for workers and managers than Germany did, relying instead on more traditional kinds of skill and initiative; it moved into the big-business age less comfortably than its new rivals did, partly because of its established pattern of family-owned factories. Industrialization in Britain continued, but its relative share declined.

Overall industrial output elsewhere in the West continued to increase. The expansion of railroads and the focus on heavy industry in Germany and the United States prompted strong growth in metallurgy and related branches such as armaments. New electrical and chemicals industries took off, the latter on the basis of new manufacturing needs and techniques in dyes, chemical fertilizers, and explosives. The organizational thrust of the industrial revolution took on new contours with the rise of big business and the development of new methods of disciplining and arranging the factory labor force. In sum, the rapid change in the cast of industrial actors made clear what British industrialization had already taught: the industrial revolution involved ongoing change, not simply an initial conversion to new techniques.

The expansion of Western industrial society also brought growing international rivalry and disruption. The British worried increasingly about competition, particularly from Germany. A major depression in the 1870s, not fully resolved until the 1890s, resulted in part from international pressures and also worsened those pressures. The "great depression" of the 1870s, as it was then called, was a new kind of slump. Traditionally, depressions had begun with agricultural failures caused by bad weather or crop disease; the resulting rise in food prices cut demand for manufactured goods. This had been true, for example, in the 1846–1847 slump that helped generate the revolutions of 1848. By the 1850s the expansion of agricultural production, plus transportation improvements that made widespread food shipment possible, reduced the prospect of this kind of collapse in the industrial areas. Recessions in the new context began with a failure of demand for other reasons, leading banks to cut their industrial loans which produced yet another reduction of industrial demand. The resulting spiral of declining production and growing unemployment caused less dire want than the old agricultural failures had, but the cycle also tended to be more prolonged. The crisis of the 1870s, triggered by several bank failures in the United States, stemmed from a growth in industrial output that often exceeded demand. Workers' wages were low. The incomes of European peasants were declining because of competition with cheap food imports from the Americas. In this context came a major industrial pause: sales plummeted and manufacturers tried desperately to find new outlets for their goods, at the same time cutting wages and jobs.

The 1870s depression did not permanently interrupt Western industrialization. It did, however, generate new demand for an increase in protective tariffs against foreign goods, a movement that swept over all industrial nations except Britain in the following two decades. The crisis also gave rise to urgent efforts, avidly supported by many industrialists, to seek new market security internationally. Interest in expanding imperialism increased, in part because of a desire to monopolize potential markets in Africa and Asia and to insulate these markets against growing international competition. Thus, the advent of new rivalries within the industrial world helped escalate the impact of industrialization in the world at large. This escalation, in turn, helped move the Western-dominated first phase of the industrial revolution into a more fully international setting.

5 The Social Impact of the Industrial Revolution

The industrial revolution was a wide-ranging experience as well as an intensely human one. Its technological and organizational core had ramifications reaching into almost every facet of society—from personal life to wider institutions and cultures. Specific impacts varied with each region. The experiences of women during French industrialization, for example, differed from those in Britain because a larger number of French women stayed in the labor force; by the late nineteenth century about 23 percent of the French labor force was female compared with about 15 percent in Britain. Nevertheless, in broad outline the social impact of industrialization was similar in most Western countries.

No society managed to industrialize without massive social dislocations. There are distinctions as well between short-term and long-term social impacts. Historians' focus has changed as the more durable consequences have become more apparent. Great debate used to center on the standard of living of the first generation or two of factory workers, particularly in Britain. There were points on the side of pessimists, who claimed deterioration, and points for the more optimistic. The debate was colored by more contemporary politics, with Marxists during the Cold War bent on showing how much workers suffered, their opponents more eager to defend capitalism. But it is also true that different groups of workers fared differently, and different aspects of material standards also varied—clothing, for example, improved, whereas housing often deteriorated amid urban crowding. And there is no question that, with time, working-class poverty decreased. Today, much greater attention is given to shifts in the nature of work and supervision, which had more fundamental and durable implications—though the initial suffering of some early workers must not be forgotten.

Early attention also seized on the heavy use of women and, in Britain, of child workers in factories. With time, however, the removal of many women from manufacturing work and the downgrading of their economic importance have appeared more significant—though again there were early abuses, including sexual exploitation, that figure into evaluations as well. In this case, changes in our own gender standards, with widespread approval of contemporary women's work, as well as better historical information on what happened to most women during Western industrialization, have changed perspectives dramatically. For children, it was the reduction of work and the historic shift to schooling that ultimately mattered most, though these results did not emerge immediately for the whole working class.

DEBATE #5: *WHAT DID THE INDUSTRIAL REVOLUTION DO TO THE EXPERIENCE OF WORK?*

When historians first began to pay attention to the history of industrial workers, they focused either on the rise of the labor movement or on a passionate debate about material conditions—whether living standards rose or fell in the first few decades of industrialization. This last debate ultimately fizzled not because it was firmly resolved, but because everyone had to agree that over the long run, real wages and standards improved for most workers.

But what might be the most important question, what happened to work itself, has been harder to deal with, from the early days on to the present. Employers argued that machines made work easier, and in terms of physical exertion that was so, though not for everyone right away. On the other hand, safety problems could be more severe.

Complications abound. Factory work was less skilled on average than traditional craft work; there was much less chance to take pride in product, when tasks were subdivided. But most people had never been craft workers. How did factory labor compare to agriculture?

Some workers found some of the new jobs enthralling. Train engineers, for example, loved the power of driving an iron monster through the countryside. But many workers resented being bossed around for their entire life, without much chance to rise to a higher position (though there was some mobility). The pace of work was a real challenge, ultimately leading to complaints about what we today would call stress [here was a feature of industrial labor that would steadily intensify].

Successful adjustments simply deepen the basic questions of quality. Workers strove, ultimately with some success, to reduce working hours and, later, to gain some vacation time. Ultimately, formal retirement factored in as well. All this made work more endurable, but did it improve the quality of jobs themselves or make it easier to ignore this issue? From the mid-nineteenth century onward, some workers fairly explicitly decided that they would press for higher earnings, admitting that they had lost control over work itself. This process of *instrumentalism*—work becoming an

(*Continued*)

instrument of a better life off the job—spread widely; but did it come at a lasting cost to job quality?

Some workers were deeply alienated by their job conditions, finding no real meaning in this major aspect of their lives. More—and this may still be true today—displayed a mixed reaction. They took pride in working well, but they did not fully identify with their jobs (as artisans once had); and when asked if they wanted their kids to follow their footsteps, their reaction was at best mixed.

So is it possible to offer a historical evaluation? What were the most enduring problems associated with industrial work? How do the plusses of the industrial work experience compare to the minuses? Have there been fundamental improvements, or deteriorations, from the early industrial period to the present? And have significant national differences emerged, depending on trade union power and the pervasiveness of a narrow work ethic? Finally, looking ahead to more recent industrializations like the Chinese, have some of the same basic issues arisen in terms of jobs quality, and if so why?

Further reading: Peter N. Stearns, *From Alienation to Addiction: Modern American Work in Global Historical Perspective* (London, 2008); for fascinating, and diverse, commentary from modern workers themselves, Studs Terkel, *Working* (New York, 1974).

Life on the Job

One fundamental transformation involved the work experience. Factory workers sometimes faced an increase in poverty, as wages were kept low and prices of some goods rose. But other workers won modest benefits from the industrial revolution, partly because the prices of manufactured goods fell, and certainly the tendency after the initial decades was for standards of living to improve. Constraints remained very real. The new working class had little margin over subsistence, and various crises such as illness, a recession, or old age had the potential to bring extreme misery. Furthermore, reactions to other features of the industrial revolution often were colored by initial suffering. Nevertheless, the exiguous standard of living was not in itself the most important change that the industrial revolution brought to the labor force.

Job conditions imposed many hardships. Factory life subverted the traditional work rhythm that workers brought from craft or agricultural backgrounds. Machines worked quickly, and employers believed (or professed to believe) that hard work was the stuff of life. New shop rules attempted to bring a new pace of work to the factory hands. Workers had to arrive when the factory whistle blew; if they were late, they would be locked out, lose half a day's pay, and be fined as much in addition. The enforcement of clock-based time was a new experience for many. Beyond this, rules stipulated that workers could not wander around the factory, chatter, or sing (even if the constant din of the new machines had permitted). The typical unevenness in the traditional work pace was explicitly attacked: work was meant to be steady as well as fast, with no whimsical interruptions, for if one worker stopped, a whole machine might shut down. Rules, fines, and layers of supervisors were devices aimed at imposing an unfamiliar sense of time and coordination on the factory hands.

The development of factory supervision followed from the struggle to reshape a whole labor force. Many early factories decentralized supervision considerably. A skilled spinner might directly hire the two or three assistants he required, often employing members of his own family. If the crew did not work well, the spinner himself would lose pay, so he had a stake in proper discipline. Fairly quickly, however, this system was replaced by more formal direction. Decentralized operations did not ensure fast, regular work, given the huge increase in pace that employers sought. Further, many workers lacked adequate knowledge of their machines to tend them reliably; more skilled, technical direction was required—not for the sake of workers or safety but for the machinery itself. (One French factory owner decorated the most productive machine in the plant with a garland of flowers each week, a clear indication of where priorities lay in the new work process.) Thus, most factories after a decade or two introduced foremen to hire and fire workers and to keep the work going properly. Many of these foremen were drawn from the worker ranks, but they were expected to represent management interests and to drive their workers hard. With this innovation, the factory system not only introduced a new pace and discipline but also a new experience of being bossed. For the first time in Western history (aside from American slavery), a growing minority of people were working under the daily control of someone else, and not simply for a few years of youthful apprenticeship but for a lifetime. Later developments that restricted the foremen themselves, such as the rise of industrial engineering and formal time-and-motion regulations in U.S. factories, carried the loss of control over daily work life even further.

Some employers modified the sense of strangeness with active policies of paternalism. Because of humanitarian sentiments, but even more because of the need to attract and retain skilled miners or metallurgists, often in remote areas, heavy-industry firms in particular adopted such policies. Textile companies often tried the approach as well—like the Massachusetts companies that built and supervised attractive barracks for their first female factory hands. Paternalistic firms constructed worker housing, provided some medical care, and in other ways extended assistance beyond the wage to certain workers. Many workers viewed paternalism as an appropriate form of treatment, reminiscent of the attention landlords or artisans' masters had provided in the old days. Paternalism was not uniformly beneficent, however. Companies that provided housing could use the threat of eviction to discipline potential strikers. Furthermore, many paternalistic benefits proved meager or deteriorated when a company had assembled an adequate labor force. For various reasons, paternalism did not basically modify the growing formality and impersonality of direction in the factories; most workers saw themselves as separate from the employing class, and many resented this separation along with so many other novelties.

Industrial work also became steadily more specialized. As more procedures were carried out by machines, a growing number of workers did small, repetitious tasks. There were important demands for considerable skill, but the semiskilled ranks grew most rapidly overall, particularly as the industrial revolution wore on. These semiskilled workers required training, but of a limited sort, and they had little sense of contributing much to a final product that they might see as their own. This was one reason many factory workers worried about their demeaned status in society—a pervasive theme around the world during industrialization.

The new pace and discipline, a lifetime of supervision by a separate management group, and a limited sense of achievement—these were the hallmarks of the factory work experience, and they differed from the standards recalled by workers from rural or craft backgrounds. Furthermore, they tended to extend beyond the factory to other work settings. Artisans, in particular, found themselves confronted by attempts to speed up work, even when the pertinent technology had not greatly changed. And they watched their employers, once fellow workers though also owners of the shop, turn into owners of small businesses. Many artisan masters increased their shop or crew size—construction work experienced this trend especially—and withdrew from the production process to concentrate on directing work and arranging sales. Many masters also stopped housing and feeding their employees as craft workers gradually became part of a permanent working class.

Workers experimented with various kinds of adjustment to the new work setting. Some liked it, at least for a time. Many workers expected to remain in the factories for only a few years, then to return to the countryside with some savings. A few workers enjoyed gaining new skills or were fascinated by new equipment, such as the powerful railroad locomotives. A number of workers profited from the possibility of upward mobility. Although only a handful of workers actually rose from rags to riches, becoming factory owners in their own right, a larger number were encouraged to acquire greater skill or to become foremen. Mobility was not, however, open to most workers, and many did not find the prospect relevant.

A larger number of workers sought ways to modify the new work regimen and regain some control. They wandered around the factory or stole or dirtied materials, regardless of what the rules said. Many took unauthorized days off after their earnings built up a bit. Employers who expected workers to maximize their pay found that most preferred to earn less but have more free time. Artisans especially, but also some factory workers, often took Mondays off to extend their Sunday leisure—French workers called the practice "holy Monday"—and defended it for some time. Workers changed jobs frequently, particularly when they were young, single, and in their prime earning years, believing they could improve conditions and gaining an illusion of choice and defiance. Not surprisingly, many new factories faced up to 90 percent turnover in a given year as the majority of workers indulged in transience around a core of more stable personnel.

Factories during the industrial revolution formed something of a battleground between the growing labor force, with its work habits and expectations, and the new factory owners, with their demands. The owners progressively managed to reshape work habits. Many noted that even the second generation of workers, born and bred in the factory shadow and often beginning work as children, were less intractable than their parents. Certainly, specific habits, such as returning to the countryside during harvest, declined rather quickly. But employers did not win the battle to their full satisfaction. One French owner complained that his workers put in only 72 percent of the effort that his factory rules required, and although the claim was self-interested, it may have approached the truth. Workers maintained a distinctive conception of work, and they did not give up this conception entirely.

With time, workers also began to develop another strategy: accepting changes in the work situation in return for higher pay. Skilled British workers—what some have called the "aristocracy of labor" in the factory economy—began to articulate this bargain by 1850. They (and workers later in other countries) essentially conceded that they could not control their labor in traditional ways. If they had to accept a faster pace and recurrent changes in techniques, they felt entitled in return to a share in the rewards in the form of higher pay and shorter hours. This "instrumentalist" approach—so called because workers were accepting their work less as an end in itself and more as an instrument for achieving a better life off the job—was one of the novel results of the factory environment.

A serious constraint on the work experience, particularly in the early decades of the industrial revolution, came from limitations in recreational opportunities. The new industrial cities were bleak places. Hours of work were very long, and many workers had neither time nor energy for much entertainment off the job. Also, employers and other officials directly attacked many popular leisure customs. The tradition of village festivals, which had dotted the preindustrial calendar for ordinary people, faded quickly, partly because workers lived and labored among strangers and could not replicate the festival setting, but even more because city governments actively opposed traditional processions as dangers to public order. Employers, too, in their desire for regular work habits, fined workers who took traditional days off, though this tactic was not always fully successful. Police forces, newly created in European and American cities, spent up to half their time trying to regulate popular leisure habits in the interests of maintaining what was now defined as public respectability and creating a more punctual, docile working population. Much worker leisure focused on the tavern. Drink provided an escape from the tedium of work life. Even more important, the neighborhood tavern offered workers a chance for some sociability as they struggled to form new ties in a difficult environment. In sum, the period was a low point in the history of popular leisure. Only when the factory system was well established did a greater range of opportunities develop that allowed workers to define more clearly a nonwork portion of their waking hours.

Forging the Industrial Family

The industrial revolution had an immense impact on family life. Observers in all the industrial societies began worrying about the fate of the family institution early on, in what has become a consistent theme in industrial history. By some measurements many families managed to survive the transformations surprisingly well. Rates of marriage, for example, went up in western Europe during the nineteenth century because more people could hope to support a family and because marriage seemed to offer important advantages. There was no simple equation between the industrial revolution and a decay in family life. Unquestionably, however, industrialization strained many families and forced virtually every group to redefine the basic functions the family was to serve.

The biggest jolt was the progressive removal of work from the home. Families were no longer centers of production, though the transition was gradual and remnants of older domestic activity persisted into the twentieth century. Families retained a host of economic functions, which made up one reason that marriage remained vital for so many people. But the functions were more diffuse than when the family had served as the fundamental economic unit, in which husbands and wives contributed tangibly to the family's subsistence and children began to assist the family economy from an early age.

Two visions of the industrial family developed in western Europe and the United States during the nineteenth century. Middle-class commentators increasingly saw the family as an emotional haven, an essentially spiritual refuge deliberately separate from the new stresses of economic life. Home was a sanctuary in which innocent children could be taught morality. Marriage was a loving partnership between two people who shared a pure affection that could rise above petty material concerns. As an American writer put it, "True love—that which abides—has its foundation in a knowledge and appreciation of moral qualities." The family ideal offered purpose and justification for the messy competition of the business world. This sanctification of the family was a statement of ideals, to be sure. But the interest in separating family qualities from industrial life had some genuine reality among the middle class, where couples sought emotional and moral satisfactions even as family economic functions declined. Many middle-class families became centers of sedate leisure, and women enhanced family time by playing the piano and reading uplifting stories aloud. Along with the leisure function came a new interest in family-oriented consumption, for the focus on the home easily translated into a desire for better and more comfortable furnishings and decorations. Thus emerged a growing market for a variety of manufactured products, such as wallpaper, furniture, and carpeting.

The second definition of the industrial family, common in the urban working class, stuck closer to tradition. The family remained an economic unit, though it no longer was the center of production. Families could serve new economic needs by providing supplementary wage earners, particularly children. They could provide additional earnings from home-based activities such as taking in boarders or doing laundry. A more extended family that linked several adult relatives, not just the married couple, could aid with loans to help the jobless ride through unemployment and provide information about available jobs.

Both visions of the functions of the family required substantial reshuffling of familial roles. The overarching need to adjust to the removal of production from the home created even greater pressures in the same direction. The task of the man of the family was to generate primary economic support. In working-class households other family members contributed some wages, but the breadwinning capacity of the husband/father was vital. A good family man was, above all, a man who fulfilled his obligation to provide. Women had to spend growing amounts of time organizing family consumption. In the middle class this meant running a fairly complex household, usually with the aid of an employed servant. In the working class this meant shopping and trying to stretch a tight budget simply to keep food on the table. Many a working-class housewife had to feed her husband all the meat she could afford because his stamina was so essential to the family's survival. Working-class wives also took on new responsibilities for maintaining contact with other relatives, for in contrast to more traditional families, in which the husbands' relatives loomed largest, the kinship ties of wives now predominated, if only because they had more opportunity than their husbands to socialize.

Women's work roles declined substantially during the industrial revolution in Western society. They might acquire other family responsibilities—like their role as moral arbiter in the middle-class household, or their maintenance of kin networks in the working class—but their economic importance dropped. Industrial technology attacked women's work early, as it displaced domestic spinning. Because men had, on balance, performed more skilled manufacturing tasks before the industrial revolution, their work was somewhat more sheltered from mechanical competition. Furthermore, when production did move outside the household setting, many families faced a genuine dilemma: How could child care, shopping, and housework be managed? The answer, generally, was to emphasize a new and sharp kind of labor division between men and women: men worked and earned while women took care of domestic duties.

The economic decline of women was long masked by their importance in the early factories, particularly the textile centers. Well over half the early labor force in cotton production, from New England to Belgium, was made up of women. Many employers argued that women's willingness to work for lower wages, their nimble fingers amid the machines, and their docility were essential for industrial success. But the absolute numbers of factory women were small compared with the hundreds of thousands of female domestic manufacturers being pushed out of work. Furthermore, most factory women were young, in their teens and early twenties, and intended to work for only a few years before marrying and quitting the factory scene. Finally, the percentage of women in the textile factories declined somewhat with time; the mechanization of weaving, for example, brought more men into the factories. An even sharper displacement process occurred in the business class. Many early factories maintained an older tradition of family management. Women kept accounts and supervised sales, while their husbands bought supplies and directed the labor force. Very quickly, however, with any success at all, the wife was moved off the premises to direct the domestic haven.

Within a generation, a clear pattern of gendered work developed throughout the industrial West. By the 1850s, most middle-class women did not hold jobs at any point in their lives. Only unmarried adult women could, with great difficulty, find respectable work as governesses for children. Working-class women commonly held jobs from late childhood until marriage in their early twenties; their earnings contributed significantly to the family economy. The majority worked as domestic servants, for there were not enough factory jobs to go around, but the contribution of young women to manufacturing remained considerable. After marriage a minority of women continued working, particularly in the textile centers. In general, however, a wife's working outside the home was taken as a sign of the husband's failure: drunkenness, disability, and death were the obvious culprits. Working-class women did earn in the home as babysitters, laundresses, or boardinghouse keepers; some even manufactured small items like artificial flowers. But they were outside the mainstream of wage-earning labor.

Men vaunted the new economic division between the genders. This was one principle on which businessmen, middle-class humanitarians, and many male workers readily agreed: respectable adult women should not work. An increasing emphasis on women as the frail sex followed from this categorization. Because the organizations of working-class men typically excluded women, a new gender basis for protest activity arose. Early labor unions regarded women as unreliable members—for were they not willing to accept low wages? Thus emerged the start of a vicious circle: because men's groups excluded women, many female workers turned against the budding unionism, further incensing the male leadership. Additionally, many male workers hoped to gain better wages for themselves by limiting competition from women. Hence, many worker leaders joined middle-class humanitarians in urging legal limits on women's hours of work, like the twelve-hour law passed in Britain in 1847, the avowed purpose of which was to protect women from strain, to safeguard the home, and to make a source of labor competition less desirable to employers. Indeed, this kind of legislation did contribute to the replacement of women in industrial jobs.

Some working-class men also assaulted or taunted women on the job, seeking to demonstrate by means of abusive sexual prowess a masculinity that was being challenged by loss of skills and authority in the factory. Abuse in the family almost certainly increased as well, founded on the new differential in economic power between men and women and men's effort to compensate for demeaning jobs by assertiveness in other areas. A British worker stated a common theme: "I found my wife was out when I returned home after closing hours [of the local tavern], so when she did come in, I knocked her down; surely a man can do a thing like that to his wife." Middle-class gender relations were less candid, though some factory owners sexually abused their female workers. But in the middle class also, assumptions of women's weakness and irrationality followed from their loss of economic place.

The challenge to traditional roles in the family economy extended to children, for whom the industrial revolution also ushered in a fundamental transformation. Children had always begun to work early in life, both in agriculture and in craft shops; child labor was not an invention of the industrial revolution. Both employers and workers found it normal for children to labor in the early factories—workers because of the pressing need for supplementary income and a sense that early work would prepare children with skills for later use in the traditional economy, and employers because they clearly benefited from the low wages children were given.

Child labor in the factories was not, however, merely traditional—a fact various groups began to realize early. Some children were mercilessly exploited, especially in British industrialization, and the pace of work put unusual strain on young workers. Accidents were common, particularly because children often worked as the machines were operating; cotton spinning had a category of laborers called "bobbin boys," who tied broken threads while the machine ran on. As the supervision of labor became more formal, child workers were increasingly separated from their parents and other relatives and placed under the direction of strangers. Their treatment might not have deteriorated—uncles and fathers often drove children hard—but parents became increasingly uncomfortable about this further disruption of tradition.

Improvements in machinery made child labor increasingly unnecessary. Larger textile machines and more automatic processes reduced the viability of very young workers. Such changes, combined with humanitarian concerns and workers' desire to regain family control, led to a series of child labor laws, initiated in Britain in 1833. These laws limited the use of children under twelve and reduced the hours even for the younger teenagers. The laws were vigorously debated; many manufacturers in particular resisted these challenges to their authority. Nevertheless, a growing number of middle-class reformers condemned the cruelty of industrial child labor. They also insisted that children needed time for schooling to prepare them more adequately for industrial work later, because on-the-job training was declining with the dilution of the craft traditions. Many workers agreed, seeking better treatment of their children and a reduction of low-wage competition. The British example finally helped spur child labor legislation elsewhere. France passed its first law in 1841, and the German states introduced similar measures. The early laws were not well enforced—France, for example, installed paid inspectors to regulate the use of children only in the 1870s—but the trend was clear.

In the long run, obviously, the chief impact of the industrial revolution was to dissociate children from productive labor. Middle-class families did not put their sons to work until their later teens; working-class children were increasingly held out until at least age twelve or fourteen. Children's roles were redefined by the growing belief that the task of childhood was education, not contribution to the family income. By the 1830s in the northern part of the United States, and by the 1870s in France and Germany, this belief had been converted to a legal mandate in the form of compulsory primary schooling. Children were removed from much potential abuse through this shift, but they also became more and more separated from the adult world and from direct contact with the roles they would have as adults. New concepts such as adolescence came into play in acknowledgment of the in-limbo stages of development between literal childhood and a life of work.

The redefinition of childhood obviously had further impact on the family itself. A new barrier emerged between fathers and their children, as the separation of work and family meant an increasing day-to-day gap between men and their offspring. Families also had to reconsider how many children to have. First in the middle class, then after about 1870 in the working class in western Europe and the United States, birthrates began to plummet. If children were no longer a resource but an expense—the cost of maintaining them and readying them for school actually went up—parents fairly quickly realized that a smaller family made stark economic sense. The industrial revolution thus led quite directly to a population revolution—called "the demographic transition"—in which the average family size shrank to unprecedented levels. By 1900, families in most groups throughout the Western world expected to have two to four children rather than the six to eight regarded as the norm just a century before. This change had further implications for adult sexuality and birth control, for the functions attached to motherhood, and for family interactions with the children themselves. The spiral of changes launched by industrialization required a host of subsequent adaptations.

The adjustments in family roles that the industrial revolution impelled varied in duration. The first impulse to heighten the division between men and women proved not to be permanent, though it lasted well into the twentieth century. Later phases in the evolution of industrial society in the West brought a subsequent transformation in women's employment that undid much of the differentiation introduced in the nineteenth century. The man/provider-woman/homemaker distinction lingered to an extent, but the constraints it imposed lessened in the late twentieth century. In contrast, the transformation of childhood steadily intensified as the length of schooling expanded and as the dissociation of children from extensive work commitment increased. On a larger scale still, the need persisted to redefine family functions—to find a basis for stability once the family stopped serving as an essential economic unit and to generate believable definitions of family success once production moved outside the home. Even though the industrial revolution in a strict sense was completed almost a century ago, many people in Western society today continue to grapple with the huge changes it introduced into personal life and private institutions.

DEBATE #6: *HAS THE INDUSTRIAL REVOLUTION FUNDAMENTALLY ALTERED GENDER ROLES?*

Agricultural societies almost always established and maintained patriarchal gender structures, emphasizing male superiority and restricting women's public roles. Has the industrial revolution basically changed this framework?

The answer is obviously complicated by the fact that most Western societies fairly quickly sought to emphasize gender differences in new ways as industrialization developed, and some of these changes still echo today, as in arguments that it would be better for families if women did not work and in unequal pay levels. How much difference is there between initial impact of industrialization on gender, and longer-term effects?

(*Continued*)

In what ways did industrial revolutions at least potentially undermine traditional, patriarchal arrangements—not only on the job but in the family? Does mechanization impact gender differences? To what extent do machines emasculate men, robbing them of traditional identities, and open new opportunities for women? What about the seemingly inevitable changes in marriage and parenthood?

Dealing with gender and industrialization is inevitably complicated by our own changing value judgments. For example, fairly early on Western industrial societies began introducing laws to limit women's work in factories. A British law in 1841 restricted women's hours of work to twelve, and Britain continued to pass special legislation on women up until 1937. Other early industrial societies introduced similar measures. Until the 1960s, most historians (male and female) regarded these laws as a sign of progress, though of course they noted that for many decades men were not as well protected and that women faced many burdens despite the regulation of work time. In light of current assumptions, however, shaped by the kind of "second wave" feminism that took shape a few decades ago, these laws look less like progress and more like discrimination, holding women back. Is it unwise to impose contemporary standards on the complexities of early industrialization? Would women have done better without these types of laws?

It is also important to note that the initial Western reaction to the gender/industrialization relationship does not describe patterns in some later industrializers like Russia. Indeed, Russian leaders would long point to the superiority of their industrial society in dealing with gender. How can the comparative dimension be factored in?

Is the industrial revolution, at least in the long run, also a gender revolution?

Further Reading: Louise Tilly and Joan Scott, *Women, Work and Family* (New York, 1984); Janet Greenlees, *Female Labour Power Women Workers' Influences on Business Practices in British and American Cotton Industries, 1780–1860* (Burlington, VT, 2007).

Social Divisions and Protest

The industrial revolution divided Western society in new ways. Several traditional social classes saw their prestige plummet. Aristocrats suffered because their economic status derived from landownership and because they disdained giving detailed attention to commercial methods and motives. Individual aristocrats, from eastern Germany through

Great Britain, benefited from increased agricultural sales or from direct involvement in setting up new mines or metallurgical plants. As a whole, however, the class declined as both its economic base and its culture were undercut by the industrial surge. A large part of the history of western Europe in the nineteenth and even the early twentieth centuries followed from the maneuverings of these beleaguered aristocrats to compensate for their economic anachronism. The tension between the established aristocracy and the industrial revolution had some constructive results: individual aristocrats participated in many efforts to regulate some of the worst abuses of industrial labor, combining humanitarianism with social-class resentment against greedy but successful manufacturers. One reason the United States lagged somewhat in labor regulation was the absence of an aristocratic counterpoise. But the decline of the aristocracy also had negative effects. German aristocrats, for example, used their political power to win tariffs and subsidies for their production of low-quality grains, a tactic that helped to keep food prices higher for the masses than they otherwise would have been.

Other established groups were gradually reduced by the ongoing revolution. Europe's peasantry shrank in relative numbers and in economic significance. The artisan class was progressively divided between the owners of small businesses and the wage laborers. Traditional economic values and settings declined along with these social classes, and the process often was painful.

The clearest direct result of the industrial revolution involved the expansion of a new, predominantly urban working class and middle class, spurred not only by the rise of factory owners and managers in industry but also by various professional groups such as engineers. Middle-class and working-class people shared some experiences during the industrial revolution. As already noted, both groups had to reconsider the roles of women and the appropriate size of the family, though they reached somewhat different conclusions and followed a different chronology. Anxieties about change and failure affected both groups as well.

But the middle class readily saw the industrial revolution as a source of social and personal progress. These individuals accepted the ethic of hard, intense work and saw it pay off in personal achievement. Even at the end of the nineteenth century, French industrial managers, graduates of schools that had already pushed them to work extremely hard, expected to work frequently on Sundays and holidays, focusing on little beyond the job—"cold to worldly distractions" was how one industrial engineer was described. Because they had succeeded in industrial life, many middle-class people were impatient with complaint and somewhat callous toward those below them economically and socially. This relied heavily on the notion that paying a wage discharged one's obligations to the labor force; if poverty existed, it resulted from poor work habits. The thinking was distinctly self-serving: Good workers could save enough to tide them and their families over bad times. The real causes of misery were excessive drinking—as one French engineer put it, workers "understood no pleasure without a drink in their hand"—and poor family habits, including breeding too many children. Any self-disciplined person could see the benefits of industrial life and use them to advantage.

Throughout the Western world, middle-class readers regaled themselves with wildly exaggerated stories of rags-to-riches success. Horatio Alger in the United States, Samuel Smiles in Britain, and many other popular fictional characters showed how hard work and technical ingenuity would bring a poor person to the summits of the business world in a single lifetime.

Both perceptions and reality differed greatly for the growing working class. For these people the industrial revolution meant, at best, some modest and uncertain gains in living standards, but it also entailed tremendous personal disruption, an alien system of work, and a tragic loss of control. Mobility was for most a chimera. Working harder might simply lead to wage cuts so that the benefits emerged as profit for the employer, not pay for the worker. Planning for the future made little sense given the frequent recessions. Many workers found it better to work their children hard (in the interests of acquiring a small home, for example) than to promote their education and advancement. Many workers opposed the idea of intense work designed to maximize productivity and turned to a concept—called by British laborers a "lump o' labor"—that a given day and a given amount of pay demand so much effort and no more. Not only the interests but many of the basic ideas of the working class clashed with those of the middle class.

A new kind of class division was thus endemic to the industrial revolution in Western society. Unlike the traditional owning and laboring groups—aristocrats and peasants—who had shared a number of ideas about what work and life were all about, many middle-class and working-class people disagreed fundamentally. Furthermore, and again unlike aristocrats and peasants, the two groups were in daily contact because one class now regularly supervised the other. The industrial revolution established the conditions for recurrent class conflict on both ideological and material grounds. A number of theorists were quick to define the contest. As early as the 1820s groups of utopian socialists, both in Europe and in the United States, urged the establishment of new, cooperative principles of work that would replace class divisions with a new harmony. (New Harmony was, in fact, the name of several utopian communities established by Europeans and Americans in the United States.) More important still was the ideology that Karl Marx began to develop in the 1840s. Marx described the inevitable conflict between profiteering owners and the workers who created the real value of manufactured goods. He forecast a future in which the working class would continue to expand yet become more miserable and finally turn against the exploiting class. Violent revolution would produce a new state, where government would seize the property owned by the capitalists and create a cooperative society in which voluntary concord and essential equality would prevail. Unlike most utopian socialists, Marx favored the industrial revolution—machines did create the potential for greater social wealth and leisure—but he identified fundamental flaws in the version of society being created under the capitalist system of private property and the competitive pursuit of profit, with its inevitable intensification of class warfare.

Frequent protest did indeed mark the decades of industrial revolution in Western society. Many workers reacted out of sheer misery. Food riots—a traditional protest form—erupted periodically in factory cities when workers attacked bakers for raising bread prices. Other violence was directed against competing workers. Philadelphia weavers rioted against Irish immigrants who seemed to threaten their jobs, and several associations of French workers, organized around different secret rituals, frequently engaged in pitched battles. A more innovative form of protest was the strike, which withdrew labor—the only real commodity of the working class—in order to press factory owners for better conditions. Early industrial strikes broke out particularly when employers attempted to reduce wages during economic slumps. In the textile town of Lowell, Massachusetts, for example, managers announced a 15 percent wage cut in 1834. Female factory workers gathered immediately, despite company attempts to dismiss the ringleaders. Protest songs showed that basic issues transcended pay to include the kind of hierarchy being established in factory life:

> The overseers they need not think
> Because they higher stand
> That they are better than the girls
> That work at their command.

Strike movements occasionally spilled over into larger organizational efforts. Many British textile workers and miners gathered in national campaigns to set up labor unions in the 1820s and early 1830s, hoping to use union organization to counteract the power of employers to set working conditions. On a more local level, craft workers, who were increasingly alienated from their employers, frequently set up local unions that would enable them, when the economy was booming and skilled workers were in short supply, to gain real bargaining power in improving wages and limiting hours of work.

Finally, workers sometimes reached out for a larger kind of protest against the industrial order itself. Some attacked machines; Luddite episodes in France in the 1820s were expressions of many of the same interests in restoring an older order of work that had sparked the original Luddism in Britain a decade earlier. Others sought political means of redressing the new inequality that marked the workplace. Many American workers participated fervently in demonstrations in the 1820s and 1830s, seeking broader political rights that would affirm their basic equality in society. A British movement called "Chartism" gained millions of signatures in campaigns to grant political rights to the working class; the goal was a combination of practical gains (new state sponsorship of worker education, for example) and symbolic equality. A variety of workers, in particular from the craft sectors, participated in the European revolutions of 1848. Some German artisans sought a restoration of the guild system and other restrictions on the industrial order. Craft and factory workers in Paris rallied for what they called the "organization of work," by which they meant some immediate state measures against widespread unemployment and a larger rollback of the increasing mechanization and inequality of work.

By 1848, a growing minority of artisans and factory workers, especially in France and Germany, were becoming interested in socialist ideas. Some saw in socialism an alternative to industrialization itself, hoping for small, worker-led cooperative production units. Various utopian socialist schemes attracted this kind of interest. Other workers, drawn to thinkers like Marx, accepted the benefits of machines but opposed the capitalist system. A worker-run state would purge capitalism and remove inequities, leading to unprecedented freedom and general prosperity. Government repression after the revolutions of 1848 reduced socialist agitation, but it would revive in the 1860s.

Yet, despite these efforts to express physical suffering and acute moral agony, none of the protest currents succeeded in deflecting the steady onrush of industrialization. The grand labor union schemes failed. The Chartist petitions were rejected. Worker participation in the revolutions of 1848 was brutally repressed. Government troops destroyed the partisans of a new organization of work in the bloody June Days uprising in Paris. A few months later Prussian forces crushed the craft workers in Berlin and other German centers.

Workers faced impossible hurdles in seeking to slow or redefine the basic trends of the industrial revolution. Protest organizations were illegal and remained so in most Western countries until the 1870s. Troops and police were readily rallied against worker efforts. Employers had great repressive power through their ability to fire strikers and sometimes evict them from their homes. Bargaining with small groups of craft workers was necessary because their skills earned them special attention, but employers zealously attacked larger groups whose agitation challenged their authority in industry. Workers themselves were divided. Male workers tended to ignore issues affecting women. Craft workers tended to highlight their skills and traditions, rejecting the unions whose members were the growing mass of factory hands. Many factory workers relied on individual adjustments that impeded collective action. A few workers concentrated on rising to supervisory posts.

A larger number changed jobs so often that they formed inadequate ties with any set of colleagues. That most factory workers labored among strangers complicated protest planning. When a growing number of workers were also immigrants—Irish workers in Britain and the United States, French Canadians in the United States, Belgians in northern France—the problem was compounded. Finally, the goals of workers were often diffuse. Their opposition to principles of industrial work might be fierce, but their alternatives were vague. Some advocated a restoration of guilds, others sought some utopian community, and others did not know quite what to pursue.

Working-class protest slowed for two decades after 1848. In France and Germany many leaders were arrested or exiled after the uprisings collapsed. Police forces became more adept at riot control. Many so-called labor aristocrats decided to concentrate on respectable unions that would bargain calmly for improvements and strike only as a last resort and then without violence. The New Model Unionism movement developed in Great Britain, featuring skill-specific unions of craft workers and skilled factory operatives like machine builders (called "engineers" in Britain). Craft unions also surfaced in Germany and France. The first wave of working-class struggle had ended; dying with it were the most sweeping efforts to call the factory system itself into question. A new current of protest, having as its objective important gains within the industrial system, began to take shape from the late 1860s onward in the United States as well as in Europe. New organizations sought the loyalties of craft and factory workers alike; the American Knights of Labor and the Marxist Social Democratic Party in Germany were two examples. Class warfare was about to enter a second major phase associated with the ongoing industrialization of the West.

A New Political and Cultural Context

The impact of the West's industrial revolution extended well beyond work and leisure, family life, and basic forms of protest. Governments changed, though responses to the revolution were only one component in the new political systems that emerged in Western nations during the nineteenth century. The extent of state involvement in economic policy varied, from noninterventionist Britain to the much more active German government. Nevertheless, all Western governments began to participate in new activities relating to railroad expansion, industrial tariff policies, and sponsorship of technical expositions. All governments also increased their role in education, providing a growing number of primary schools for the masses and a growing array of technical schools to enhance the training of experts. Police forces expanded, particularly in the cities. With the enactment of child labor laws, governments gradually became involved in the regulation of industrial working conditions, and this involvement, in turn, ultimately produced a specialist bureaucracy capable of monitoring compliance with labor and safety laws. Finally, governments began to respond to some of the special material problems highlighted by the industrial revolution and undertook new welfare functions. To be sure, Britain during the 1830s sought to make assistance to the poor less rather than more desirable, an approach reflective of middle-class interests in revising traditional notions of charity so that people would take responsibility for themselves. City governments, however, were already beginning to distribute some food to help the poor during economic recessions. Then, in the 1880s, the German government, relatively recently centralized, pioneered state-sponsored insurance to provide modest payments to aid the sick, the injured, and the elderly; the goal was simultaneously to reduce some of the starkest problems of working-class life and to defuse growing worker commitment to socialist political parties.

Clearly, the industrial revolution prompted a major redefinition of government functions, putting state agencies and policies into more direct contact with ordinary people than ever before.

Culture changed as well. Many artists and writers turned against the ugliness of the industrial setting. Romantic painters early in the nineteenth century concentrated on idyllic scenes of nature in part to contrast with the blight of factory cities. A bit later, many artists professed a withdrawal from their larger society, urging that art was for art's sake—a stance that was a radical alternative to industrial materialism. On the more popular level, the industrial revolution stimulated interest in secular rather than religious culture. Religion survived, and the intensity of certain strands, such as Methodism among British workers and Catholicism among many immigrant workers in the United States, formed a vital part of working-class life. On balance, however, the industrial revolution encouraged pursuit of material gains and belief in the power of science and technology. Many workers turned against established churches that seemed to be allied with conservative, propertied classes. Interest in socialism or other protest ideas gave some workers an alternative loyalty, which reflected and enhanced the secularization process. No single industrial culture emerged, but the industrial revolution had a substantial impact on beliefs and tastes.

Finally, as the industrial revolution solidified in western Europe and the United States during the nineteenth century, it inevitably altered the industrial countries' relationships with other parts of the world. The power of industrial technology fed new power politics on the international scene; an explosive round of imperialism was a direct consequence of the West's industrial expansion and internal competition. Even before the imperialist outburst, however, industrialization had cut into traditional economies from Mexico to Malaya and had forced a growing number of governments to take some first, halting steps toward replicating the West's economic Goliath. Internationally as well as socially, the industrial revolution served as a generator of additional change.

6 The Industrial Revolution outside the West

Before the 1870s no industrial revolution occurred outside Western society. The spread of industrialization within western Europe, although by no means automatic, followed from a host of shared economic, cultural, and political features as well as frequent and familiar contacts. The quick ascension of the United States was somewhat more surprising: the area was not European and had been far less developed economically during the eighteenth century. Nevertheless, extensive commercial experience in the northern states and the close mercantile and cultural ties with Britain gave the new nation advantages in its rapid imitation of Britain. Abundant natural resources and extensive investments from Europe kept the process going, joining the United States to the wider dynamic of industrialization in the nineteenth-century West.

Elsewhere, conditions did not permit an industrial revolution, an issue that must be explored in studying the international context for this first phase of the world's industrial experience. For almost a century, the West held a virtual monopoly in the industrial domain. Yet the West's industrial revolution did have substantial impact. It led to a number of pilot projects whereby initial machinery and factories were established under Western guidance. More important, it led to new Western demands on the world's economies that instigated significant change without industrialization; indeed, these demands in several cases made industrialization more difficult.

Pilot Projects: Russia

Russia's contact with the West's industrial revolution before the 1870s offers an important case study that explains why many societies could not quickly follow the lead of nations like France or the United States in imitating Britain. Yet Russia did introduce some new equipment for economic and military political reasons, and these initiatives did generate change—they were not mere window dressing.

More than most societies not directly part of Western civilization, Russia had special advantages in reacting to the West's industrial lead and special motivations for paying attention to this lead. Russia had been part of Europe's diplomatic network since about 1700. It saw itself as one of Europe's great powers, a participant in international conferences and military alliances. The country also had close cultural ties with western Europe, sharing in artistic styles and scientific developments—though Russian leadership had stepped back from cultural alignment because of the shock of the French Revolution in 1789 and subsequent political disorders in the West. Russian aristocrats and intellectuals routinely visited western Europe. Finally, Russia had prior experience in imitating Western technology and manufacturing: importation of Western metallurgy and shipbuilding had formed a major part of Peter the Great's reform program in the early eighteenth century—though the tsar had carefully avoided a full effort to imitate Western economic and social structure, for example, in protecting the system of serfdom.

Contacts of this sort explain why Russia began to receive an industrial outreach from the West within a few decades of the advent of the industrial revolution. British textile machinery was imported beginning in 1843. Ernst Knoop, a German immigrant to Britain who had clerked in a Manchester cotton factory, set himself up as export agent to the Russians. He also sponsored the British workers who installed the machinery in Russia and told any Russian entrepreneur brash enough to ask not simply for British models but for alterations or adaptations, saying "That is not your affair; in England they know better than you." Despite the snobbery, a number of Russian entrepreneurs set up small factories to produce cotton, aware that even in Russia's small urban market they could make a substantial profit by underselling traditionally manufactured cloth. Other factories were established directly by Britons.

Europeans and Americans were particularly active in responding to calls by the tsar's government for assistance in establishing railway and steamship lines. The first steamship appeared in Russia in 1815, and by 1820 a regular service ran along the Volga River. The first public railroad, joining St. Petersburg to the imperial residence in the suburbs, opened in 1837. In 1851 the first major line connected St. Petersburg and Moscow, along a remarkably straight route designed by Tsar Nicholas I himself. U.S. engineers were brought in, again by the government, to set up a railroad industry so that Russians could build their own locomotives and cars. George Whistler, the father of the painter James McNeill Whistler (and thus the husband of "Whistler's mother"), played an important role in the effort. He and some U.S. workers helped train Russians in the needed crafts, frequently complaining about their slovenly habits but appreciating their willingness to learn.

Russian imports of machinery increased rapidly; they were over thirty times as great in 1860 as they had been in 1825. Whereas in 1851 the nation manufactured only about half as many machines as it imported, by 1860 the equation was reversed, and the number of machine-building factories had quintupled (from nineteen to ninety-nine). The new cotton industry surged forward, most production being organized in factories using wage labor.

These were important changes. They revealed that some Russians were alert to the business advantages of Western methods and that some Westerners saw the great profits to be made by setting up shop in a huge but largely agricultural country. The role of the government was vital: the tsars used tax money to offer substantial premiums to Western entrepreneurs, who liked the adventure of dealing with the Russians but liked their superior profit margins even more.

But Russia did not really industrialize at this point. Modern industrial operations did not sufficiently dent established economic practices. The nation remained overwhelmingly agricultural. High-percentage increases in manufacturing proceeded from such a low base that they had little general impact. Several structural barriers impeded a genuine industrial revolution. Russia's cities had never boasted a manufacturing tradition; there were few artisans skilled even in preindustrial methods. Only by the 1860s and 1870s had cities grown enough for an artisan core to take shape—in printing, for example—and even then large numbers of foreigners (particularly Germans) had to be imported. Even more serious was the system of serfdom, which kept most Russians bound to agricultural estates. Although some free laborers could be found, most rural Russians could not legally leave their land, and their obligation to devote extensive work service to their lords' estates reduced their incentive even for agricultural production. Peter the Great had managed to adapt serfdom to a preindustrial metallurgical industry by allowing landlords to sell villages and the labor therein for the expansion of ironworks. But this mongrel system was not suitable for change on a grander scale, which is precisely what the industrial revolution entailed.

Furthermore, the West's industrial revolution, although it provided tangible examples for Russia to imitate, also produced pressures to develop more traditional sectors in lieu of structural change. The West's growing cities and rising prosperity claimed rising purchases of Russian timber, hemp, tallow, and, increasingly, grain. These were export goods that could be produced without new technology and without alteration in the existing labor system. Indeed, many landlords boosted the work-service obligations of the serfs in order to generate more grain production for sale to the West. The obvious temptation was to lock in an older economy—to respond to new opportunity by incremental changes within the traditional system and to maintain serfdom and the rural preponderance rather than to risk fundamental internal transformation.

The proof of Russia's lag showed in foreign trade. It rose, but rather modestly, posting a threefold increase between 1800 and 1860. Exports of raw materials approximately paid for the import of some machinery, factory-made goods from abroad, and a substantial volume of luxury products for the aristocracy. And the regions that participated most in the growing trade were not the tiny industrial enclaves (in St. Petersburg, Moscow, and the iron-rich Urals) but the wheat-growing areas of southern Russia, where even industrial pilot projects had yet to surface. Russian manufacturing exported nothing at all to the West, though it did find a few customers in Turkey, central Asia, and China.

Russia's lag showed most dramatically in a new military disadvantage. Peter the Great's main goal had been to keep Russian military production near enough to Western levels to remain competitive, with the huge Russian population added into the equation. This strategy now failed, for the West's industrial revolution changed the rules of the game. A war in 1854 pitting Russia against Britain and France led to Russia's defeat in its own backyard. The British and French objected to new Russian territorial gains (won at the expense of Turkey's Ottoman Empire), which had brought Russia greater access to the Black Sea. The battleground was the Crimea. Yet British and French steamships connected their armies more reliably with supplies and reinforcements from home than did Russia's ground transportation system, with its few railroads and mere 3,000 miles of first-class roads. And British and French industry could pour out more and higher-quality uniforms, guns, and munitions than traditional Russian manufacturing could hope to match. The Russians lost the Crimean War, surrendering their gains and swallowing their pride in 1856. Patchwork change had clearly proved insufficient to match the military, much less the economic, power that the industrial revolution had generated in the West.

After a brief interlude, the Russians digested the implications of their defeat and launched a period of basic structural reforms. The linchpin was the abolition of serfdom in 1861. Peasants were not entirely freed, and rural discontent persisted, but many workers could now leave the land, and the basis for a wage labor force was established. Other reforms focused on improving basic education and health, and although change in these areas was slow, it, too, set the foundation for a genuine commitment to industrialization. A real industrial revolution lay in the future, however. By the 1870s Russia's contact with industrialization had deepened its economic gap vis-à-vis the West, but it had also yielded a few interesting experiments with new methods and a growing realization of the need for further change.

Pilot Projects: Asia, Latin America, and Africa

Societies elsewhere in the world—those more removed from traditional ties to the West or more severely disadvantaged in the ties that did exist—saw even more limited industrial pilot projects during the West's industrialization period. The Middle East and India tried some early industrial imitation but largely failed—though not without generating some important economic change. Latin America also launched some revealingly limited technological change. Only eastern Asia and sub-Saharan Africa were largely untouched by any explicit industrial imitations until the late 1860s or beyond; they were too distant from European culture to venture a response more quickly.

Prior links with the West formed the key variable, as Russia's experience abundantly demonstrated. Societies that had regular familiarity with Western merchants and some preindustrial awareness of the West's steady commercial gains mounted some early experiments in industrialization. Whether they benefited as a result compared with areas that did nothing before the late nineteenth century might be debated.

India and the Middle East

One industrial initiative in India developed around Calcutta, where British colonial rule had centered since the East India Company founded the city in 1690. A Hindu Brahman family, the Tagores, established close ties with many British administrators. Without becoming British, they sponsored a number of efforts to revivify India, including new colleges and research centers. Dwarkanath Tagore controlled tax collection in part of Bengal, and early in the nineteenth century he used part of his profit to found a bank. He also bought up a variety of commercial landholdings and traditional manufacturing operations. In 1834 he joined with British capitalists to establish a diversified company that boasted holdings in mines (including the first Indian coal mine), sugar refineries, and some new textile factories; the equipment was imported from Britain. Tagore's dominant idea was a British-Indian economic and cultural collaboration that would revitalize his country. He enjoyed a high reputation in Europe and for a short time made a success of his economic initiatives. Tagore died on a trip abroad, and his financial empire declined soon after.

Other early industrial ventures included some factory cotton production, around Bombay, which among other things began to support training for some Indian textile engineers—ultimately reducing dependence on foreigners. By the 1870s cotton cloth made in Indian factories began to replace British goods in Chinese markets. And a British entrepreneur set up some metal production in southern India.

These first tastes of Indian industrialization were significant, but they brought few immediate results. The big news in India, even as Tagore launched his companies, was the rapid decline of traditional textiles under the bombardment of British factory competition; millions of Indian villagers were thrown out of work, even though some manual textile production would survive past 1900. Furthermore, relations between Britain and the Indian elite worsened after the mid-1830s as British officials sought a more active economic role and became more intolerant of Indian culture.

A further step in India's contact with the industrial revolution took shape in the 1850s, when the colonial government began to build a significant railroad network. The first passenger line opened in 1853. The principal result, however, was not industrial development but a further extension of commercial agriculture (production of cotton and other goods for export) and an intensification of British sales to India's interior. Coal mining did expand, but manufacturing continued to shrink. There was no hint of a full industrial revolution in India. Among other things, the British colonial government had no real interest in Indian industrial growth, even purchasing weapons from England rather than supporting the rich tradition of Indian arms manufacturing.

Imitation in the Middle East was somewhat more elaborate, in part because most of this region, including parts of North Africa, retained independence from European colonialism. Muslims had long disdained Western culture and Christianity, and Muslim leaders, including the rulers of the great Ottoman Empire, had been very slow to recognize the West's growing dynamism after the fifteenth century. Some Western medicine was imported, but technology was ignored. Only in the eighteenth century did this attitude begin, haltingly, to change. The Ottoman government imported a printing press from Europe and began discussing Western-style technical training, primarily in relationship to the military.

In 1798 a French force briefly seized Egypt, providing a vivid symbol of Europe's growing technical superiority. Later, an Ottoman governor, Muhammed Ali, seized Egypt from the imperial government and pursued an ambitious agenda of expansionism and modernization. Ali sponsored many changes in Egyptian society in imitation of Western patterns, including a new tax system and new kinds of schooling. He also destroyed the traditional Egyptian elite. The government encouraged agricultural production by sponsoring major irrigation projects and began to import elements of the industrial revolution from the West in the 1830s. English machinery and technicians were brought in to build textile factories, sugar refineries, paper mills, and weapons shops. Ali clearly contemplated a sweeping reform program in which industrialization would play a central role in making Egypt a powerhouse in the Middle East, equal to the European powers. Many of his plans worked well, but the industrialization effort failed. Egyptian factories could not, in the main, compete with European imports, and the initial experiments either failed or stagnated. More durable changes involved encouragement of the production of cash crops like sugar and cotton, which the government required in order to earn tax revenues to support its armies and its industrial imports. Growing concentration on cash crops also enriched a new group of Egyptian landlords and merchants. But the shift actually formalized Egypt's dependent position in the world economy, as European businesses and governments increasingly interfered with its internal economy. The Egyptian reaction to the West's industrial revolution, even more than the Russian response, was to generate massive economic redefinition without industrialization, a strategy that locked peasants into landlord control and made a manufacturing transformation at best a remote prospect.

Spurred by the West's example and by Ali, the Ottoman government itself set up some factories after 1839, importing equipment from Europe to manufacture textiles, paper, and guns. Coal and iron mining were encouraged. The government established a postal system in 1834, a telegraph system in 1855, and steamship building and the beginning of railway construction from 1866 onward. These changes increased the role of European traders and investors in the Ottoman economy. Again, the clearest result of improved transport and communication was a growing emphasis on the export of cash crops and minerals to pay for the necessary manufactured imports from Europe. An industrial example had been set, and as in Egypt, a growing, though still tiny, minority of Middle Easterners gained some factory experience, but no fundamental transformation occurred.

DEBATE #7: *ASSESSING DELAYS IN INDUSTRIALIZATION*

Reactions to industrialization outside the West during most of the nineteenth century raise a difficult and painful question, that has some applicability for the twentieth century as well: why did other regions innovate so slowly, despite the example of European power and success?

It is of course possible to argue that this is an inappropriate question: industrialization was very new, and it may not be at all surprising that most societies, many with limited prior connections to the West, did not immediately respond. The fact that, by the later twentieth century, much of the world was industrializing may support this approach.

But we have seen that some countries, like Russia and Egypt, did understand that some fundamental realignments were occurring, and yet had difficulties in creating effective strategic reactions. And other places, like China with its rich manufacturing tradition, did not seem to wake up to the new threat.

Aside from an understandable lag in reaction to developments both so new and so foreign, explanations logically divide into two main approaches (which may however be combined).

Approach #1: the power position of the West, combined with increased attempts to exploit other parts of the world, undercut

(*Continued*)

effective reactions. Industrialization gave Western governments and businessmen new ability to exploit the rest of the world, and they responded greedily. Their factories undercut local industries. Their companies pressed for greater access to resources and food exports, providing rewards for a few local intermediaries but pressing more and more workers into low-wage sectors. Western banks encouraged foreign governments to take out loans, crippling their independence. The cruelties of nineteenth-century imperialism, specific developments like the pressure to open China to opium imports, legitimately call attention to West's eagerness to exploit and extend its economic advantage.

Approach #2: granting the difficulty of quickly matching Western innovations, much of the explanation must rest with internal factors: with governments and aristocracies that discouraged business initiatives; with cultures that were hostile to innovation and often focused more on religious than on secular goals. In many cases, lack of widespread literacy was combined with other popular habits, for example, in resistance to a modern sense of time or punctuality, that would complicate effective participation in an industrial labor force.

What is the right balance to strike between these two approaches? For many contemporary students aware of the undeniable evils of imperialism, criticizing the West may be most palatable stance, but does it provide a full explanation? Is there a different balance between Western exploitation and local traditions depending on the particular region involved? Is it accurate to lump Muhammed Ali's failures, China's "century of humiliation" by the West, and Africa under imperialism under a single explanatory framework?

Further Reading: Michael Gasster, *China Struggles to Modernize* (New York, 1984); Immanuel Wallerstein, *World-Systems Analysis: An Introduction* (Durham, NC, 2004).

Latin America and Africa

Latin American nations, newly independent after 1820, had strong historical ties with western Europe. Although cultural links to Spain and Portugal did little for industrialization—these areas lagged within Europe—the broader European connection was solid, and Western merchants, led by the British, expanded commercial ties. Because of economic disorder following the independence wars, little imitation was possible until about 1850; more pressing problems of political consolidation commanded greatest attention. A steam-driven sugar mill was set up as early as 1815 in Brazil, however, and the number of engines, all imported, had risen to sixty-four by 1834. Coffee processors began acquiring steam equipment at this time also, and by 1852 the nation boasted 144 engines in all. Individual businessmen also established some cotton textile factories, meeting about 10 percent of national demand. These were interesting developments; they enhanced the operations Brazilians performed on some of their leading export crops, but they served largely to confirm Brazil's concentration on these sectors. The effort led neither to a more general industrial development focused on internal demand nor to a balanced set of innovations that would foster Brazilian industries in machine building and metallurgy. Nor did great interest arise on the part of the government at this point. As was true elsewhere, the difference between important technical imitation and a real industrial revolution, even if partly imitated, remained clear. Most Brazilian workers and most sectors of the Brazilian economy did not move toward industrialization. Change was real but came mainly in the form of a growing emphasis on export crops and raw materials.

Patterns elsewhere were even more diffuse. Cuba had first built a rail line in 1838 (from Havana to Guines), and other Latin American nations began to sponsor railroad development in the 1850s, using capital borrowed from European banks and equipment purchased from Europe. Twenty years later Brazil had 800 miles of track. Paraguay inaugurated steamship and rail lines after 1858; the nation also built Latin America's first iron foundry. The country was unique in the region in hiring British technicians using tax revenues, thus avoiding dependence on foreign loans. This promising start was cut short by loss in a war with Argentina, Uruguay, and Brazil. Chile inaugurated its first rail line in 1852 after some previous development of steam-powered flour mills, distilleries, sawmills, and coal mines. Mexico lagged in rail construction, with only 400 miles in 1876. And many other Latin American nations envisaged only short lines connecting seaports to the interior, not nationwide networks. Overall, early rail development helped spur mineral and food exports—the cash-crop economy—while increasing reliance on foreign banks and technologies.

Developments of preliminary industrial trappings—a few factories, a few railroads—did provide some relevant experience on which more intensive efforts could build (mainly after 1870). A few workers became factory hands and experienced some of the same upheaval as their Western counterparts in new routines and pressures on work pace. Many sought to limit their factory experience, leaving for other work or for the countryside after a short time; transience was a problem for much the same reasons as in the West: the clash with traditional work and leisure values. Some technical and business expertise also developed. By the 1850s a number of governments were clearly beginning to realize that some policy response to the industrial revolution was absolutely essential, lest Western influence become still more overwhelming. On balance, however, the principal results of very limited imitation tended to heighten the economic imbalance with western Europe, a disparity that made it easier to focus on nonindustrial exports. This, too, was a heritage for the future.

Sub-Saharan Africa, in contrast, avoided any significant contact with the industrial revolution until the late nineteenth century, ignoring or shunning even modest imitation. The region faced great economic changes after 1820, mainly because of the effective ending of the Atlantic slave trade. This reduced tremendous pressures on Africa's labor force (though the East African slave trade with the Middle East actually accelerated for a time), but it also cut the revenues available to West African merchants and governments. Some attempts were made to expand traditional industries, but there was no basis for major technical change, and no capital was available for venturing in new directions. African societies had long-standing experience with ironworking and other relevant technologies, and they had a substantial commercial tradition. Weakened governments and major economic dislocation, however, made quick response to Europe's transformation virtually impossible. Economic innovation focused on agriculture, particularly the area of vegetable oil production, where there were export possibilities that brought in some earnings to compensate for the loss of the slave trade.

China

Chinese industrial history has generated a huge scholarly literature in recent years because it has become increasingly clear that, in principle, an industrial revolution could have occurred in China almost as readily as in the West. Chinese production levels and living standards in the eighteenth century were essentially on the same levels as in places like Britain. The giant nation continued to introduce important technological changes, for example, in spinning. Also, until late in the nineteenth century, China was not significantly affected by competition from European-made factory goods. Rather, what seems to have happened was a focus in government policy on military defense, particularly against the threat of land-based invasions from potential enemies, such as Russia. Internal unrest and a major famine in the 1870s provided further distraction. Overall, the costs of maintaining an overextended empire forestalled additional economic innovation for a crucial century—the same century that saw western Europe now racing ahead. Furthermore, given a long tradition of hostility to most outside influence, the Chinese were slow to register opportunities that might result from imitation of Western technologies. All this added up to a situation in which Chinese leadership sought to deal with the growing evidence of Western industrialization mainly by avoiding it.

As a result, early steps toward industrial change depended on pressures from the outside. Britain, which acquired the port city of Hong

Kong in the 1840s, set up some initial factories in its new territory. No railroad was constructed until 1876, when a Western company built a line without government authorization. (The government's response was to tear up the line and let the remnants rust away.) The first successful railroad was opened in 1882 to carry coal from the Kaiping mines to a port. No textiles were produced by machinery in China proper until 1890, though some sluggish planning efforts preceded this project. In effect, until almost the end of the nineteenth century, the industrial revolution passed China by, partly, of course, because traditional manufacturing remained strong. The same held true for much of Southeast Asia and, until the 1860s, for Japan.

Restructuring the International Economy

Direct contact with industrial organization and technology formed a significant facet of world history during the middle decades of the nineteenth century, but it was overshadowed by a more general reorientation in international economic relationships as the West began to display its industrial muscle. Already the world's premier commercial society, the West, now including the United States, greatly increased its world role as a direct consequence of industrialization. Economic inequalities among major world societies accelerated, and some economies were durably redirected in response to Western pressure. The significance of international trade expanded as well, and several new institutions were created to facilitate this exchange.

The West's industrial revolution meant a flood of cheap manufactured goods directed toward world markets. Some societies could absorb new imports of textiles and metal products without facing massive dislocation. Russia, as we have seen, increased its imports, but its internal manufacturing sector, which included production of a wide array of goods in individual villages for local consumption, was sufficiently large that its overall manufacturing performance improved. Its relative economic position in the world declined because the country failed to keep up with Western gains, but its absolute levels held strong, aided by a modest amount of new technology in a few sectors.

The impact of Western imports in other cases was more disruptive. Latin American nations had gained their independence from Spain by 1820, but the attendant wars and internal strife inevitably weakened the domestic economies for a time. Simultaneously, the withdrawal of Spanish regulations had opened Latin American markets to massive imports of machine-made textiles from Britain. What had been a growing industry in the manual production of textiles at home was virtually crushed. Tens of thousands of people, urban and rural, were thrown out of work. Urban women were particularly hard hit as a major source of supplementary income disappeared. Poverty and prostitution increased rapidly as a result. Similar disruption of the traditional manufacturing sector occurred in India, where Britain had, even before outright industrialization, manipulated tariff regulations to discourage the once-thriving Indian cotton industry. These were cases in which the crippling of manufacturing thrust important economies backward toward fuller concentration on agriculture and mining.

The combination of Western industrial growth and the resultant disruption of the internal economies of many other areas steadily increased the inequalities in international economic performance. In 1800, Mexico's per capita income was about a third of that of Great Britain and half of that of the United States. Because of growing Western competition and internal disarray following the wars of independence, Mexican per capita national income actually fell until 1860; at that point it stood at a mere 13 percent and 14 percent respectively. It was a graphic illustration of the new balance sheet between industrializers and most of the nonindustrial regions.

Disruption and decline were not the whole story. The West's industrial revolution provided new economic opportunities for some regions outside the industrial orbit. A herding economy in the Mosul region of northeastern Turkey expanded rapidly in the mid-nineteenth century. Demand in the West for raw wool for its growing factories spurred a host of trade representatives to seek new sources of supply. Both the British and the French governments, through their local consular officials in this part of the Ottoman Empire, kept tabs on wool production, and Turkish merchants and urban authorities did the direct bargaining with the tribespeople. The British directly encouraged expansion of cotton production in Egypt because they sought a more reliable and cheaper source of supply than the southern United States offered, particularly after the disruptions of the U.S. Civil War. And of course opportunities to sell food to urban western Europe increased. Russia increased its grain exports, and other areas in east-central Europe, like Hungary, did the same. Latin American nations found new opportunities for export earnings by expanding their production of cash crops such as coffee, which added to existing commercial agriculture in sugar and tobacco. Brazil saw a massive increase in the production of rubber, a crop not native to the country and responsible for considerable environmental damage.

A commercialized export economy expanded steadily in a growing number of regions in Africa, Latin America, and Asia. Local merchants and landlords found substantial profits in their changing economies. They helped press a growing number of workers, in particular former peasants but also immigrants, to change their work habits in a fashion not entirely dissimilar to patterns developing in the West's factory centers. Latin American landlords, backed by liberal governments, pried land from traditional Indian or mestizo villagers in order to expand coffee and sugar production. They then attempted to alter the work habits of these new agricultural laborers, trying to reduce the time spent on festivals and drinking and urging more regular and efficient work routines and a new sense of time. Along with local labor, immigrant workers fueled this new commercial economy. Brazil and Argentina began to recruit growing numbers of Spaniards, Italians, and Portuguese. In Brazil the many immigrant workers directed to the coffee-growing regions helped to propel this sector to a commanding position in the world coffee trade by the 1880s—56 percent of the total market share. Workers from India and Southeast Asia were sent under long-term indenture contracts to work on commercial estates in the Caribbean region and elsewhere.

Changes of this sort were vitally important, and they brought important profit opportunities to several local groups, merchants and landowners in particular, but also some other elements like the herders in Mosul. At the same time, however, these shifts increased vulnerabilities on the world market, and they most definitely failed to generate any sort of economic parity with the industrial West. The simple fact was that the goods exported to the West—agricultural and mineral products almost exclusively—were not as valuable as the manufactured products that the West exported. The terms of trade favored the West. Furthermore, Western capitalists controlled many operations directly. They ran the shipping and most of the international trading companies. With their greater capital resources, they bought many mines and estates outright. For example, Westerners, including entrepreneurs from the United States, owned most railroads, banks, and mines in Colombia and Chile by the late nineteenth century.

The fundamental imbalance showed in many ways. Cash-crop and mineral exports involved little new technology, except in the transport systems used to get them out of their originating countries. These sectors were much more dependent than Western factories on very cheap labor, often kept in semi-servitude by indenture contracts or company stores. The new working class being created around the world had some features in common with the workers of the industrial West, but it was far more miserable.

Local governments and businesses, seeking to develop their export opportunities and in some cases sincerely hoping to generate more diversified economies, frequently went into debt. The construction of modern port and rail facilities in Latin America, though vital to expanding the export sector, cost more than the exports easily paid for. The solution was to borrow from eager, capital-rich banks in western Europe and the United States; the result was a growing indebtedness that made additional investment more difficult and that invited Western interference, including military threats on occasion, in basic economic policy.

Impoverished workers and growing foreign debt made it difficult to imagine a real industrial revolution, though by the late nineteenth century some Latin American leaders saw industrialization as a valid goal.

Latin America became a classic area of economic dependence, importing manufactured products and luxury goods from the West while trying desperately to stay afloat with low-cost exports.

Industrialization did have some role in a potentially positive development in nineteenth-century labor history: the abolition of the leading forms of slavery and serfdom, particularly in the Americas but ultimately on a global scale. Western reformers had pushed for abolition out of genuine humanitarian sentiment, though also, perhaps, to distract factory workers in their own societies from their miseries by calling attention to more degraded labor elsewhere. It was also true that slavery was too inflexible for certain economic operations now that world population growth ensured an adequate labor supply in the Americas. Ex-slaves welcomed their freedom. But low wages and more subtle forms of servitude, through debts to company stores, for example, constrained the impact of change in all the regions selling raw materials to the West. Work in the economies producing cheap export goods was typically unprotected and miserable—even in the southern United States.

Economic change created new gaps between Asia and Europe. How could an industrial revolution even be contemplated in nineteenth-century India? Even though India, unlike the Latin American nations, was still ruled from Europe—by an English government that had no interest in creating a new industrial rival—the result of Western industrialization had impoverished large stretches of the nation. Cotton manufacturing had drastically declined by 1833, with millions of Indian women and men, domestic spinners and weavers, thrown out of work by machines half a world away. The peasant economy became increasingly dependent, and it harbored unprecedented numbers of unemployed people. In the 1850s the British turned from a concentration primarily on sales to India to a new, parallel interest in cheap supplies. The railroads were introduced in the 1850s not only to facilitate the sale of British goods but also to encourage the production of raw materials such as jute and cotton. As commercial estates expanded with the aid of huge reserves of cheap labor, India became increasingly locked into a dependent position in the Western-dominated world economy.

Western industrialization further exacerbated the military imbalance of world power. Even earlier, Western armaments had ensured predominance on the seas and had allowed Europeans to establish colonies in a number of ports and on islands such as Java, Borneo, and the Philippines. With industrialization, Western forces gained even greater maritime potency by virtue of larger ships and bigger cannons; new advantages in land wars accrued as well, with factory-produced weapons. In the 1830s this growing military superiority, plus the insatiable thirst for new markets and sources of supply, began to usher in a new age of European expansion. To be sure, the Americas were now largely independent, though economic penetration continued nevertheless. But

Africa, Asia, and the Pacific Islands offered almost irresistible allure. It became obvious that Polynesian islands such as Hawaii, discovered by Europeans in the eighteenth century, could be made over into additional sources of sugar and other goods; it was logical to take over the government as well. China, long proudly resistant to Europe's economic overtures, was forced open during the Opium Wars that began in 1839. European gunboats, backed by small forces of well-armed soldiers, did the trick. The carving of North Africa began. France seized Algeria beginning in the late 1820s. Britain and France disputed control of Egypt. In 1869 a French industrial concern completed construction of the vital Suez Canal, a major improvement in access to India and the rest of Asia, but it was the British who gained effective control in the 1870s. By this time also, European expeditions in Southeast Asia and particularly in sub-Saharan Africa were adding huge swaths of territory to Western empires old and new.

The industrial revolution directly prompted this last and greatest imperialist outburst from the West. Steamships enabled Europeans to sail upriver, giving them new entry into China and particularly into the previously unnavigable rivers of central Africa. Mass-produced repeating rifles provided new advantages in gunnery, and by the 1860s early versions of the machine gun offered even more deadly fire. When this basic muscle was added to the quest for secure markets and cheap supplies, the age of industrial imperialism was at hand. Completion of imperialist conquest and full economic exploitation of new holdings, particularly in Africa, came only after 1880, but the stage was clearly set as a direct result of the first phase of the industrial revolution. And the consequence of the new imperialism, in turn, was an even greater economic and political imbalance in the world at large.

Structural imbalance intensified Western scorn for peoples who seemed incapable of mastering advanced technology and modern organization. A variety of factors fed growing racism, but a rooted belief that performance in economy and technology measured the worth of a society played a growing role.

Finally, the first decades of industrialization's entry onto the world stage brought the West's initial attempts to create an international infrastructure. Forming part of this structure were international trading companies and shipping lines, which were expanded by the technology of the steamship. After 1850, telegraph lines were laid across the Atlantic and then to other regions outside the West; this development was vital to the transmission of commercial as well as political information. Also in the 1850s and 1860s international conferences (effectively confined to the Western powers) began to discuss world postal arrangements and worked to standardize some agreements on patents and commercial law. The world postal union, established in 1878, greatly facilitated international mailings; international copyright rules on works of literature and art were set in 1886. The globe was shrinking because of industrial technology and new levels of world trade, and unprecedented arrangements to reduce disputes and ease communication both reflected and furthered this contraction. Western control of the initial agreements was inevitable and ensured their application in other parts of the world as well; some of the consequences in terms of spreading new ideas and technical knowledge ultimately led in less predictable directions.

The Two Faces of International Impact

The most important short-term global result of Europe's hold on industrialization was the growing economic imbalance between the small number of industrial powers and most of the rest of the world. Beyond that, more and more regions had to alter their economies to produce low-cost goods for export to the industrial centers, hoping to stay afloat in a global economy that was out of their control. Important residues of these changes persist today, in continued imbalances and economic dependence. Even countries now achieving industrial success remember their period of weakness, and often push even harder in consequence.

But there was another outcome as well. The small industrial steps taken in Brazil, Russia, and India were the seeds from which later industrialization would sprout. They did not generate a full process of change at the time; they could not prevent growing weakness, including reliance on cheap exports. But from the standpoint of the twenty-first century, when countries such as Brazil and India loom as the world's next economic giants, the quiet first steps may have been more important, historically, than the brief but vivid exacerbation of inequality. Both patterns—the short-lived global hierarchy with the industrial West on top, and the small first moves toward industrial change in key nations in Asia and Latin America—mark the first stage of the industrial revolution in the world arena.

The first stage was certainly unique in one respect, for the growing imbalance created by the West's exploitation of its industrial lead would not be permanent. More striking modifications of the West's industrial monopoly would help set up the second phase of the industrial revolution in world history.

Part 2

The Second Phase, 1880–1950

The New International Cast

7 The Industrial Revolution Changes Stripes, 1880–1950

Three major developments defined the second phase of the industrial revolution in world history from the late nineteenth century to the mid-twentieth: industrialization outside the West, redefinition of the West's own industrial economy, and growing involvement of nonindustrial parts of the world, along with an overall intensification of international impact. This phase began to take shape in the 1870s and 1880s, though no firm markers divided it from previous trends. Several Western societies, including Germany and the United States, were still actively completing their basic transformation, becoming more fully urban and committed to the factory system as their manufacturing power presented new challenges to Britain, the established industrial power. Large numbers of new workers, fresh from the countryside, still poured into German and, particularly, U.S. factories, experiencing much of the same shock of adjustment to a new work life that earlier arrivals had faced a few decades before. But even as many trends continued, the phenomenon was changing shape (see Map 7.1).

Second-Phase Trends

In terms of long-range impact, international developments were particularly striking. Several major new players began to industrialize by the 1880s and were the first clearly non-Western societies to undergo an industrial revolution. Russia's industrial revolution had a massive impact on global power politics. Japan's revolution altered world diplomacy as well and ultimately had an even greater effect on the international balance of economic power. The focal point of the second phase of the industrial revolution involved the transformation of these two key nations. By 1950, when their revolutionary phases were essentially complete, neither had matched the West's ongoing industrial strength. But a key measure of these later industrial revolutions—like those of the United States and Germany before—was the capacity of these societies to grow more rapidly than the established industrial powers. Later industrial revolutions could allow newcomers to begin to catch up, and this feature marked many aspects of world history from 1880 to the present day.

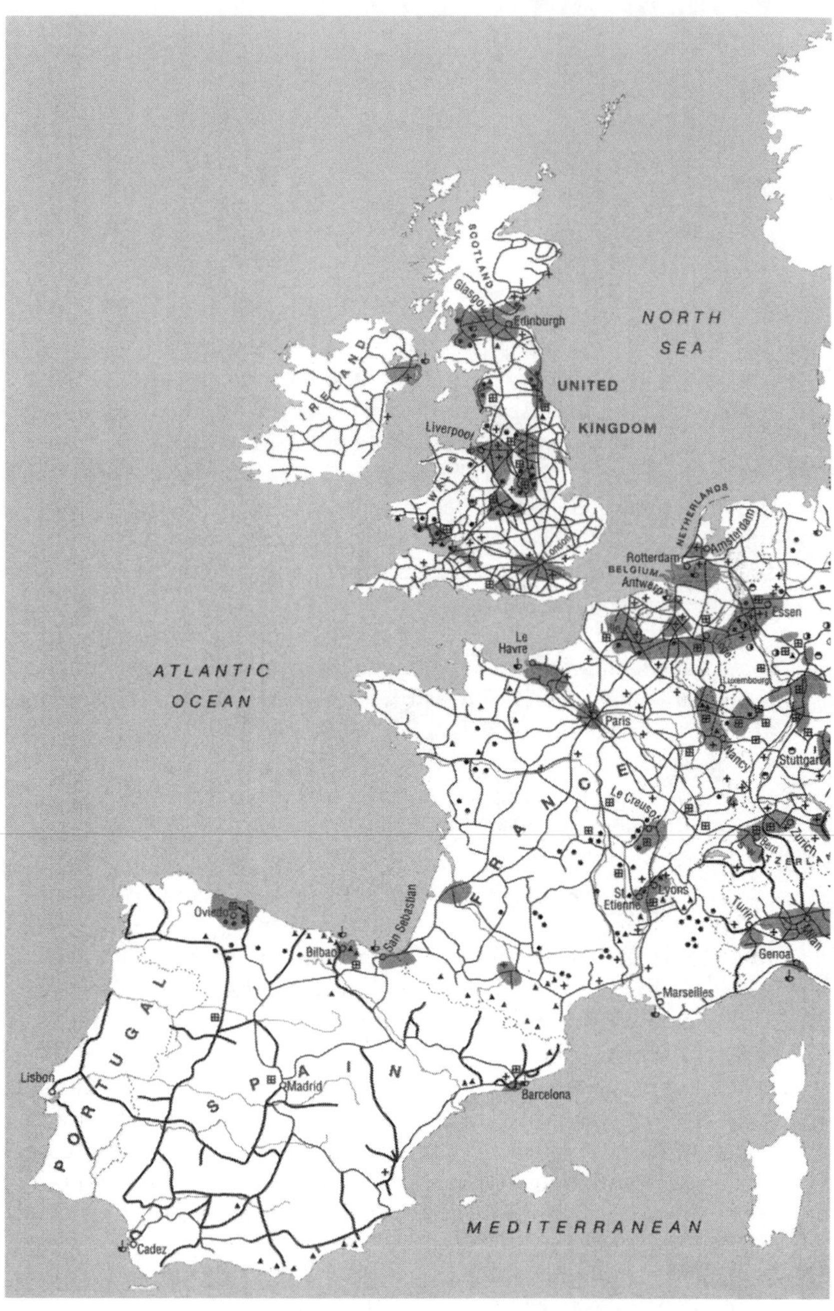

Map 7.1 The Industrial Revolution in Europe, 1870–1914.

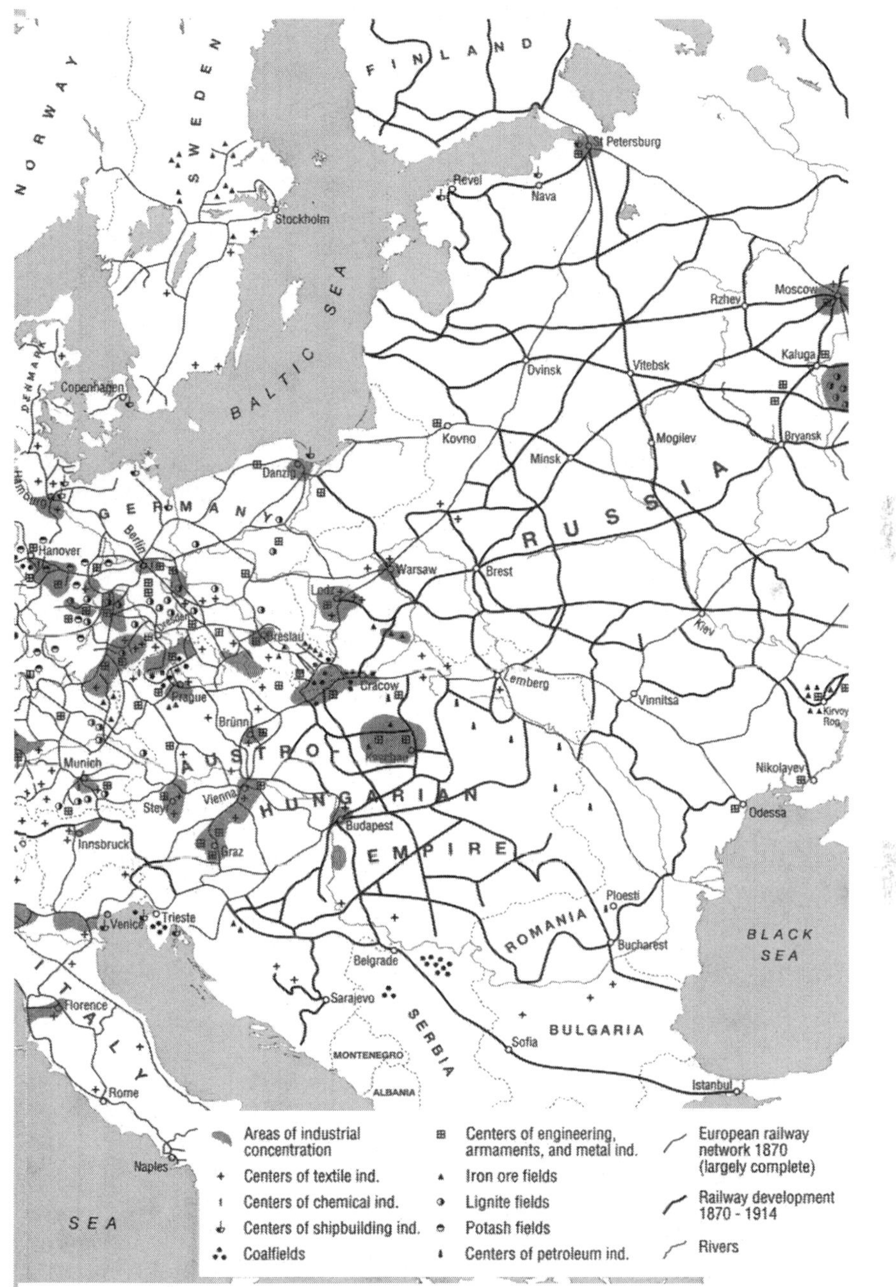

Map 7.1 (Continued).

Map 7.2 The Industrial Revolution in the Wider World by 1929.

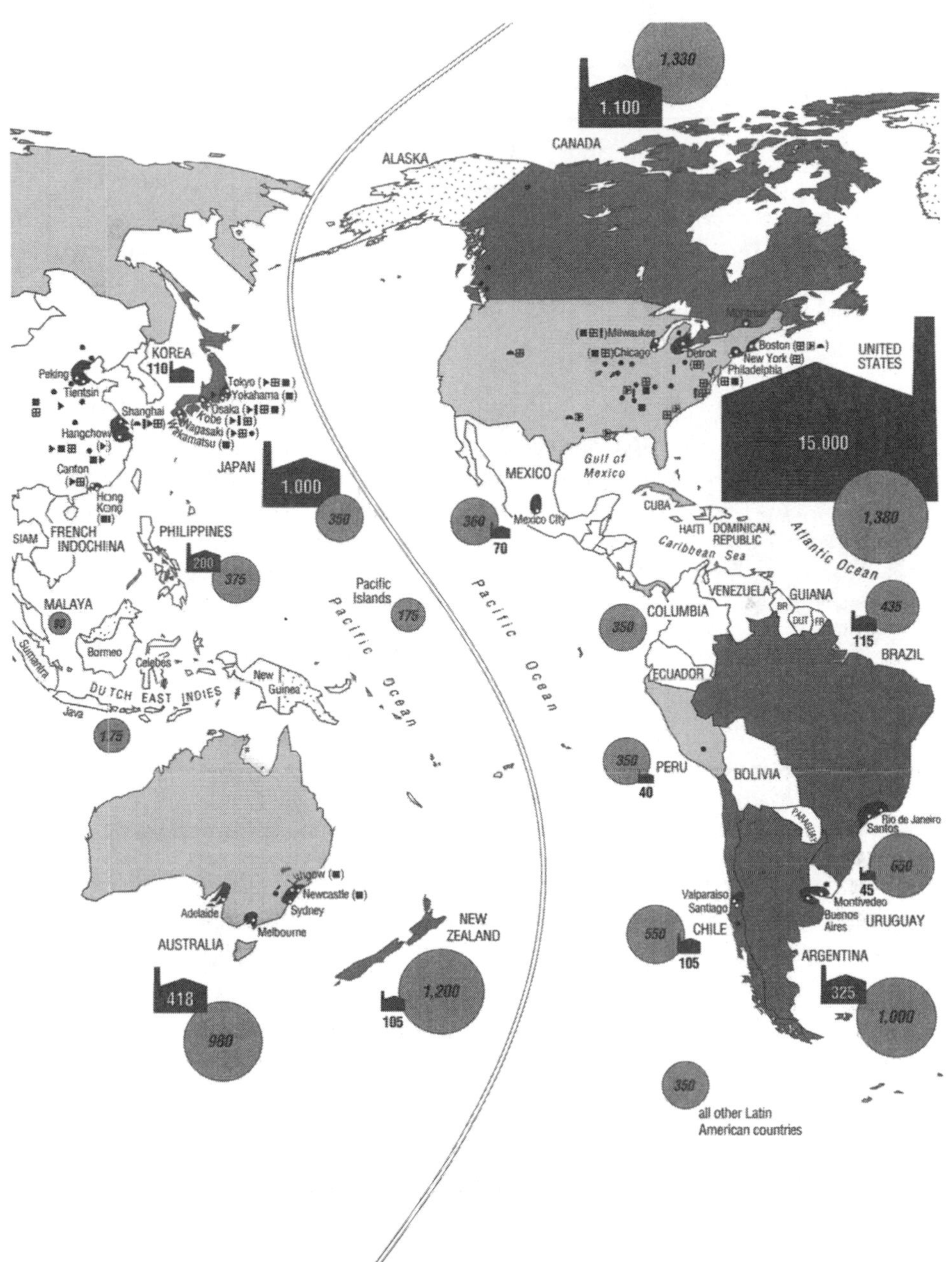

Map 7.2 (Continued).

While industrial revolutions in Japan and Russia constituted the most striking additions to the roster of transformed economies, several British dominions industrialized as well. Canadian industrialization, which had many features in common with the process in the United States, began in the 1870s, and by 1950 had propelled the country to a ranking among the world's ten leading industrial powers. Like the United States, Canada would emphasize continued production of agricultural and mineral products, but with advanced technologies and relatively high wages, along with factory output. Also important, though still overshadowed by Western industrial dominance, a number of societies, including India and Brazil, enhanced their fledgling industrial sectors during this period, which would ultimately prepare a more rapid process of change in the later twentieth century.

Expansion of the international roster of industrial societies and also limitations to this expansion require renewed attention to causation: Why were some newcomers able to advance but not the world as a whole? There are other questions as well: How did these later industrial revolutions compare with earlier Western versions and with each other? Later industrial revolutions had many elements in common with the basic phenomenon in the West. They involved massive technological and organizational change and huge shifts in the experience of work and the nature of family life. But later industrial revolutions also revealed the effect of different chronology: the newcomers had to find the means to compensate for initial backwardness and to react to the relatively advanced industrial forms already established elsewhere. Finally, later industrializations outside the West reflected different preindustrial cultures and institutions. They emerged from somewhat different strengths and weaknesses and took distinctive forms in the process. Most obviously, Japan fairly deliberately sought to industrialize without becoming fully Western, either in culture or in politics. These challenging issues must be addressed in interpretations of the second phase of the world's industrial revolution.

Other changes surfaced during the same decades. The West, in important ways, began to transform its own transformation. The late nineteenth century is sometimes referred to as a "second industrial revolution" in western Europe and the United States, and although the term may be misleading—many fundamental trends simply intensified—it invites inquiry into the recurrent shifts in direction that the industrial revolution set in motion even when most of the basic features were already established. A changing industrial West also affected the rest of the world, including, of course, the areas now industrializing for the first time, making it even harder—though not impossible—to catch up.

The third development involved a partial redefinition of how the industrial revolution affected areas not involved in the process directly. Here, too, many prior trends persisted. New levels of Western economic exploitation of resources in Africa mirrored many patterns visible earlier in Asia and Latin America. Economies in Latin America and several parts of Asia expanded food and mineral production to serve industrial areas. It also became apparent that some societies might develop small, low-cost industrial sectors without really changing global patterns of economic inequality. Certain kinds of factories, with cheap labor and modest technology, often provided an additional source of export goods to the West, without yet clearly leading to a wide-ranging industrial sector.

Certainly, the global impact of the industrial revolution intensified, and this had widespread effects. New kinds of international economic crises emerged, most notably the Great Depression of the 1920s and 1930s. The industrialization of conflict emerged on an international scale in the world wars of 1914–1918 and 1939–1945. Industrial impact on the environment gained greater visibility and prompted some new concern. While the initial industrial revolution had generated local environmental impacts, with smoky cities and fouled waterways, the late nineteenth century saw more extensive damage, and not just in the industrial centers. The industrial revolution was entering a new world phase, often in troubling ways.

DEBATE #8: *HOW MANY INDUSTRIAL REVOLUTIONS IN ONE PLACE?*

Many observers today talk about four industrial revolutions, including of course the original one based on steam power. There is the second industrial revolution, further defined later in this section but focused strongly on heavy industry and new sectors like chemicals, along with use of petroleum and electricity. A third is sometimes staked out for the later twentieth century, involving greater use of scientific research but also growing automation and digitization. And some now claim we are entering a fourth revolution, based on cyber systems, more robotics, (hopefully) more clean energy, and so on.

Is the idea of four revolutions within basically two centuries useful, or does it confuse any sense of what the industrial revolution is about in the first place? It is clear that industrialization generates periodic surges of further technological change, and each surge will displace workers and earlier industrial centers, causing distress. By the later twentieth century, the "third" revolution was dramatically reducing the number of workers in manufacturing, while rapidly expanding the service and information technology sectors—potentially a particularly dramatic change. On the other hand, basic contours of industrial society persist even

(*Continued*)

today—including urbanization, low birth rates—the list of continuities is considerable.

Confusing the issue still further is that fact the newly industrialized societies—like Japan and Russia during the "second" upheaval—would combine some of the features of the most advanced systems—like big factories in the Russian case, or rapid electrification in Japan—with some of the growing pains of initial industrialization. India today participates strongly in the "third" phase even while just beginning to industrialize extensively in other respects (for instance, in retaining a large agricultural population).

Were the effects of "later" industrial revolutions, in societies that had already industrialized, as substantial as the initial experience? What are some good ways to evaluate this comparison?

Is each of the four revolutions equally transformative? How does the "second" compare to the "third," and are there really fundamental differences between #3 and #4, or are we risking falling victim to hyperbole?

Granted the obvious and important fact that societies, once industrial, don't hold still, is the idea of multiple revolutions useful or confusing in dealing with the results? And just to add to the mix: some observers, instead of talking about multiple revolutions, have tried to define a "postindustrial" economy and society. Again, what kind of case can be made, and what are the arguments against? How much have societies like Japan or the United States moved away from the basic patterns established by the initial industrial revolution?

Further Reading: Jeremy Rifkin, *The Third Industrial Revolution: How Lateral Power Is Transforming Energy, the Economy and the World* (London, 2011); Daniel Bell, *The Coming of Post-industrial Society* (New York, 1984); James Hull, "The Second Industrial Revolution: History of a Concept," *Storia della storiografia* 36 (1999), 81–90.

Why Japan and Russia?

The engagement of two nations outside the West in the industrial process was the most striking new element in the world's industrial panoply by the late nineteenth century. Why were Japan and Russia and not others able to participate? Neither country shared many of the factors that had prompted the West's industrial revolution a half century earlier. Further, neither country had such obvious advantages in approaching industrialization that their lead over several other areas should be viewed as automatic. Japan, particularly—long isolated from much international trade and lacking crucial resources for an industrial economy, notably coal—would not have been on any 1850 observer's list of the countries most likely to succeed industrially. Thus, it is essential to undertake a new assessment from the standpoints of both causation and comparison.

Areas held as outright colonies were not likely candidates for full-fledged industrial revolutions in the late nineteenth and early twentieth centuries. Although significant factory industry existed in India by 1900, the dominant thrust of British colonial control emphasized the maintenance of India as a source of cheap goods and a market for Britain's manufacturing. While British industry was distracted during World War I, new tariffs protected Indian industries and a significant metallurgical sector emerged, with new sales opportunities. Still, the Indian economy continued to emphasize low-cost exports for the most part, while also sending streams of emigrant workers into the labor market from the Caribbean to southern Africa. The colonial exploitation of Southeast Asia and Africa aimed even more single-mindedly at preserving the imbalance between hinterland and industrial homeland. Portugal, for example, began pressing its colony of Mozambique to produce cotton for the developing Portuguese factories; this pressure came at the expense of balanced agricultural practice and secure local food supplies and reduced any chance of expanding an urban manufacturing base in this part of southern Africa. Widespread population growth in many colonial territories also provided so much ready, cheap labor that extensive mechanization could be avoided. To reduce labor costs even further, some European companies in Africa used essentially forced recruitment into labor gangs. Many Asians migrated as indentured servants to several different regions.

Latin America, though no longer literally colonial, was similarly dominated by the industrial West, including the United States. Heavy foreign indebtedness, lack of local capital and entrepreneurial drive, cheap labor, and a long tradition of the production of specialty foods and raw materials for export to the West blocked most of Latin America from a full leap toward an industrial economy. Foreign ownership of key sectors, such as the copper mines of Chile, further inhibited the emergence of a corresponding manufacturing sector. Significant change occurred, including the expansion of some industry, but full industrialization was not yet possible.

China and the Ottoman Middle East raise different analytical problems. These two societies were not held as colonies, though European seizures cut into the territory of both states. Both areas, though China in particular, continued to be beset by political weakness and ongoing population pressure during the nineteenth century, both of which inhibited their response. Both China and the Ottoman Empire remained suspicious of outside example and consequently, even while recognizing the West's growing industrial power, tended to concentrate on modest, piecemeal reforms. Both states, for example, sought to improve their military technology and organization without constructing an industrial foundation. Their economies changed but were increasingly penetrated by Western business interests. Outright industrialization proved to be an elusive goal.

What did Japan and Russia offer that made them more successful second-wave industrializers? Russia had extensive coal and iron holdings. Also, its prior contacts with the West could be put to good use. Many Russian leaders knew Western languages (particularly French), and although Westerners frequently thought of Russia as economically backward, they did include the nation in their frame of reference. Japan had an extensive merchant class, though it was based entirely on internal trade. It had developed an important urban culture and a productive, market-oriented agricultural sector, which one scholar has described as an "industrious revolution" before the mid-nineteenth century. The Japanese population also boasted a high rate of literacy, thanks to Confucian-led programs in the seventeenth and eighteenth centuries. Although Japanese education had to be rethought extensively in direct preparation for the industrial revolution, a relevant tradition and substantial skills were already available.

Japan and Russia also shared some very general characteristics that differentiated them from most other societies outside the West in the late nineteenth century. Neither was a colony, and neither had an economy that had become dominated by Western-directed commercial patterns. The Japanese had virtually no foreign trade, though a vital contact with Dutch merchants was preserved at the port of Nagasaki; during the previous two centuries Japan had focused strongly on internal commercial growth. Russia's trade ties were more extensive; Western merchants controlled most of the trade with the West, and the terms of trade were potentially to Russia's disadvantage in their emphasis on cheap labor and unprocessed goods exported in return for finished products from western Europe. But Russia's internal economy was not totally skewed toward this trade—in contrast, for example, with the economies of parts of Latin America. In sum, Japan and Russia brought considerable economic independence to their encounters with the industrializing West.

Both countries also had reasonably strong governments. Russian tsars claimed vast authority, and they ran an active government with considerable confidence. Recurrent territorial expansion, particularly at Turkey's expense, revealed Russian vigor well into the nineteenth century. Administrative efficiency was on the rise (along with enhancement of a repressive political police). Japan's shogunate had introduced an active bureaucracy during the seventeenth and eighteenth centuries, preserving feudalism in name but supplementing it with a reasonably effective central state. The shogunate had lost some of its vitality by the early nineteenth century, and it lacked a consistently secure tax base, but its effectiveness was considerable even so. Compared with China's political deterioration—the ability of its imperial administration to command loyalty was plummeting by the mid-nineteenth century—Japan and Russia were both in good political shape. Not surprisingly, government directives in each instance helped set the industrialization process in motion.

Russia and Japan also knew from experience the salutary results of well-planned imitation of other societies. Russia, of course, had been selectively learning from the West for several centuries and even before that had borrowed from the Byzantine Empire. Japan had gained greatly from earlier imitation of China. It had renounced its willingness to copy—by establishing an isolationist policy early in the seventeenth century, after a flurry of active interest in sixteenth-century Western merchants and missionaries—but it had a tradition of successful borrowing that its leaders could recall. Further, contact with Dutch merchants kept interest alive within a small group capable of pushing for a change in direction. The so-called Dutch school of trained translators began to press for more elaborate contacts with Western culture by the late eighteenth century, pointing particularly to Japan's inferiority in science and medicine, and attacking Confucian traditionalism. This debate did not by itself reorient Japanese culture, but it provided some precedent for later change. The basic point was clear: both Russia and Japan knew that learning from outsiders could be profitable and need not overwhelm their own distinctive values.

For all their advantages, neither Russia nor Japan spontaneously decided upon an industrial revolution in the nineteenth century. As late as the 1850s both had regimes that would have preferred to maintain the status quo. But Western assertiveness abruptly removed that option. The British–French victory over Russia in the Crimean War in the 1850s convinced the tsarist regime, after only brief hesitation, that it had to sponsor bolder initiatives lest its independent foreign policy be hopelessly compromised and the country become captive to superior Western economic and military strength. During the same years, Japan faced an even more direct threat to its internal control. In 1853 a U.S. fleet sailed into Edo Bay, near Tokyo, demanding that Japan open its markets to trade—or face bombardment. Commodore Matthew Perry's return to Japan in 1854 was bolstered by a visit from the British fleet. Japan had no choice but to open two additional ports to foreign trade. Britain, Russia, and Holland quickly won additional trading rights, and Western merchant enclaves were set up that operated under their own laws. Several bombardments of Japanese forts by Western naval vessels drove the point home further. Japan's isolation had become impossible; the only issue was whether the country could master the terms of change.

Both Russia and Japan responded to the challenge by making explicit commitments to major reforms, and these reforms quickly included the early stages of industrialization. Intent alone was not enough, to be sure, as many countries later discovered in the twentieth century. Both Russia and Japan faced immense strain and no small amount of internal disagreement in implementing their fundamental decision to meet the Western challenge by adopting key features of the Western economy. Nevertheless, conscious policy choice formed the first step. Japan and Russia soon took different paths as they followed up their choice—indeed, Japan tested its industrial achievement in outright war with Russia in 1904. Developments in the two countries conjoined, however, to break the West's industrial monopoly, and this break, in turn, marked the emergence of a decisive new phase in the world's industrial history.

The international expansion of industrialization hardly passed without notice. Various Western observers, noting Japan's new economic and military strength by 1900, began talking of a new "yellow peril" and of still more industrial competition. On the surface, however, it was the continuation and even enhancement of Western industrial strength that continued to dominate, drawing attention to the new round of innovations and to the continued rise of the United States and Germany. The second phase of industrial history still saw the world's population divided between a minority of outright industrializers and a majority of societies strongly shaped by the interests of the industrial powers. Only a few hints of greater latitude opened up, aside from Japanese and Russian advances.

The second industrial period lasted until after World War II. It cut across a host of significant events, including the world wars and the depression. Of course industrial patterns were affected by the big events, and helped shape them in turn. But a decisive shift to yet another broader, international phase and yet another redefinition of what characterizes the most advanced industrial economies would emerge only in the later twentieth century. For several decades from the later nineteenth century onward, Western economic strength, now further refined, jostled with the addition of the new entrants in shaping the industrial history of the world.

8 The Industrial Revolution in Russia

Russia and Japan, beginning their industrial revolutions at least a half century behind most of the West, had to meet a number of special challenges. They had to acquire Western technical expertise. Outright invention was not necessary, but the process of imitation in societies not accustomed to such rapid technological change was at least as demanding. Both societies had to make reasonably explicit decisions about how to further but also how to control the process of foreign imitation. These new industrializers had to provide capital; this had been true in the West as well, but for societies that had scanty preindustrial capital resources, trying to catch up imposed special burdens. Both societies had to provide motivation. Neither Russia nor Japan had a large preindustrial merchant class that was burning to set up factories; Russia had little merchant class at all. The two nations proved capable of producing vigorous entrepreneurs and managers, but government played a greater role in launching the process in the first place. Certainly the state's ability to guarantee loans and to invest tax resources was crucial to early industrialization, given the distinctive conditions of Russia and Japan. In broad outline, industrializing as a latecomer required more explicit policy decisions and a more careful shepherding than had been necessary in the West in the early nineteenth century. This was true in the two great industrial revolutions that took shape around 1900; it would be true later for post-1950 industrializers as well.

Both Russia and Japan moved to industrialization in stages. A tentative experimental phase—which Russia had already experienced to an extent before 1870—included larger reforms that helped make way for economic change. This preliminary period was followed by more rapid growth in a society still overwhelmingly agricultural. Russia and Japan had well-developed industrial sectors by the early twentieth century, but both lagged well behind the West. Both also needed some serious structural adjustments before they could move further, and these were introduced in the 1920s and 1930s, as the specific characteristics of the Japanese and Russian versions of an industrial society were more clearly delineated.

Finally, both nations had to cope with extraordinarily rapid change because their industrial revolutions had to be combined with a wider set of reforms, all initially introduced in response to the West's growing military and economic power. In this aspect, too, latecomer industrialization displayed some features not present, at least in such intensity, in the West itself.

Yet Russia and Japan took very different industrial paths, and many of the differences survive to the present day. The diversity resulted from preindustrial traditions, including the structure of rural society, from varied kinds of contacts with the West, and from distinctions in the way the industrial revolution was initiated. Most obviously, Japan was able to industrialize without massive collective unrest, whereas Russia became the only society to date to experience full-fledged political and social revolution after the industrialization process was well under way. Japan's industrial revolution followed a somewhat more consistent style than Russia's, though there was substantial revision of Japanese policy in the 1920s. Russia tried two formats, one before its 1917 upheaval and one after; only in combination did they produce a genuine, if unusual, industrial economy.

Early Industrialization: Before the Revolution

The Russian reform period that began in the 1860s brought limited freedom for the serfs and produced a host of other political changes, some of which involved economic policy. Government budget procedures were regularized, and a state bank was created in 1866 to centralize credit and finance. New law codes adopted soon thereafter standardized commercial law and facilitated business operations. Government policy also encouraged more foreign investment.

Russia's reform era ended in 1881, after which highly conservative, even repressive, policies went into effect in most quarters. The Ministry of Finance, however, maintained a commitment to change. The resultant tension was no small factor in the ultimately revolutionary impact of Russian industrialization, as Russia tried to combine industrial dynamics with a stagnant political context and, even then, had to contend with resistant conservatives who objected to the social danger of continued industrialization. Nevertheless, vigorous economic policies were sufficient to propel growth despite the political recalcitrance. The minister of finance during the 1890s, Serge Witte, was a genuine economic planner of a type that rarely had been seen in Russian bureaucracy at the time. Witte devoted his great talents to the stabilization of Russian finance. Among his goals for the country were the acquisition of a considerable gold reserve, the rapid growth of railroads, and the promotion of heavy industry.

Witte's background was as a railroad official, and he advocated rapid additions to the Russian network. Mileage doubled between 1895 and 1905, the additions including almost the whole of a line

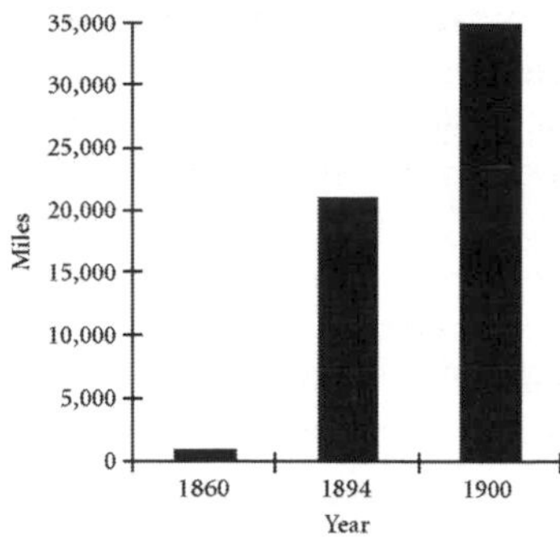

Figure 8.1 Railroads in Russia, 1860–1900.

across Siberia that opened the vast resources of this region to industrial use (see Figure 8.1). In 1860 Russia had boasted less than 700 miles of railroads, but by 1894 the total was already 21,000 miles, and by 1900 it had soared to over 36,000. Private companies, working under government concessions, did much of the work, but after 1880, state control increased. Most new lines were built and operated directly by the government. Some private lines were purchased; the rest were strictly supervised. The Russian railroad boom encouraged fuller utilization of Russia's considerable resources in coal and iron and of its extensive production of wool. The boom also directly induced increased output in heavy industry to create the rails and rolling stock and to provide the necessary fuel. As in the United States, railroad development became integral to the further advance of industry.

The Russian government assumed an unusually extensive role in investment banking. Private banks, though they were virtually unknown before the reform period, did exist; the first corporate commercial bank was founded in 1864, and the number of institutions grew steadily thereafter. In addition, the government operated not only a state bank for commerce but also a number of other special credit institutions. Regularization of Russia's monetary system was another crucial government contribution. Russia's paper money had been nearly worthless in foreign exchange during the 1850s. Gradually the gold backing of Russian currency was increased, so the ruble became more stable and more open to international trade. Further, as part of improvements in commercial law, the government facilitated the formation of joint stock companies, or corporations. Only eighty corporations had existed in the whole of Russia before 1860. From 1861 to 1873, 3,547 new companies were formed, and this trend accelerated in later decades. Finally, the government enacted high tariffs on industrial products, protecting nascent Russian industry and encouraging still more manufacturing.

A key ingredient in Russia's early industrial revolution, along with increasingly focused government planning and railway development, was foreign entrepreneurship, from which Russia gained much-needed capital and technical knowledge. Yet the Russian government retained enough power over foreign entrepreneurs to limit the sort of outright exploitation that marked Western operations in many parts of Africa and Latin America. The line between foreign participation and foreign intrusion was a fine one, but on the whole Russia's industrialization process benefited from considerable openness in the early decades.

West European industrialists were quite aware of Russia's vast potential. The huge population, though largely impoverished, presented a tempting market to target. Still more obviously, the rich reserves of coal and iron begged for rapid exploitation. There were clear profits to be made, potentially at higher yield rates than in the more crowded industrial sectors of western Europe. Foreign enthusiasm about Russia rivalled that about the United States, another huge nation heavily dependent on European capital. But the smaller business class in Russia made the foreign presence there even more noticeable and its role in guiding industrialization even greater.

Foreign capital was absolutely essential to Russian industry. It constituted at least 20 percent of all capital invested before the 1890s and then began to expand even further, accounting by 1914 for a full 47 percent of all corporate investment in the nation. Because the government was not actually pumping much funding directly into industry—even railroad construction commanded only about 5 percent of the total budget—the West European component effectively compensated both for Russia's poverty and for the state's commitment to wide-ranging military and bureaucratic programs that strained its resources. France, Belgium, Germany, and, after only a slight lag, Britain all developed extensive interests in Russian industry.

West European activities spread across Russia's industrial map. A number of French and Belgian metallurgical firms set up Russian branches. A French steelmaker, Eugene Verdie, established a steel company in Russian Poland in 1877 as an extension of his French firm, and then, with a St. Petersburg ironmaster of Scottish origin, formed a Russian company in order to supply 30,000 tons of steel rails to the Russian government. Another branch of the same operation provided metal to a navy shipyard. A variety of Belgian firms, including the Cockerill firms, operated in specialty steels, encouraged in part by their desire to penetrate the Russian market and break through the nation's high tariffs. Allgemeine Elektrizitaets Gesellschaft and Siemens, the two great German electrical firms, dominated the same industry in Russia through wholly owned subsidiaries; the Westinghouse company of Pittsburgh, Pennsylvania, operated as well, through a French subsidiary. German companies were also active in textiles, sometimes in partnership with Russians or Poles.

French and Belgians joined the textiles parade as well; Company of Myszkov, for example, was founded with in 1911 and claimed an improved process for treating ducing rayon. Western subsidiaries in public utilities, c ucts, medicinal drugs, explosives, and even mirrors range of Russian industrialization. Finally, Western en a number of operations in Russia, for example in ship confident assumption in their superiority in technological knowledge could place real burdens on Russian workers—though in some cases a handful of skilled Western workers helped ease the transition.

Not surprisingly, failures and disputes in Russia were common, and some foreigners pulled out after extensive problems with their workforce or clashes with local property owners, deriving from the foreigners' unfamiliarity with Russian property law. Foreign managers were themselves not always of top quality, and mistakes in equipment installation or business calculations were frequent. A French cotton manufacturer described a pattern in a 1903 report to his firm:

> The workers showed themselves hostile to all progress, and never succeeded in reaching normal production. We vainly tried to introduce piece work to stimulate their ardor; yet this only increased their dissatisfaction. We returned badly disillusioned, if not completely disheartened ... Shortly after our return a strike followed persistent agitation and after three weeks rioting broke out. The mills were stormed three times by the rioters ... The entire French and Belgian personnel fled for their lives, and left the government to protect the mills.

In fact, the company did prosper modestly, after hiring a Russian managing director, expanding on the basis of reinvestment of profits. Its decision to turn to an increasingly Russian staff was part of a general trend after 1900 toward reliance on local management. This trend was furthered by a growing number of contests with government officials. Russian bureaucrats, keenly aware of the need to keep powerful foreign interests under control, frequently blocked company merger plans or demanded that discontented workers be granted concessions for the sake of public order. Foreign investments continued until 1914, and government encouragement persisted as well—hence the steadily increasing percentage of capital investment provided from abroad. The process not only brought money and technology to Russia but also contributed to the expansion of a pool of Russian managers and technical experts.

A number of individual Russians seized on new industrial opportunities from the 1860s onward. Certain groups, such as the Old Believers, a religious minority that had clung to older Orthodox traditions and gained state disfavor in the eighteenth century, provided disproportionate bers of entrepreneurs. As in western Europe earlier, minority status as often a spur to seeking achievement in this new field. A surprising number of former peasants launched industrial operations; some even got started before their emancipation in 1861. This group was particularly important in setting up small textile operations in spinning, weaving, and cloth printing.

Russian industrial growth increased steadily and then had its first extraordinary spurt in the 1890s. A worldwide recession early in the twentieth century slowed development, but growth resumed at a rapid pace from 1908 until the outbreak of World War I.

Exploitation of Russia's iron mines and coalfields began slowly in the 1850s, pioneered by individual Western industrialists. Coal deposits in the Donets district of south Russia had been discovered late in the eighteenth century, but there was no extensive mining until after 1850—the effective beginning of a modern coal-mining industry in the nation. Oil was discovered in the Caucasus around 1870, and a growing petroleum industry took shape soon thereafter. By 1900, Russia was second in the world in production of petroleum, supplying about one-fourth the total. Heavy industry in general grew rapidly. During the 1890s the number of industrial companies grew by a full 216 percent. Oil production rose 132 percent; pig iron 190 percent; coal 131 percent; manufactured iron 116 percent; and cotton manufactures 76 percent. Overall industrial growth rates, held at 6 percent per year during the late 1880s, soared to 8 percent during the 1890s and then resumed a 6 percent level after 1908.

International comparisons show a similar Russian story. Russia's overall industrial growth rate between 1860 and 1913 matched that of the United States (though it started from a lower base). By this measure, the country expanded almost twice as fast as Germany in the same years, over three times as fast as France, and over four times as fast as Britain—though again the starting point was much lower. In a host of industries, Russia had become the fourth or fifth largest producer by the early twentieth century; it ranked fourth, for example, in steel output. To be sure, these achievements are somewhat misleading, given the unusual size of Russia's population; per capita industrial production was less impressive, and it included some technologically backward sectors as well as relatively advanced heavy industry. Even textiles, however, showed the usual symptoms of industrialization: increasing mechanization, greater use of cotton (Russia increased its homegrown cotton supplies accordingly by encouraging production in central Asia), and decreasing average prices for manufactured goods.

By 1914 there was no question that Russia had passed through a first industrialization phase. It had concentrated particularly on heavy industry because of native resources, foreign interest, and the government's military needs. The military emphasis helped generate a substantial number of large factories and encouraged relative neglect of the consumer-goods sector despite the growth in textiles and other light industry. Technology development had also been impressive, in part because of the input from abroad. Expansion of the number of trained Russian engineers had helped maintain the pace of change; the availability of skilled workers grew, though it lagged somewhat behind the levels in western Europe and the United States. Russia's previous lack of an extensive artisanal tradition limited the available manufacturing skills. The factory labor force expanded rapidly. Skilled workers accumulated in St. Petersburg and Moscow, and there were old hands in metallurgy in the Urals region. The rapidly growing Donets Basin, however, seemed chronically short of workers of any sort and of skilled operatives in particular. Some foreign companies compensated by importing the most up-to-date equipment that could be operated by semiskilled workers, but the problem of matching a labor force to industrialization—a considerable hurdle in any industrial revolution—was greater than average in Russia. There was progress in this quarter nevertheless. The number of experienced miners and metallurgists more than doubled in the Donets area in the decade after 1904. The emergence of St. Petersburg and Moscow as multifaceted manufacturing centers that combined factories and smaller crafts was another sign of Russia's move toward the type of industrial economy common in the West. Overall, rapid urbanization rates paralleled the spurts of industrial growth around 1900 and resembled the patterns in Germany or Britain a half century or more before.

Russian involvement in World War I, however, strained industrial capacity. Russia was attempting to fight an established industrial power—Germany—by using advantages in numbers to compensate for less abundant war material. The war not only interrupted Russia's industrial growth but also ripped its social fabric, bringing political revolution and, after this further dislocation, a radically altered framework for the resumption of industrialization.

DEBATE #9: *COMPARING INDUSTRIAL REVOLUTIONS*

The spread of industrialization raises one obvious problem, for scholars and students alike: since industrial revolutions by definition share many common elements, like new technology and growth of a working class, why not simply say "Russia and Japan industrialized" and leave it at that. Why go into another set of details?

There are two responses, though it really is true that once you know one industrial revolution, you know something about all the others. First, a focus only on Britain or the West simply

(*Continued*)

shortchanges crucial parts of the world, as if their industrial histories are somehow inferior just because they came later. At a time when Asian industrializations, most obviously, are shattering previous patterns of world power, a largely Western approach is indefensible—again, even if some of the framework is familiar.

But the second response deserves more explicit debate: while all major industrial revolutions were similar, each had a distinctive set of characteristics. How can industrial revolutions be compared? What are some of the leading differentiators?

Certain factors may be fairly obvious: for example, the fact that in "latecomer" industrializations governments played a leading role. Other comparisons are more subtle, but intriguing: what kinds of preindustrial cultures would affect attitudes of the new middle and working classes? (Example: compare industrializations that occur in a partially Confucian framework with those in the West.) What about prior levels of commercialization (a key factor in the Russian context, compared say to Britain or Japan)?

Then there is the undeniable fact that, for various reasons, each industrial revolution had a certain flavor of its own: different balances between heavy industry and consumer goods production; different labor policies in the leading companies; different degrees of reliance on exports, and so on. Some of these distinctions emerged early on, others would take shape only as the industrial revolution matured, as in the 1920s in Russia and Japan. Why and how was Russian industrialization distinctive, compared to other cases both before and after? This is the question that, by definition, cannot be answered simply through knowledge of the standard components.

Further Reading: Alexander Gerschenkron, *Economic Backwardness in Historical Perspective* (Cambridge, 1962); Dmitry Verkotorov, *The Industrial Revolution of Stalin* (Moscow, 2006).

Social Impacts: Industrialization and Revolution

Russia is the only nation to have experienced massive political revolution after starting a successful industrialization effort. Its working class played major roles both in the Revolution of 1905 and then in the great uprising of 1917, in which workers' councils, or soviets, formed the backbone of the revolutionary effort. Russian workers became unusually successful at expressing moral outrage. Despite the substantial internal differences in most of the industrial working groups—urban artisans, workers in heavy industry, more isolated coal miners, and less skilled and often largely female labor forces in textile factories—a sense of class consciousness emerged by the early twentieth century. Workers in many Western countries had felt some of the grievances the Russian workers articulated; there had been a labor ingredient in the revolutions of 1848 in France and Germany. But industrial workers as part of a sustained, successful revolutionary effort constituted a first.

The rapidly growing Russian working class faced many material problems. Child labor was widely used and abused in some cotton factories. The emancipation of the serfs, combined with substantial population growth, unleashed a flood of potential urban workers, and wages in many early factories were quite low in consequence. Moscow industrialists, slower to mechanize than their colleagues in St. Petersburg but able to draw from a densely populated rural hinterland, compensated for their shortcomings through cheap labor. Factories in the Urals, where traditional heavy industry had already attracted many workers, paid low wages. To be sure, places that had to recruit new workers, like St. Petersburg or the growing Donets area, offered high pay at least to a skilled minority. Even in these regions, however, conditions were worsened by employer imposition of company stores or shoddy worker barracks. Housing conditions in factory centers were typically crowded, and a stark iron bedstead with a straw mattress was the only furnishing. Housing in the rapidly growing cities deteriorated as construction failed to keep pace, and foul sanitary conditions added to worker woes. Many employers reduced pay by arbitrary fines. Safety conditions were dreadful; textile factories were dusty, chemical works filled with noxious fumes. Hours of work were long, ranging up to fourteen a day. Family life was often disrupted. Many male workers left their families back in their villages as they wandered in search of temporary factory work. Considerable use of women in textiles and other industries cut into family time. Sexual habits loosened. Workers with some experience in the factories began to engage more commonly in sexual intercourse before marriage, and working-class attitudes toward sexuality—particularly for men—relaxed traditional peasant standards. Finally, there was the new work regime itself to come to terms with. Russian peasant labor had not been joyous, but the pace and regimen of the factories came as a tremendous shock.

Workers reacted to their new environment in many ways. Changing jobs and leaving factory centers altogether to return to the countryside were endemic. Many companies worried about the long absence of workers for four or five months in the summer. Drinking, already a popular pastime among the Russian peasant masses, often increased in a group that had few other regular leisure outlets.

The unusual foreign involvement in Russian industrialization played some role in stimulating grievances beyond the levels prevailing earlier in the industrializing West. The privileges of foreign workers often drew attack. In 1900, after a mutual name-calling incident, two hundred workers burned all the buildings and possessions of sixty thoroughly frightened Belgian workers at a glass factory. Western managers were an obvious target for some labor leaders, who associated foreignness with exploitation.

The speed of Russia's industrial development placed many former peasants in large and technically sophisticated factories, without the benefit of any intermediate stage of smaller plants and less demanding equipment. In 1900, when Germany had only 14 percent of its manufacturing labor force in factories with over 500 people, Russia had 34 percent—and nearly a quarter of all Russian workers labored in factories with over 1,000 people. The likelihood of disorientation and alienation in these settings was particularly great for workers who came from the highly personalized context of village life. To be sure, earlier Russian factories had created a minority of workers with substantial industrial experience, and a second or even third generation of factory hands existed by 1900. But the confrontation with novelty was unusually great and helped to propel even badly paid transient workers toward a broader class consciousness.

The speed factor affected craft workers as well. Growing factories and cities meant a need for new numbers of urban bakers, construction workers, and printers. Some of these groups, such as printers in St. Petersburg, briefly displayed some of the preindustrial cohesion characteristic of artisans earlier in the West, in part because some of them had been recruited from Germany. Journeymen and masters gathered for joint ceremonies such as feasts and gift giving and expressed thanks for the employers' "paternal concern"; employers responded in kind by invoking their "love for their younger brothers." This collegial atmosphere lasted into the 1880s, but it was soon shattered by the growing size of printing establishments, more complex equipment, and a definite class consciousness on the part of the employers—including those espousing fraternal affection just a decade before. By 1905, workers were attacking their employers' "arbitrary authority," and erstwhile fraternalists were responding, "I am the boss, and I can dismiss workers from my shop if I don't like them." This transition from familial atmosphere to sharp employer-worker division had occurred in western Europe also, but over a longer period of time and without the newness of the craft itself adding to the confusion. Not surprisingly, the St. Petersburg printers, briefly a moderate voice among Russian workers, helped fuel the radicalism of the revolutionary era.

Worker protest also reflected the unrest of the Russian countryside. New workers brought in peasant grievances against landlords and the state, and the heady experience of urban life and association with other workers helped enliven isolated villages when workers returned. In no other large industrial revolution were peasants still so aggrieved as in Russia. (The only comparable case was Catalonia, in Spain, which was drawing from peasant migrants in the south at precisely the same time.) Unquestionably, grievances of the related sections of the Russian populace fed each other.

Furthermore, Russian workers had a more abundant array of ideological inspirations than Western workers had enjoyed in a comparably disruptive phase of industrialization. As Russia imported factory techniques, its discontented intellectuals also imported Western socialist ideas, and a largely homegrown anarchist movement added another source of ideological fuel. Urban workers gained rapid access to radical doctrines and leaders. Indeed, they learned socialism at precisely the same time that many Western workers were converting to it—in the 1880s and 1890s. But by then Western workers were in a more advanced industrial stage and able to see some improvements, at least in material conditions. They absorbed socialism but on the whole discounted its literal revolutionary content. Russian workers were more likely to buy the whole package.

Finally, Russian workers felt keenly their isolation from urban society and from the state. This feeling added to their resentment and also built their sense of mutual cohesion. Workers in the cities were addressed condescendingly by their social "betters," treated, in fact, as peasants when many of them were quite proud of having cast off that former life. The government was remote and repressive. A few factory laws were passed, one of them as early as 1845 limiting child labor, but they were largely unenforced. Workers knew the government best as the repressor of strikes and unions, both of which were firmly illegal. As workers, particularly in St. Petersburg and Moscow, learned new ideas and horizons from the radical intellectuals, they gained a sharp sense of their powerlessness.

All these factors operated in combination. They reflected not only the conditions common to early industrialization but also the rigidity of Russian politics and social hierarchy and the larger agitations of Russian society. The amalgam differentiated Russian workers from their counterparts in earlier Western industrialization and from workers in Japan, with whom they shared many problems but in a different cultural context. When further mixed with growing peasant and liberal protest, the combination produced a major worker revolution.

Organizations among industrial workers began in the 1870s, though there had been important strikes even before then. Unions in Odessa and St. Petersburg were broken up by the police. A great textile strike occurred in 1878, and strikes began to pepper the industrial landscape. Many resulted in arrests and trials, but these, in turn, publicized the hardships of factory life and spread a message of potential liberation. The government issued a new factory law in 1866 to protect workers from unsafe conditions, but it also reaffirmed the prohibition on worker organizations and increased the penalties for striking. Employer pressure brought a softening of the factory law in 1890, but workers were gaining new ground. By the 1890s Vladimir Ilyich Lenin and other Marxist leaders were spreading socialist doctrines in the cities, forming the Social Democratic Workers Party in 1898. The economic slump after 1900 caused widespread unemployment and new unrest, including strikes in many centers.

From this context emerged the general strike of 1905, triggered by Russia's loss to Japan in the 1904 war. Unions, or soviets, were established in many factory centers. Workers briefly won the vote and the legality of strikes for economic (but not political) goals. Employer resistance stiffened, however, creating growing class antagonism. The government banned the Marxist party, jailing or exiling many leaders. Workers were briefly cowed, but a new and more determined strike wave resumed in 1912. Several strikes led to brutal confrontations with police and many arrests and injuries. When the hardships of World War I added still greater incentive, workers were ready to rebel in 1917. Again the soviets formed, and this time they served as the basis for the new communist regime headed by Lenin, which overturned the short-lived middle-class government that had initially replaced the tsar. The world's most genuine working-class revolution had triumphed.

The Industrial Revolution under Communism

The Russian Revolution and subsequent civil war, following on the heels of World War I, dealt a blow to the country's economy. Manufacturing output declined, and many workers left the cities to scour the countryside for food. Lenin's government probably compounded the difficulties by nationalizing all the great factories and soon nationalizing small business as well. Management was disaffected, and production faltered further. The communist regime also renounced all foreign debts, seizing the factories that had been built in part by foreign capital. These actions provided the new Soviet Union with substantial industrial assets, but in the short run it both antagonized foreign investors and further disrupted established management.

During the early 1920s Lenin modified his policies through the New Economic Program, which gave some leeway to private business while maintaining government management of the big factories. Lenin and his colleagues were committed to extending the industrial revolution. Marxist doctrine assumed an industrialized economy capable of abundant production; it attacked capitalism, but not industry or technology. Further, Soviet leaders, isolated from the rest of the world, saw the need for industry to ensure the nation's defense.

In pursuing further industrialization, the communist state expanded several themes that had already developed in Russia's first industrial decades. It relied still more extensively on state guidance and control. It emphasized heavy industry, a sector in which the Soviet Union had a resource advantage and considerable ongoing momentum and that had a particularly close relationship to military strength. Industrialization under Soviet communism also maintained the emphasis on big factories and management hierarchies, though the managers were largely new faces. Private ownership was banned in industry, but a managerial class gradually assembled that was closely linked to the Communist Party. Issues of recruiting and supervising workers, though affected by propaganda praising the working class and by prohibitions on strikes and independent unions, continued to demand considerable attention.

The communist version of an industrial society also placed great emphasis on women's work. In the 1920s Soviet society began to display some of the same family adjustments that had occurred earlier in the West. The new focus on schooling led to the withdrawal of children from the labor force, and families reacted by cutting their birthrate, through either birth control or abortion. Lower birthrates meant protecting the family standard of living (now that children were an expense rather than an income source) and lavishing concern on children as individuals. These same elements had developed in the Western response to industrialization, and the result was the same as well: rapid slowing of overall population growth. But the Western pattern of withdrawing married women from the labor force did not widely apply. The need for additional workers was too great, particularly because mechanization was only selectively introduced. Many women did jobs performed in Western society either by unskilled men or by machines, such as hauling and street cleaning. Communist leaders proudly made a virtue of women's work, arguing that Soviet society avoided imposing the domestic inferiority on women characteristic of the industrial West.

The new regime also explicitly departed from a number of prior industrial policies, even aside from the vast expansion of government control and the new rhetoric surrounding women's work. It reduced dependence on foreigners. Lenin imported some engineers and skilled workers from the United States and western Europe, and he was eager to introduce up-to-date technologies and organizational schemes like the assembly line. But foreign expertise was now clearly supplementary to an impressive Soviet effort. The recruitment of talented managers from the peasantry and working class and the rapid expansion of the educational system, including technical training, provided the necessary skills internally.

The Soviet economy was substantially cut off from the rest of the world. It exported little and imported little. This was the first case in which industrialization was completed in such isolation, though of course it could be argued that prerevolutionary Russia's earlier start, although under extensive foreign guidance, also facilitated this pattern. Finally, although the new regime emphasized big factories, it was far more attentive to worker demands and interests than had been the case before. Worker protest was forbidden again, and the working class was enrolled in unions led by party members. Strikes were considered an attack on the state. But the government knew that its practical and ideological roots were in the working class, and it listened informally to potential grievances. Elaborate welfare measures—medical care, old-age pensions, and leisure and vacation facilities—began increasingly to supplement industrial life; these services were provided by the communist state.

Industrial production reached prewar levels by about 1926, an impressive achievement given the earlier disorder and the removal of most foreign experts and many previous Russian business leaders. Urban living standards improved as well. New communist managers gained increasing competence in running factories and other enterprises. Then, in 1927, Joseph Stalin came to power and effectively ended the long debate over the proper structure for the Soviet economy. The Communist Party congress in 1927 approved the first Five-Year Plan, a scheme designed to go beyond mere economic recovery to build state-run industrial growth and fuller self-sufficiency vis-à-vis the outside world.

The Five-Year Plans emphasized heavy industries, big factories, and technological modernization. (The first one was declared complete in 1932, ahead of schedule, and it was followed by other plans prepared by the State Planning Commission [Gosplan].) Vast state funds were poured into new plants; from 1933 to 1935 over half of all state construction money was devoted to industry, and of this, 78 percent went to heavy industry as opposed to consumer-goods sectors. Agriculture was collectivized in a system that led to great brutality against the wealthier peasants but increased the mechanization of agriculture and freed growing numbers of peasants for work in the factories (see Photo 8.1). The labor force expanded rapidly once again, creating a new set of problems that arose from incorporating former peasants into big, impersonal factory settings. Work efficiency remained inconsistent, and there was an endemic shortage of skilled operatives. Because the focus was on heavy industrial technology, other manufacturing operations depended on large numbers of workers using less advanced equipment, and even some of the big industrial factories employed larger numbers of workers in relation to output than was true in the West or in Japan.

Resources were allocated by state boards, independent of market forces. Conscious policy, not profits or direct competition, was intended to guide this industrialization process. This approach sometimes reduced waste and redundancy. It allowed the state, and not consumer demand, to set the tone for the economy. It also produced serious imbalances even within the favored industrial sectors. Not all state operations were effective. Planning impeded the easy delivery of goods. The state itself sometimes tried shortcuts in order to pour money into heavy industry. A lag in railroad development, for example, created transportation bottlenecks across the giant nation.

Photo 8.1 Sowing on a Collective Farm on the Steppes of the Ukraine, USSR (Union of Soviet Socialist Republics) between 1930 and 1940 (Photo 12 / Alamy Stock Photo).

The most obvious drawback of the new approach to industrialization involved worker motivation. Deliberate neglect of consumer goods meant that workers were confronted with few attractive options for purchase. Even food production often broke down, for farm collectivization did not ensure rapid agricultural growth. Subsequent Five-Year Plans trumpeted increased attention to consumer goods, but the stress on heavy industry continued, and scarcities of food, clothing, and housing made life in the cities extremely difficult. Working wives, particularly, had to spend much of their free time in long shopping lines, in what became a daily reminder of the limitations of Soviet industrial life. On the brighter side, workers had considerable security. They were ensured full employment, and the Soviet Union's massive industrial growth during the 1930s contrasted vividly with the miseries of the Depression in the West. Not only educational levels but also opportunities for mobility increased. Health and life expectancy improved also, a basic measure of standard-of-living gains.

The communist regime spared no pains to create a sense of dignity for the working class and to reverse its previous sense of being scorned and isolated. Art and drama glorified the heroic worker. Special programs were also created to deal with some of the characteristic goals of an industrializing economy. The government, taking a page from capitalist factories but in an appropriately communist context, introduced a series of incentive schemes in the 1930s to try to stimulate harder work. Particularly productive workers, called "Stakhanovites," were given bonuses and hero-of-labor pins. Aleksei Stakhanov, a miner in the Donets Basin, had developed a new method of extracting coal in 1935, which allowed him to exceed greatly the established rates of output. Within a few weeks his example was given tremendous publicity by the government and was emulated by workers in a variety of trades—partly from patriotic devotion, partly to win higher wages.

The system had a dark side. The Soviet regime imprisoned millions of people for a variety of political offenses as part of its enforcement of rigid political orthodoxy, including the ban on open labor dissent. Many of these prisoners were used in forced labor, essentially as slaves, particularly for big construction projects like dams and canals and in some isolated mines. Exactly how extensive forced labor was remains controversial. But although it was not the primary ingredient of industrial success, it did play a role. Russian industrialization also imposed considerable environmental damage, not only in the factory centers but other parts of the country pressed to produce minerals or textile fibers. Damage was particularly great in portions of central Asia.

By the standards the government most cherished, the new industrial system worked. Output expanded rapidly. In 1928, as the first Five-Year Plan began, the Soviet Union stood fifth in the world in manufacturing output. In scarcely more than twenty years, and despite the tremendous toll exacted by World War II, it moved to second place, behind only the United States. Coal production of 35 million tons in 1928 escalated to 109 million tons in 1935. Pig iron production almost quadrupled, and steel production tripled. Chemical and machine-building industries, poorly developed before, came into their own. By 1936 the Soviet Union was producing more tractors than any other nation in the world. New regional centers that developed, particularly in Siberia, were important in both mining and metallurgy. Electrification proceeded rapidly. In fifteenth place internationally in the generation of electric power in 1913, the nation moved to third place by 1935. Lenin had said, "Electrification plus Soviet power equals communism," and the mechanical power came with a vengeance.

Although Soviet production figures were sometimes inflated, the massive industrial growth of the 1930s was one of the great surges in the history of the industrial revolution anywhere. The quality of goods was sometimes dubious; particularly in the neglected consumer sector items were not only hard to find but frequently shoddily made. A whole host of problems lurked within the Soviet industrial system, and the world did not become fully aware of them until the late 1980s. Yet the achievements at the time were breathtaking. The industrial labor force tripled, to about 6.5 million workers. Gigantic industrial complexes were built from scratch in resource-rich centers like Magnitogorsk in the Urals and

Kuznetsk in western Siberia. Magnitogorsk acquired an industrial population of a quarter million in just a few years, a reminder that industrial revolutions still had the same power to entice people to relocate, as they had demonstrated in the days of Manchester or the Ruhr Valley. Over 1,500 new Soviet factories were built during the 1930s.

As opposed to the government's unreliable claims of 20 percent annual industrial growth, Soviet industrial output does seem to have expanded between 12 and 14 percent per year during the 1930s, unquestionably one of the best sustained records in the world's industrial history. To accomplish this expansion essentially alone—the Soviets had only modest outside technical expertise and almost no outside financing—simply magnified the achievement. By the 1950s, when the Soviet economy had recovered from World War II and resumed impressive growth, and when a full half of the population was urbanized, the Soviet Union had completed one of the few full industrial revolutions in world history and certainly one of the most unconventional.

9 The Industrial Revolution in Japan

Japan's industrial revolution began to take shape in the 1870s. A host of developments ushered in the new phase, some of them familiar echoes of earlier industrialization processes, others reflecting a distinctive national signature.

A National Approach: government, former feudal lords, entrepreneurs—and some foreigners

As in Germany and Russia, railroad building both symbolized and caused a more general pattern of rapid industrial growth. The story of early Japanese railroads also suggests some of the patterns involved in later industrial revolutions, including the immense constraints of early initiatives.

The reform-minded Meiji government launched a major railroad development plan in 1870, only two years after the regime had consolidated its hold and abolished feudalism. Railroads were considered necessary for the overall economic unification of Japan and as a basis for further modernization. The state initially hoped to rely on private capital, guaranteeing a dividend rate of 7 percent on any capital invested and asking the Mitsui firm to raise funds for a line between Osaka and Kyoto. But when few capitalists stepped forward, and the company did not materialize, the government acted directly, establishing an important precedent for state involvement in the industrialization process as a whole. Between 1870 and 1874, railroad building accounted for nearly a third of all state investments in modern industry. Foreign loans added to the mix. An initial line between Tokyo and Yokohama, completed by 1872, was built with a million-pound loan from the British Oriental Bank. The government initially hoped to use U.S. contractors, but British pressure forced ultimate reliance on the British option.

Whatever the birth pains, government lines proved to be immediately profitable, and after 1874, official subsidies were sufficient to attract private investment. By 1892 Japan had a total of 1,870 miles of track, 550 miles of it government-owned and 1,320 miles in private hands. An early private company formed by a group of nobles had problems completing its plans but opened a line between Tokyo and Aomori in 1881; capitalized with 20 million yen, this company was the largest enterprise in Japan. The government guaranteed 10 percent dividends and employed 256 engineers (under the Ministry of Industry) to provide necessary technical expertise. After the success of this first company, other firms formed, and private railway investment increased fiftyfold between 1881 and 1891. Japanese heavy industry was unable to supply equipment until after 1900, so Japan continued to depend on imports from Europe, even for basic items like the necessary engines. In 1907, however, the Kawasaki shipyard began to produce the first locomotives and coaches in Japan's brief industrial history.

The government also pioneered the development of new mines for iron, lead, copper, gold, silver, and coal. Private mines existed, but only the state enterprises—there were six by 1881—operated on a large scale with modern, imported machinery. The government invested heavily in the technical modernization process. It put 2.4 million yen into the Kamaishi iron mines, but the effort failed and the mines were put out of operation and ultimately (in 1887) sold to a private investor for a mere 12,600 yen. A copper mine also sputtered along and finally was sold for a fifth of what the government had invested. The Miike coal mines, however, were successful and turned a good profit when they were sold—six times the state's outlay.

Other mines developed through Western investment. A feudal lord cofounded a mine with the British firm Thomas Glover. The agreement was that Thomas Glover would provide the money to open the mine and run it for seven years, paying a royalty on any coal produced; the mine would be returned to the lord thereafter. The Meiji government soon intervened, taking over the mine and selling it to a businessman, Goto Shojiro. Goto made another deal with the British firm to acquire capital, pledging that Thomas Glover would have exclusive sales rights on the coal—as "monopoly sales agent for the coal in East Asia." Profits would be divided equally between the two partners. But the mine failed, and Goto went bankrupt; Japanese courts distributed his assets among Japanese creditors but awarded very little to Thomas Glover, which sold its share in the mine to the Mitsubishi shipping company in 1877. Western investment, in this and in other instances, helped launch Japanese industry, but under strict controls and with many setbacks. The contrast to the more open situation in Russia was obvious.

Shipping and shipbuilding attracted government attention early on. Japan was an obvious candidate for maritime activity, despite over two centuries of governmental restrictions on seagoing ventures. The focus on shipping proved a crucial move in helping Japan escape Western control of its commerce. The Mitsubishi company began operations after a complex evolution from a semifeudal armaments arrangement. A feudal samurai, Iwasaki Yataro, had managed armaments procurements for a regional lord, buying foreign weapons and ships; he proved efficient in reorganizing older feudal enterprises and procuring funds for arms purchases. After the Meiji regime was established, his firm became an independent company, though it was still supposed to help the feudal lords and provide jobs for samurai. Iwasaki converted the company into his personal property in 1873, renaming it Mitsubishi. He developed a loyal staff of former samurai—much of his success stemmed from the high morale and group solidarity among these lieutenants. Mitsubishi competed directly with a government shipping line, the Nippon Postal Steamship Company, which carried both passengers and freight, including rice, along the coast. Mitsubishi's ships were more modern and its bureaucracy was less cumbersome. Iwasaki's firm soon drove the Nippon Company out of business and went on to become a major government carrier. In 1874–1875 the government bought eleven iron steamers for military transport, loaning (ultimately giving) all of them to Iwasaki; major government subsidies also poured in. The condition was that Mitsubishi engage in direct competition with foreign lines, opening a regular route between Japan and China, where the Americans and British had established domination. By 1877 Iwasaki had badly beaten the Americans' Pacific Mail Company and an English steam company. By this time the huge conglomerate had also established a stake in coal mining and shipbuilding, borrowing the Nagasaki shipyard from the government in 1877 and buying it outright in 1887. Big business entered early in Japan's industrialization.

The Japanese government stimulated the textile industry as well. In 1877, when only three modern cotton-spinning mills were operating in Japan, the Meiji government owned two of them. This sector also required large amounts of capital, and the government was one of the only available sources. But the Japanese state played just a modest role in light industries. It supported no construction of textile equipment, for example, relying entirely on imports for the few modern factories that existed. By 1910 the government was sponsoring the construction of the world's largest battleship, the *Satsuma*, but had yet to develop an overall plan to modernize textile production.

Some historians have argued that the Japanese government sensibly focused on investments that inherently involved a large scale and technological complexity and, further, that Japan's limited resources dictated leaving other areas to private hands, even at the cost of much slower technological change. Others have contended that the government concentrated on heavy industry simply because of its direct bearing on military production, essential not only for defense but for imperialist adventures—which Japan began to experiment with as early as the 1870s in an expedition against Taiwan and undertook more seriously in the 1890s with a successful war against China. Whatever its mix of motives, the state played a vital role in early Japanese industrialization, as these initial impressions clearly demonstrate.

Government involvement in early industry far exceeded that in Russia before the 1917 revolution—correspondingly, foreign investors were much more successfully limited. Government operations blended readily with private business, however, and the boundary lines were far fuzzier than in the Western or Russian traditions. Private use of government assets had certainly occurred in the West—as in the huge public land grants to U.S. railroads—but the Japanese movement of investment funds and business management back and forth was distinctive. Within big private firms, a modified feudal tradition built intense group loyalty, which coexisted with intense profit seeking on the part of individuals like Iwasaki. This was another way in which a vigorous preindustrial culture fed into successful, unique industrial management style. Even today Japanese industry is famous for the close collaboration of business and government, in contrast to the somewhat more adversarial relationship in the West.

The Context for Industrialization

Japan was in many ways an unlikely candidate for a quick response to the new industrial challenge of western Europe and the United States. The nation, long isolated, faced many problems in trying to comprehend the West, even as it began to realize that some imitation of Western ways was essential (among them, of course, an industrial revolution). Japanese visitors to the United States commented, for example, on the bizarre lack of veneration for leadership; most Americans in the 1860s seemed to have no idea of what had happened to George Washington's descendants. Political parties baffled them: How could groups dispute so bitterly yet manage to sit in the same legislative chamber? To be sure, these same visitors saw the centrality of Western technology early on. They proudly noted that Japan learned how to build a steamship very quickly. They also realized the importance of science in Western education and began to incorporate it into Japanese training fairly rapidly, jettisoning Confucian traditionalism, though not the larger Confucian emphasis on group harmony and devotion to society.

Not surprisingly, as in Russia, a number of Japanese continued to oppose even the limited westernization that occurred. Several leading feudal lords hoped to restore isolation in the 1860s rather than industrialize; they lost, and on balance anti-industrial sentiment was lower in Japan than in Russia. But a broader concern about the direction of change complicated aspects of the industrialization process.

Japan was also poor in the relevant natural resources. It had some coal and copper and traces of other minerals, but it quickly recognized the need to trade not simply for complex equipment from the industrialized nations but for the raw materials that were the sinews of industry. Textile fibers appropriate for mechanization, notably cotton, also had to be imported. In short, understanding the resource problems that guided Japanese industrialization almost from the start is an aid to understanding several distinctive features of the process: why the government subsidized mining ventures so quickly—and also why several failed; why there was an early and lasting attempt to develop a large export sector—to pay for vital supplies as well as new technology; and why Japan engaged in early imperialist expansion—to acquire territory that could provide secure, cheap supplies of needed materials.

Japan also faced the burdens of established Western competition. This is one reason both Japan and Russia required extensive government involvement in the industrialization effort—as a way to compensate for backwardness and to provide guidance and capital designed to speed the process of change lest catching up become impossible. Japan, however, had to deal with far greater constraints than those faced by Russia. It could not impose high tariffs on industrial imports. British and U.S. pressure, backed by military threats, forced largely open markets; only in 1911 did Japan regain control over its tariff policy. Western businesses operated in parts of Japan under Western, not Japanese, commercial law. In this context the Japanese government had to work even harder than its Russian counterpart to achieve the same result: adequate national control over the economy and adequate national monitoring of the necessary borrowing from Western experts and financiers. Japan managed to prevail: Western investments were limited to a far greater extent than in Russia. Government subsidies and guarantees on investment earnings made up part of the difference. Japan also early established a policy of encouraging Japanese business to "buy Japanese" rather than to import from abroad. Some imports were technically imperative, but where there were options, the government pushed native pride in Japanese distinctiveness and cultural traditions of social solidarity to prevent overreliance on foreign economies. This pride was another distinctive feature inserted in the industrial economy that continued to affect policy into the late twentieth century.

Recent research has emphasized another angle: the need for the government to consciously provide the cultural retooling needed for a national commitment to industrialization. It did this by making a quick commitment to mass education, with a science component unprecedented in Confucian culture. It began sponsoring technology shows to push the same message. In 1872 it required national conversion to Western clock time, arguing that Japanese traditions here were "uncivilized." It force fed, in other words, a cultural context similar to that which had helped generate Western industrialization. But it overlaid this with strong emphasis on national pride and loyalty, and community cohesion—a distinctive overall mixture.

Japan's industrial achievement against formidable obstacles was unquestionably impressive. The energy and focused policy that would push the nation toward the top of the world's industrial leadership in the late twentieth century were absolutely essential in getting the industrialization process launched in the first place. Every available asset, from elements of prior culture to high levels of education to the sweat of Japanese workers, had to be brought to bear. At the same time, Japanese industrialization inevitably advanced slowly at first because of the special impediments Japan faced.

DEBATE # 10: *CONFUCIANISM AND INDUSTRIALIZATION*

This is a rather focused debate, but arguably quite important. Western historians (and other observers) often criticized the Confucian tradition for its resistance to technological change and indifference to science. Confucian values could contribute to explicit resistance to industrialization, as when Chinese leaders ordered the destruction of an initial railway line. Japanese reformers explicitly urged that major cultural adjustments were essential if industrialization were to proceed.

But the same reformers carefully argued that large elements of Confucianism remained vital and valid. And, as things have turned out by the early twenty-first century, the "Confucian zone" of the world—not only Japan, but the Pacific Rim and China—has been the leading center of global industrialization after the West itself (despite huge differences within the zone, as between Japan and China).

So is a modified Confucianism a vital industrial factor, compared to other cultural traditions? Here is another important area where assessing the role of culture in industrialization seems unavoidable. And if Confucianism plays a role—despite the obvious fact that it was in no way designed with this in mind—what are its relevant features? How does it compare with the Western cultural values that seem to have promoted the industrial revolution a bit earlier? What are the main differences between industrialization in a revised Confucian tradition, and industrialization in the Western cultural context? Or alternatively, is East Asian industrial success due to non-cultural factors entirely, so that Confucianism is not really relevant?

There may be another, contemporary implication to all this: a leading scholar suggested a decade ago that the next framework for world history will feature competition and conflict among leading culture zones, with both the Confucian heritage and a Western heritage high on the list: will rival definitions of industrial values push tensions beyond economic competition alone?

Further Reading: Wei-Bin Zhang, *Confucianism and Modernisation* (London, 2000); Samuel Huntington, *Clash of Civilizations and the Remaking of the World Order* (New York, 1996).

The Early Stages

Japan's early commitment to industrialization began in the 1860s. In contrast to Russia, Japan revamped political as well as social structures, though without revolution, thus reducing some of the tensions industrialization created when inserted into a traditional political fabric. The abolition of feudalism did not eliminate the powerful nobility, however, and finding outlets for samurai energies continued to be a preoccupation. Many samurai were able to adapt their values to successful industrial management, and the way was left open for other kinds of leaders, notably successful businessmen, to join elements in the former nobility in creating a new elite. The Russian dilemma—seeking industrialization while trying to preserve the political dominance of the tsar and the nobility—was thus avoided.

Initial Meiji reforms brought additional gains. With the abolition of feudalism came freedom of occupations. Farmers were able to trade directly. The elimination of earlier monopolies on regional trade meant open access to urban markets and the abolition of tax barriers on roads. A fully national economy emerged for the first time. Most traditional merchant houses—and preindustrial Japan had developed a large merchant class and big trading companies—were tied to the finances of feudal lords and proved unable to make the transition to a new economy. Many business failures occurred. But new commercial ventures proliferated, bringing a host of new small businesses and a few potential giants to the fore. What was happening by the 1870s, even before much outright industrialization, was a liberation, an unshackling of the Japanese economy. The resultant dynamism fed easily into new industrial ventures.

Agriculture changed as well. Rural society was increasingly divided between market-oriented landowners and tenants and laborers. The owners, including progressive landlords, began to introduce fertilizers and farm equipment. The government provided technical assistance, setting up a faculty of agriculture at the Tokyo Imperial University. Production soared. Rice output more than doubled between 1880 and 1930. At the same time, the Japanese government quickly copied some Western public health measures. The result, along with greater food supplies, was a rapid population increase, from about 30 million in 1868 to 45 million in 1900 (and on to 73 million in 1940). Because the numbers of people needed on the land did not increase, vast new labor supplies were available for factory and other urban jobs.

This was the context in the 1870s in which the government began to sponsor pilot industries. The Ministry of Industry was established in 1870 under Ito Hirobumi and quickly became one of the leading agencies of the state. The government expanded arsenals and shipyards, built telegraph lines, and of course made the start on railroads and new mining. The railroad network was absolutely vital, since Japanese commerce previously had depended on very expensive coastal shipping. In 1868 it cost as much to ship goods 50 miles inland as to transport them to Europe. Railroads gave Japan an internal circulatory system, opening up previously isolated areas both to sales and to purchases. The state also set up a few model factories in textiles, cement, glass, and machine tools. These early factories generated little output, but they helped train Japanese technical experts and labor. New roads and ports, more suitable commercial laws, and a new banking system helped round out the government-sponsored infrastructure.

The first truly industrial phase of growth began in the 1880s. Big businesses emerged, the forerunners of *zaibatsu*, the great industrial conglomerates. Would-be industrial giants faced obvious problems in finding capital. A few won some loans from Western banks. Still more, like the Mitsubishi founder, gained capital from political connections, serving government shipping and military needs. Other new entrepreneurs were mavericks, rising from the growing group of commercial farmers and winning success through business acumen. Shibuzawa Eiichi was born into a peasant family that produced indigo. He became a merchant and won a government post in the Finance Ministry by backing the right side in Japan's 1860s conflicts that led to the establishment of the Meiji regime. In 1873 he made the so-called heavenly descent from government to private business. He founded the First Bank and began to develop an uncanny knack for using his depositors' money to launch new industry. His initial success was the Osaka Cotton Spinning Mill, created as a corporation in 1880. It was a big mill, for Shibuzawa had decided that smaller mills were uneconomical. Huge profits resulted, and it became easy to find investment funds in additional plants. Between 1896 and 1913 the yarn output of the company rose tenfold. The company turned to cloth production after 1900, here experiencing one hundredfold growth, from 22 million square yards in 1900 to 2.7 billion in 1936.

With operations of this sort established, Japan enjoyed a rapidly growing, industrialized textile sector by 1890. Textile growth also gave Japanese industrialization a more rounded quality than existed in the contemporaneous process in Russia. Consumer goods drew considerable attention in Japan, despite the government's urgent interest in shipbuilding and other industries more directly relevant to military strength. During the 1890s modern industries were established in construction goods—cement, bricks, and glass—and in food processing (including beer), match production, and chemicals. These industries drew a variety of new Japanese entrepreneurs who operated within the solid context for growth the government had established.

By the 1890s a vast increase in education that had been launched in 1872 was beginning to pay off in terms of the technical expertise available in Japan and also the quality of the factory labor force. In 1890, primary schools had 64 percent of boys and 31 percent of girls in attendance, figures that rose to 96 percent and 90 percent respectively by 1905. Increasing numbers of primary school graduates, in turn, went on to middle and higher education. These developments steadily increased Japan's ability to assimilate the latest Western technologies. The nation was not yet producing new inventions of its own (as opposed to making appropriate adaptations of Western devices), and virtually all of the technology used in industries like textiles was foreign. But Japan's capacity to absorb innovations from elsewhere was becoming legendary.

Study trips abroad, often government-sponsored and launched even before the Meiji regime, continued, providing the information flow on which the leading Japanese industries depended to stay up-to-date. By 1900 many Western companies had also established engineering staffs in Japan to promote their product sales. A British company, for example, sold virtually all of the textile-spinning equipment used in Japan until 1925, and it had personnel on hand to explain the equipment's use. Arrangements within Japan also facilitated information exchange. There were lags, to be sure, and small companies in particular found it difficult to keep up with their bigger rivals. The government, of course, actively assisted in providing technical expertise to all branches of modern industry. Associations formed among Japanese companies also helped. Given the cooperative spirit in Japanese culture, cartels that reduced internal competition formed even more rapidly than in Germany. Boren, the cotton-spinners trade association, issued technical publications and exchanged engineers among companies to keep knowledge current. Very few companies established monopolies on technology, and when cooperation did not suffice, experts were hired away from other firms.

A second major industrial spurt took shape after 1905 and extended to 1918. The boom centered on light industries, but there was growth in shipping, coal, chemicals, and electric power as well. It was at this point also that Japan installed a significant metallurgical sector, developing the ability to produce its own locomotives and other heavy equipment besides ships. By 1921, machinery, just 3 percent of total Japanese manufacturing output in 1880, had soared to 14 percent. Generation of electric power, virtually nonexistent before 1910, rose sevenfold between 1910 and 1920. Whereas Japan's first industrialization period in the 1880s and 1890s had featured the displacement of human and water power by steam engines, in this second growth period electrification replaced steam engines. These successive developments—first the widespread adoption of steam power, and then the rapid conversion to electricity—occurred much more rapidly in Japan than in other industrial countries, including Russia and the West.

If Japan's industrial revolution displayed unusual vigor, along with some unusual characteristics, it was a gradual process, not an overnight conversion. Well into the twentieth century Japan's economy was by no means fully industrialized. Like the West a half century earlier, Japan continued to depend on a large agricultural sector and on a host of small operations. Factory workers formed only a small percentage of the total labor force. Japan also had an unusually large number of small businesses along with the more visible giants. In 1900 Japan's agricultural population was still 67 percent of the total (down from 80 percent in

1870). Thereafter the percentage fell rapidly—more rapidly than in most Western industrialized nations, including the United States, and much more rapidly than in the agriculture-plagued Soviet Union. By 1920 Japan's rural population was only 51 percent of the total. More surprising were the numbers of small businesses; Japan ranked well above all industrial nations in the percentage of small business into the 1930s.

The importance of small business, in turn, reflected more than Japan's late start in the industrial revolution—a late start that made it virtually inevitable that traditional branches would retain vitality for some time. Substantial consumer needs for processed foods and other goods normally produced by small units sustained modest establishments. But Japan's early industrial decades also featured an unusual reliance on exports, not of factory goods but of goods produced in small shops with relatively modest equipment. In this regard, Japan's economy long bore some resemblance to that of other nations that depended on earnings from sales to the industrial West: Japan needed a cash specialty, and it needed a low-wage labor force that could make this specialty pay off (see Figure 9.1).

The overall problem was obvious. Despite rapid industrial growth, Japan depended heavily on machine and raw-materials imports from the West and elsewhere. As a result it needed to earn foreign exchange. In this respect, too, Japan's situation differed considerably from that of Russia. The Japanese worked hard on the problem, trying to limit

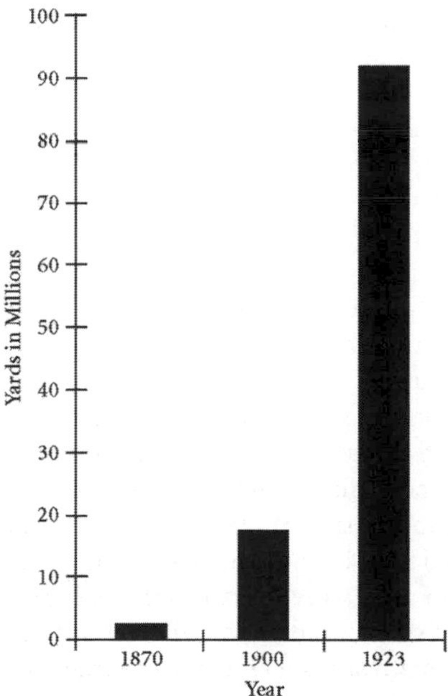

Figure 9.1 Evidence of Japanese Industrialization: Silk Production.

imports to basic industrial necessities. They developed internal production to replace imports relatively quickly. And they rapidly extended international shipping (and shipbuilding) operations to prevent a loss of earnings to foreign traders—a key move that already distinguished early industrial Japan from many nonindustrial areas.

But still, there had to be goods to sell abroad to win the needed foreign earnings: an export focus was vital. The early answer was silk, a traditional Japanese industry that with government assistance was quickly modernized. During the 1870s the state introduced mechanical reeling, developed in Europe, which allowed a higher output of silk production per worker. Silk looms were not expensive (small businesses thus dominated the sector), and technological demands were not high, but the rewards were considerable. Mechanized silk production enabled Japan to capture export markets from China, which still relied on manual silk-making methods. Silk output rose from 2.3 million pounds around 1870 to 16 million in 1900 and to 93 million in 1929. A full two-thirds of this production was exported and gave Japan vitally needed foreign exchange. The labor force in textiles expanded rapidly as a result, doubling between 1909 and 1930 and vastly overshadowing the number of workers in machine building and heavy industry.

Japan's industrial advance between the 1870s and the 1920s was startlingly swift. The commitment to change had parlayed industrial growth into imperial expansion with its successful wars against China and Russia. Lacking several obvious ingredients for an industrial revolution, Japan had compensated by means of government direction—converting prior habits like group solidarity into industrial assets and fostering an active export sector. Inevitably, the same thrust brought tensions and vulnerabilities to Japanese society. Rapid industrialization had many familiar consequences, but it also had several special features resulting from the speed and the precise emphases wrapped up in the Japanese surge.

Social Impacts

Many results of Japan's industrial revolution followed familiar patterns. Work was redefined. Preindustrial Japan had featured an urban artisanry with rich traditions. Artisans had substantial skill and a considerable penchant for leisure—"wine, women, and gambling" were entertainments characteristic of this group when resources permitted. Individual crafts had important rituals and guild organizations. The rise of factories, many of them government-run at first, cut into these traditions. High wages were offered to skilled workers, whose attraction was essential, but the work was far more strictly regulated than in the past. Rigid timetables for starting and stopping work and for taking breaks were imposed. Japanese management strove to create a new definition of work habits. In return, some benefits were offered at the start, including compensation for job injuries. Such government involvement made Japanese benefit programs more systematic at a comparable stage of the industrialization process in the West. Private factories, however, established lower wages than those in government enterprises; and female silk workers were heavily exploited.

Some skilled workers early developed a sense of pride and status that perhaps cushioned the adjustments to more rigorous working conditions. On the one hand, because of a culture that urged people to revere government officials, the important role of government pilot projects encouraged some docility among these workers in return for certain kinds of preferential treatment. On the other, as factories spread, conditions tended to deteriorate for the skilled workers, as the expansion of education generated larger numbers—another familiar theme. Many skilled factory workers began changing jobs with some frequency, seeking temporarily better deals from new employers. This transience enhanced employer nervousness about forming a stable corps of skilled operatives, but it did not improve living conditions, which were often difficult in the factory centers. Workers had to borrow or pawn their furnishings periodically just to get by—another echo from earlier industrial revolutions.

Leisure decreased notably, in part because of low wages, in part because workdays increased to twelve hours or more, in addition to commuting time. Going to public baths, drinking sake, and occasionally visiting brothels or gambling establishments constituted the recreation of many skilled workers. As one contemporary noted:

> They returned home, and after eating and drinking they read about half the paper, and if they took a bath it was past ten. If they didn't get up the next morning, they would be late to work; they could barely rest their bodies.

Middle-class critics, as in Europe earlier, lambasted wasteful habits, but in fact, outlets for leisure declined even as work became more arduous. Workers found protest organization difficult. Although some observers claimed to find close camaraderie among factory workers—"because each has experienced difficulties of his own and thus has become considerate of others"—in fact, early unions were small. An ironworkers' union in 1899 boasted only 3,000 members.

Coal miners suffered unusually poor conditions. Most were drifters from the villages, and they had low status in society's eyes and their own. Many employers hired subcontractors, who had an interest in getting as much work for as little pay as possible, and who supervised the miners literally twenty-four hours a day. Some miners ran away. Others were beaten by thugs the employers hired. Labor turnover was high; in

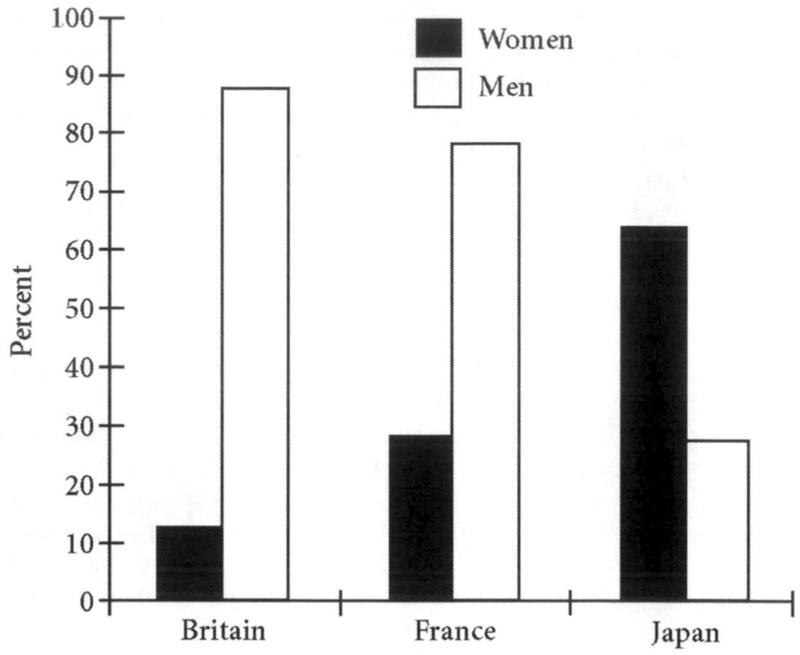

Figure 9.2 Men and Women in the Late Nineteenth-Century Labor Force in Britain, France, and Japan.

1906 one survey showed that 45 percent of the coal miners had been on the job less than a year. Few unions developed.

Japan's early industrialization was also marked by its unusual reliance on female workers (see Figure 9.2). This was the result of the prominence of textiles and uneven levels of mechanization, along with the drumming need for low wages in order to ensure export sales. In 1909 Japan's factory labor force was 62 percent female compared with 43 percent in France at a comparable stage of industrialization (in 1866). In the extent of its dependence on female factory workers, Japan surpassed the American South, Italy, and even India. Most of these women worked in small shops. They were young and usually unmarried. Many were imported from distant farm villages, where a father or brother signed them into what often amounted to industrial servitude. They had very low social status. Most were housed in dormitories entirely under their supervisors' control. They worked at least twelve hours a day, sometimes much more. After electrification in the 1920s, which illuminated the factories at night, hours often increased. Factories had full say over when and how wages were paid, and workers were often cheated. Managers argued that women wasted their money, so their wages were saved up by the factories; in fact, the managers worried that if the wages were paid out, the women would run away. Ill health was rampant, not only because of low pay but also because of dusty conditions in the plants. An 1897 report revealed that 84 percent of all the young women working in the cotton industry were either sick or suffering from injuries. Virtually no leisure activities were possible. Many workers developed irregular sexual liaisons, and some became prostitutes.

The problems female workers (and low-paid workers in general) encountered were not of course unique to Japanese industrialization. The sheer numbers, however, were startling, as women formed the majority of the factory labor force. Most intended to work only a short time, and transience was very high. Almost half of all cotton textile workers in 1897 had served in their current job for a year or less, and the figure grew worse with time. Japan's female labor force was more unstable than that of other industrial countries. Indeed, an unusual number of women simply ran away.

The toll of forming an industrial labor force showed in Japanese family life around 1900. The industrial revolution had a familiar impact in forcing families gradually to separate home and work. Many metalworkers left their wives at home, though because of low pay the latter often had to do some cheap craft production in the household. Workers' frequent movement disrupted family life still more directly. So, too, did the confusion surrounding women workers. Although many women hoped to return to village life and a traditional marriage, their lowered status and their removal from key local traditions often made this goal difficult to achieve. For a time Japan had the highest divorce rate in the world, particularly in the lower classes. In a society with strong traditions of family life, this instability was profoundly troubling, not least to those directly involved.

Formal labor protest, however, was infrequent. Because workers were strangers to each other and changed jobs often, organizing potential was reduced. Women thought more of escaping factory life than of protesting to improve it. Employers showed some talent in treating skilled workers separately, such as enrolling them in benefit societies that provided funds in case of illness or accident. The government also moved quickly to suppress any signs of unrest. A socialist party was formed by some Christian idealists in 1901, but the government immediately banned it. Other socialist movements arose in the 1920s, but most were quickly crushed by the police. Workers did not have the vote until the 1920s in any event, so their protest potential was further limited.

Nevertheless, strikes were not unknown. In 1914 the male workers in a Tokyo cotton factory voted a strike after half their number had been dismissed and the rest received a pay cut of 40 percent in reaction to a decline in sales. The company rescinded its measures in response to the general walkout, but female workers continued their protest, demanding shorter hours and better food. A union was formed, and although its charter proclaimed goals of mutual aid and "progress for the company," the company fired the twelve union leaders and the police arrested the leader of a mass meeting. The workers' resolve crumbled, and the union disbanded. Shipyard workers struck several times early in the twentieth century, often appealing for social respect and self-improvement in addition to making other demands; commonly heard was a call for more dignified titles of address. Again, however, the organizational efforts failed. The Public Order Police Law, though it did not ban unions outright, gave government wide policing powers against leaders, and these powers played a major role in failure of unionization attempts.

The lack of substantial labor unrest or organization during the early phases of Japanese industrialization bore some similarities to earlier conditions in the West, including the participants' newness to the industrial scene, Japan's relative tranquility was nevertheless surprising. It contrasted even more obviously with the revolutionary mood in early industrial Russia. The stern repression by a government controlled by a confident oligarchy of former aristocrats and new entrepreneurs was responsible for some of Japan's distinctiveness. There was less dispute or uncertainty at the top than in Russia and many Western countries, and state control was stricter. Lack of a consistent precedent of peasant unrest before industrialization certainly differentiated Japan from Russia. Major rural agitation had taken place in eighteenth-century Japan, but it had lessened by the mid-nineteenth century, and thus, new workers brought little protest baggage with them to the factories. Perhaps some larger traditions of obedience played a role. Certainly labor's collective capacity was reduced by the high percentage of women in the labor force, in a strongly patriarchal society in which women exercised no public leadership functions. The absence of protest did not result from workers' easy adjustment to industrial life, for the signs of strain were numerous. Rather, it forced workers to handle their discontents individually. Transience and family instability showed the tensions endemic to the industrial revolution and yet perhaps made protest all the more difficult.

The Industrial Economy Matures: 1920s–1950s

Many features of Japan's industrial revolution persisted into later decades, including the balance between light and heavy industry, the importance of government involvement, strong but group-oriented management, and the lack of consistent or vigorous labor protest. Yet something of a turning point occurred between 1920 and the mid-1930s that altered several key policies and furthered Japan's industrial drive.

The most obvious trigger for change came first in the form of a pronounced economic stagnation during much of the 1920s and then the catastrophic impact of worldwide depression early in the 1930s. Japanese leaders had to widen their definitions of industrialization or risk the nation's collapse. Japan's economy slumped after World War I, as did most industrial economies in the West. Recovery was hampered by the rise of the massive competition that Japan's silk industry faced from the development of artificial fibers such as nylon and rayon by Western chemical companies. Silk retained prestige, but for women's stockings and a host of other consumer products the cost and difficulty of silk began to seem a drawback. The decline in exports to the West not only threatened employment levels in Japan but also limited the earning of foreign currency. Agricultural problems also surfaced, and Tokyo's massive earthquake in 1923 had required a costly reconstruction that strained the economy. Several banks had failed in 1927.

When the worldwide depression hit, signaled by the U.S. stock market crash in 1929, the West's luxury market collapsed, cutting further into sales of silk. Between 1929 and 1931 the value of Japanese exports fell by 50 percent. Workers' real income dropped by a third, and there were over 3 million unemployed. Compounding the Depression were poor harvests in several regions, which led to widespread rural begging and near-starvation.

By 1932, however, recovery was under way. The Japanese government increased military purchases, which supported shipbuilding and heavy industry. Exports also rose as Japan stepped up its sales to other parts of Asia and reduced its dependence on Western markets. These two developments were linked to Japan's renewed involvement in war: the nation attempted new conquests in China and pushed for greater influence throughout eastern and southeast Asia. The result was unquestionably useful to the home economy. Not only did the nation bounce back from the Depression far more quickly than the industrial West, but it also moved to a new stage of industrialization as mechanization accelerated and a larger metallurgical sector emerged.

During the 1930s the production of iron, steel, and chemicals doubled. For the first time Japan gained the capacity to build its own machine tools, scientific instruments, and electric power stations; imports of manufactured products declined rapidly. By 1937 the expansion of shipbuilding had given Japan the third-largest merchant fleet in the world and by far the newest. Cotton manufacturing outstripped that of wool, though textiles began to decline in all factory sectors. The quality of Japanese goods also rose. Japan still exported only a small amount of the world's manufacturing total—about 4 percent in 1936. It still had to focus on a variety of novelty items, including cheap souvenirs for sale in the United States and western Europe, in its desperate quest for foreign earnings to pay for imports of fuel and other materials. But it could now compete in quality manufactured products as well.

The maturation of the industrial economy was reflected in the composition of the labor force. New male workers poured in from the farms to take jobs in metallurgy, machine building, and mining. The number of workers in metals and machine building rose sevenfold between 1930 and 1940, a phenomenal increase, even as the total manufacturing labor force more than doubled.

These industrial changes also moved big business to greater prominence, for it dominated the most rapidly growing sectors. The political power of the *zaibatsu* expanded accordingly. The experience of the working class was increasingly shaped by big-business policies. Large factories introduced assembly-line methods and other scientific management procedures modeled after those in the United States—just as the Soviet Union was doing in the same years.

The transition involved more than new industrial balance and big business. Attitudes toward the labor force were revised, and Japanese industrialization developed a more distinctive social orientation—a characteristic that has been largely preserved to the present day. Relevant policies had begun to shift in several related areas even before the 1930s boom. Concerned about social instability, in 1919 the government started promoting more active patriotic loyalty among Japanese citizens, workers included. Themes of duty, national glory, and loyalty to the emperor gained ground steadily. This set a context for relatively modest levels of labor unrest—despite recurrent political crises—and for a new devotion to work and productivity. More directly important were new policies adopted by the big industrial firms. These companies paid better wages than average anyway, in part because they needed more male skilled workers. They also began to expand their welfare facilities. Further, in the 1920s they launched a distinctively Japanese policy known initially as *fukaiko-shugi*, or "no dismissal" (now called *shushin koyo*, or "lifetime employment"). Under these policies, regular workers hired by large factories would not be dismissed. They might suffer pay cuts in a recession, but basic job security was ensured. Furthermore, bonuses and wage increases were tied to seniority, as was the lump sum paid out on retirement. Japanese industry was bent on tying a growing minority of the labor force to the firm as a way to reduce the job changing and transience associated with the first industrial decades.

Many factories supplemented these new policies with rituals designed to promote group solidarity. Some conducted calisthenics for all workers before the working day began. Others promoted group singing or other cooperative activities. Some of these routines recalled older Japanese paternalism and group loyalty, though the policies themselves were new. Japan was certainly inventing a new set of industrial traditions that tied many workers more firmly to their company and might well have improved morale. The contrast with the more individualistic and conflict-ridden industrial atmosphere of the West was striking. Many workers, to be sure, were excluded from these security arrangements, and thus manufacturers had much flexibility in augmenting or reducing their labor force and altering pay levels. Emphasis on company loyalty, however, prompted many workers to develop a new commitment to hard work. Daily hours of work did decrease slightly, but leisure interests expanded too. Many companies set up libraries, game rooms, and sports facilities to associate leisure with the firm and to preempt separate labor organizations. Regular workers joined company organizations at a rate of nearly 100 percent—in sharp contrast to separate unions, which gained only modestly, winning at most 8 percent adherence. Hard work seemed a logical complement to devotion to the firm, and many Japanese workers and white-collar employees, either because of an internalized work ethic or management-manipulated peer pressure, continued to accept much longer work weeks than their counterparts in the West.

Changes in both industry and policy reduced the percentage of women in the labor force. Growing prosperity and a desire to regain more family stability prompted the Japanese increasingly to emphasize the importance of women's domestic functions. Through industrial policies, firms with female workers increasingly tried to improve their status. Courses on sewing, etiquette, flower arranging, and tea ceremonies were designed to improve later marriageability—while also drawing a more reliable, less transient labor force in the short run. Japanese workers themselves pressed for more commitment to family life, accepting work by women for a period before marriage but assuming their primary commitment to household and children thereafter. Even in the 1950s, when white-collar employment for women increased in the West, the Japanese commitment to lower work rates for women persisted. In this, as in other respects, Japan seemed on a somewhat different industrial trajectory from that of the West or even more obviously the Soviet Union.

By the 1930s most workers were benefiting from the industrial revolution in a material sense. Standards of living improved. Diets became more varied, as did leisure opportunities. However, real wages did not catch up to Western levels, and Japanese culture as encouraged by employers and the government tended to divert workers from a full commitment to an individualistic consumer ethic. Longer work hours than in the West and a high savings rate reflected somewhat cautious personal values.

Japan's industrial surge was set back by its losses in World War II. The standard of living dropped well below 1930s levels, recovering only by 1953. U.S. occupation forces pushed for a breakup of the old *zaibatsu* on the grounds that their power inhibited Japanese democracy and promoted militarism. A more democratic political structure encouraged the growth of labor unions, which pressed for better working conditions. They also attempted, with some success, to improve the status of blue-collar workers. Workers' wives, for example, were now to be called by the same term as the wives of white-collar employees rather than the less polite title previously used.

After a brief adjustment, however, most of the trends visible previously in Japanese industrialization resurfaced. Unions largely supported the lifetime security policies and other measures that tied workers to their firms. The government abandoned policies aimed at reducing big business and returned to active support of large firms, restoring close mutual links and intimate ties between the government and industry. Growth rates quickly resumed as well, and by the 1950s Japan was demonstrating (as it had in the periods 1905–1919 and 1931–1940) a more rapid expansion of productivity and manufacturing output than almost all other industrialized nations.

Clearly, by midcentury, Japan's industrial revolution had been successful at implanting a solid industrial economy in what had been an isolated, largely agricultural nation such a short time before. The same revolution had built distinctive organizational policies and worker habits that proved deeply ingrained in Japan's ongoing development. Finally, the revolution continued to generate an unusual level of dynamism, making the nation by the end of the twentieth century the second-largest economy in the world, behind only the United States.

10 New Developments in Western Societies

A Second Revolution? Redefinitions of the Industrial Economy

Changes in the industrial economies of western Europe and the United States were not as decisive as those surrounding the advent of industrialization in Russia and Japan between the 1880s and the 1950s. To speak of a second industrial revolution in the West may be misleading, for it downplays the unique significance of the initial conversion from an agricultural to an industrial economy that had already occurred. Instead, a number of developments simply completed the basic revolution in countries like the United States and Germany. (Only Britain had in any real sense fully converted to an industrial economy before the 1880s.) It was only in about 1900 that Germany became half urbanized (the marker Britain had achieved in 1850); the United States and France reached this crude measurement of extensive industrialization by 1920. Rapid growth of the industrial labor force through immigration ended in the United States only during the 1920s, and even then rural movement, including the great migration of African Americans from the South, continued to provide newcomers to the basic experience of factory work. Thus, the overlap between the essential industrial revolution and new trends surfacing in the early twentieth century was considerable.

Nevertheless, several important innovations transformed the Western industrial scene between 1880 and 1950. Earlier trends intensified to the point of unrecognizability; the pace of work, for example, accelerated well beyond anything imagined during the early industrial revolution. Furthermore, several outgrowths of initial industrialization were rethought, producing a substantially different version of the larger industrial experience.

Obviously, the process of industrialization in the West guaranteed further change even after the initial phase had ended. Geographic balances continued to shift within the industrial West. Britain's position declined in relative terms throughout the second major phase of the industrial revolution, as Germany and particularly the United States gained ground. British iron resources were less appropriate for steelmaking, so the nation faced new challenges when steel began to predominate over iron; technical training and organizational coordination within big business lagged. Devastating losses during both world wars further hampered

Britain's standing. British industrialization proceeded, however. There was no retreat, and the British even pioneered in some new product development, establishing the first version of the television industry in the late 1930s. But the laurels of overall leadership passed elsewhere.

The industrial revolution also continued to fan out from earlier Western centers. Northern Italy and Catalonia, in northeastern Spain, accelerated their industrialization in the late nineteenth century. Catalonian factories emphasized textiles as industrialists combined relatively advanced technology with somewhat cheaper labor, in competition with earlier industrializers such as Britain. Industrialization also began to spread to the American South; the industries that grew were those in which new techniques and cheaper labor drew businesses from earlier factory centers such as New England—notably, in the manufacture of shoes, clothing and furniture.

Two crucial developments in the industrial West overshadowed the geographic refinements. First, more powerful technologies and production organizations spurred industrial output. Second, thanks to higher output and cheap goods from other societies, a large service sector began to emerge. Both developments effectively continued the dynamic that the initial industrial revolution had already established, but both involved new specifics and new intensities. Both, finally, had obvious international repercussions: strengthening the West's economic role in the world and setting more demanding competitive standards for new industrializers such as Russia and Japan.

Machines and the Drive for Organizational Change

The two new developments were, simply, the latest versions of the industrial revolution's essentials: technology and organization. A new round of technological innovation had in some senses begun with the Bessemer process for steelmaking in the 1850s, and there followed in the 1870s other new furnace designs that made a wider range of iron ores readily usable. Also in the late nineteenth century came the introduction of new engines that supplemented and ultimately overshadowed the steam engine: Electric turbines generated energy from coal, hydroelectric power, and petroleum, and internal-combustion engines generated power from petroleum.

Both new engine types had a number of implications for the further development of industrial economies. They competed with older industrial forms; by the early twentieth century coal-mining districts were beginning to suffer because less coal was needed for power as a result of the rise of internal combustion and petroleum. Along with the eclipse of earlier factory textile centers caused by competition from new areas, this decline in the coal industry offered the first example of the industrial revolution's capacity to destroy prior achievements. Just as the revolution had displaced earlier domestic manufacturing, so, too, subsequent developments forced the gradual, painful deindustrialization of some prior industrial strongholds. Even before 1900 some of the less efficient mining districts in France were losing jobs. By the 1920s the industrial north in Britain, whose economy was based on steam and textiles, was suffering, and here, as in many instances, workers found it difficult to respond rapidly, creating durable regional pools of unemployment—and considerable resentment.

The new machines also facilitated the dissemination of powered equipment to a wide range of production sectors, for electric motors and gasoline engines did not require concentration in a factory. The manufacture of clothing, previously a household or craft occupation, began to move into sweatshops, thanks to the use of electrically powered sewing machines. A host of crafts faced direct technological innovation for the first time. Commercial bakeries introduced mechanical kneading machines. Construction work was transformed by the use of mechanical saws and gasoline-powered cranes and by new materials such as preformed concrete. Canning machines and refrigeration changed the food-processing industries. Technology spread beyond manufacturing, particularly with the use of gasoline-powered tractors, harvesters, and other devices on the farm. Even housework was altered by the introduction of washing machines and vacuum cleaners in the 1920s. Almost every type of work could now, in a technological sense, be mechanized. Thus, hundreds of thousands of people, many of whom had already come to terms with the initial industrial revolution, had to adjust to further shifts in methods—some more fundamental than anything that had come before.

Ongoing technological change did more than create new excitement and uncertainty. It tended to homogenize the experience of work. Artisans, particularly, became more like factory workers, even when, as in the construction industry, their jobs did not literally move into a factory setting. Skills remained important, but they were no longer likely to be purely traditional, and because of the mechanization of many operations, they were more likely to be easily learned. At the same time, unskilled jobs decreased in number. Sheer physical strength counted for less than before, since there were machines to do the lifting and hauling. Semiskilled work, already the category most characteristic of the industrialized labor force, increasingly predominated.

Renewed technological change also increased the pace and specialization of many important sectors of production. Shoe manufacturing shifted from craft to factory, thanks to the sewing machine. Textile workers saw their machines steadily expand in size and pace. Machine builders, including shipbuilders, were affected by an even greater transformation around 1900, as automatic drilling and riveting machines displaced older skill categories and thus enabled semiskilled workers (including some women) to take over key operations.

The technological changes in advanced industrial economies focused on a steady proliferation of new product lines. Even before 1900 the chemical industry had begun to develop a host of novel products, including new kinds of explosives and dyes, and also the material called "plastic." These innovations continued after World War I, with such achievements as the production of artificial fibers, like the nylon and rayon that provided disturbing competition for Japan's silk exports. Electrical equipment was another area of product development, involving not only a steady stream of new household appliances but also unprecedented consumer items such as the radio.

Finally, in the early twentieth century, technological development became wedded to the other basic facet of the industrial revolution: the growing size and sophistication of organizational structure (see Figure 10.1). Major industrial corporations began explicitly to sponsor research and development, seeking additional gains in mechanization, per-worker productivity, and in product diversification. German industry led the way, even before 1900, and benefited from some close links with university-based chemical research. New medicinal drugs and chemical fertilizers were among the diverse results of this self-conscious organizational thrust toward innovation. Shortly after 1900, major firms in the United States began tentative experiments with regular research staffs.

Growing organizational sophistication involved more than technology, however. The assembly line became both the symbol and the reality of the increasing application of systematic organization to the workplace. Pioneered in the United States, particularly by automobile manufacturer Henry Ford after 1910, the assembly line crystallized earlier efforts to measure and routinize work. With the assembly line, semiskilled workers using electrically powered equipment repeated simple operations such as riveting bolts while an engine block or chassis moved by them on a conveyor belt. The goal was, as Ford's engineers put it, to make workers as much like machines as possible—to remove any need for thought or reflection (see Photo 10.1). These developments not only intensified

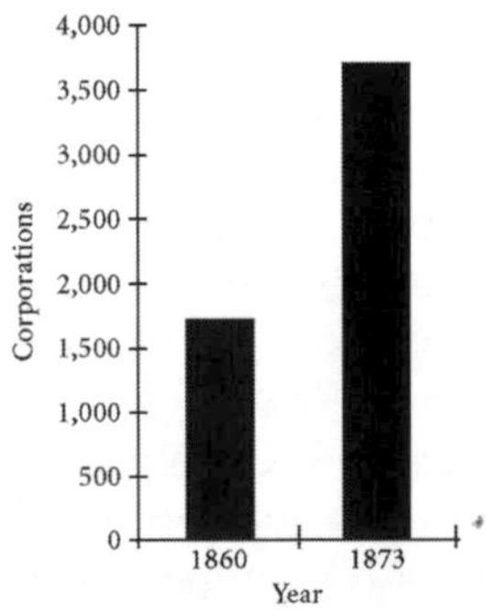

Figure 10.1 Corporations in western Europe, 1860–1873.

Photo 10.1 Workers on an Early Assembly Line at the Ford Motor Company. The Growing Automobile Industry Contributed to Economic Prosperity in the United States during the 1920s (Chronicle/Alamy Stock Photo).

the industrial experience in places such as the United States and France, where work had already been substantially transformed, but also were built into the very process of industrial revolution in newcomers such as Russia, where the effort to incorporate advanced organizational features from the West ran particularly strong after the 1917 revolution.

With larger and more sophisticated organization came the spread of giant corporations—a trend already intrinsic in industrial economies by the 1880s but extended steadily thereafter. Hundreds of new corporations formed each year in countries such as France and the United States. Some of them were small, but by selling shares to the public, they acquired considerable resources for expansion. Huge firms strengthened their hold in heavy industry and chemicals and the process spread. Newer industrial sectors, such as the burgeoning automobile industry, initially opened the way for small-scale industrialists. Car companies proliferated throughout western Europe and the United States between 1900 and 1914, but competition drove many under and yielded a handful of big conglomerates. New technologies, including the assembly line, increased the investments required, which favored larger units. Many companies were bought up or merged with the growing giants. By the 1920s big business was well on its way to predominance in this industrial branch as well.

Increasingly also, big business now meant international links. Major industrial companies had set up sales operations internationally even before the 1880s; British textile firms, for example, had agents in Latin America. Some companies had also spun off manufacturing operations. French textile firms had sponsored subsidiaries in New England and Latin America by the mid-nineteenth century, and U.S. firms had set up international subsidiaries by the 1870s. With further growth and increasing interest in international investment, these trends accelerated after 1880. German chemical companies established branches in the United States to exploit its market for their growing array of products. U.S. car manufacturers were returning the favor by the 1920s. Multinational business was beginning to come into its own.

Both technological and organizational changes rapidly increased the size of the average work unit. Small businesses still had a chance in retailing and in new branches of industry, but their role measurably declined after about 1900. Even many small firms—like the automobile repair shops that sprang up widely in the 1920s and that seemed reminiscent of a craft atmosphere—were effectively controlled by the large manufacturing operations on which they depended for supplies or orders. Formal, rationalized organization increasingly became the norm. Team play, rather than freewheeling entrepreneurship, began to be emphasized. This trend even reached boys' games: American football gained in school popularity because it simultaneously enhanced masculinity and taught the importance of cooperation. For many workers, the growth of big business meant the need to deal with increasingly impersonal organization and with generalized work rules. U.S. corporations in the 1920s began to sponsor personnel research conducted by trained industrial psychologists; the goal was to find ways to manipulate the work environment to raise output and reduce friction. Soon music was being played over loudspeakers in many settings because it had been discovered that its soothing impact increased productivity. And foremen were being taught that if they prompted an aggrieved worker to repeat a complaint several times, the worker would ultimately become embarrassed and often reluctant to press the grievance further.

These developments, extending fairly steadily through the decades after 1880, continued the rapid alteration of economic structure and working life. Many workers argued that the changes they faced were greater than those the initial factory workers had encountered. They may have been wrong: after all, they were not the ones moving from farms to factory. But their anxieties certainly reflect the fact that, whether or not the idea of a "second" revolution is really useful, the industrial revolution featured recurrent change. By the 1890s British workers were claiming that an earlier ability to sneak naps in the corner, unnoticed by a foreman, had been eliminated by a much more intense pace. Complaints about nervous exhaustion increased. A German worker lamented that, because of the concentration required on a fast-paced assembly line, "my eyes burn so that I can hardly sleep." Americans in the 1880s discovered a new disease, neurasthenia, which they claimed afflicted middle-class businessmen who drove themselves too hard. This was the first of a host of ailments that gained currency in industrial countries—including stress and burnout by the late twentieth century—and that highlighted the disparity between industrial pace and human capacity. Even after the industrial revolution was well established, its intensification and its commitment to persistent change continued to have recurring unsettling effects. The fundamental trends were not novel, but their changing incarnations often seemed startling as the industrial economies matured.

The Service Sector

The ramifications of the ongoing redefinition of technology and organization opened up several new facets of the industrial experience. More than simple intensification was involved; significant new trends were being added to the mix.

During the industrial revolution proper, the growth of the factory labor force provided the most dynamic change in social composition. The numbers of urban workers and miners expanded faster than those of any other employment group. This situation began to change as the industrial economy matured from the 1880s onward. The factory labor force continued to expand, but its rate of growth was surpassed by a new service sector.

The service sector was fueled by the expansion of commerce and the growth of business and government bureaucracy; it responded to rising levels of organization. Accelerating industrial output necessitated new sales outlets, and the department store, already introduced during the initial industrial revolution, was an obvious response. Larger stores needed larger sales forces, and sales clerks began to come into their own. Growing banks needed tellers. Hotels for business travelers or vacationers needed staff. A growing white-collar workforce serviced a variety of commercial establishments and leisure facilities.

Large organizations needed secretaries, file clerks, and low-level managers. Technology also spurred new opportunities; the occupation of telephone operator joined the list of available jobs in the late nineteenth century. The steady growth of government functions brought a proliferation not only of clerks but of schoolteachers, factory inspectors, and police officers. These jobs varied in status, but people holding them shared with other lower-middle-class workers a dependence on wage earnings, the intent to avoid outright manual labor, and a lack of high professional standing. Growing hospitals, whether public or private, produced another growing set of service employees in addition to professional doctors: nurses and medical technicians.

The rate of growth was staggering. Britain had 7,000 female secretaries in 1881; 22,200 in 1891; and 90,000 in 1901. By 1900 the British lower middle class included a full 20 percent of the total population, double its relative size a mere thirty years before.

In many respects the growth of the service sector constituted a slightly novel twist on the emergence of industrial work more generally. White-collar personnel operated under the supervision of others. Department store supervisors could bully workers just as much as their factory counterparts. One German store manager in the 1920s even installed a steam jet in the toilets, timed to go off every two minutes, so that the clerks could not linger out of sight. Efforts to speed the pace formed part of many white-collar operations. New technology added its own contribution. By the 1880s the skill levels of many clerks were being altered—some said reduced—by the advent of typewriters; handwriting no longer counted for so much. Cash registers reduced the arithmetic requirements for sales personnel and speeded the work. Schoolteachers during the early twentieth century faced little new technology, but they directly encountered the general trend toward organizational control. City school boards in the United States imposed standardized curriculums and texts throughout the schools and thus reduced teachers' autonomy as part of the same rationalization that dominated big business.

If the growth of the service sector exemplified important trends in industrial work, it also added undeniable complexity to the labor force. Service work attracted far more women than factory work did. The rise of the service sector had not yet reversed the limitations on women's jobs that the industrial revolution had imposed, but it did begin to modify them. Women quickly dominated the typewriter, partly because male clerks were too proud to learn to use the new machines. Women also gained ground in occupations like librarianship and social work, service-sector jobs par excellence. The basic life course of most women was not yet revolutionized: only a minority of women worked after marriage, and only a handful of women worked instead of marrying. But the respectability of work for women was rising. More and more, young middle-class women, like their working-class sisters, held a job for a time before marriage. By the same token, men working in the service sector were far more accustomed to the presence of women than were most of their factory-worker counterparts. The stage was being set for some larger redefinitions of women's roles in the labor force after their substantial withdrawal during the initial Western industrialization.

Furthermore, male and female white-collar workers did not think of themselves as part of a larger industrial labor force. They felt separate from blue-collar workers. They touted their ability to wear middle-class clothing to work, rather than the dirty outfits of the factory. They liked to think more in terms of potential mobility than most blue-collar workers did, though they sometimes exaggerated their real opportunities.

Employers, for their part, deliberately treated white-collar employees differently. They paid them a monthly rather than an hourly wage and gave them different (usually somewhat better) benefit packages. One of the first private pension schemes was introduced in the United States in the 1870s by the American Express travel firm for its white-collar personnel.

Even some of the drawbacks of white-collar work kept the group separate. White-collar workers were pushed to control their emotions in the interests of ingratiating themselves with customers or managers. Secretarial manuals urged, "The secretary should never forget that in order to please people, he needs to exert himself." Sales personnel were told to learn the "satisfaction of controlling [your] temper, the satisfaction of returning kindness for an insult." Department-store clerks were taught middle-class ways, regardless of their origins, so that they could deal with the best clientele. A level of emotional control and even self-manipulation was involved in many facets of service work that industrial labor could largely ignore.

Certainly the bulk of service-sector workers proudly proclaimed their membership in a wider middle class, not the working class. They either shunned unions and strikes or at least organized separately. Even many industrial workers agreed that elevation into the white-collar ranks was a step upward; thus, the growth of white-collar work, whatever its real constraints, seemed to add to status potential. Upward mobility was an important new development in the social implications of an advancing industrial economy.

Leisure and the Consumer Economy

Although more powerful technology and work organization, plus the rise of the service sector, were the big structural developments, the redefinition of the industrial economy had other sweeping implications. Mass affluence and leisure time increased, substantially modifying the work-dominated tone of the industrial revolution proper. Work became more intense, and many of the West's leaders continued to tout the importance of a vigorous work ethic. But for most people the waking hours now provided a definite division between work time and other time, and for many there was some margin of income above subsistence to help define what that other time involved.

Reductions of workday hours had been painfully won. Many workers had had to strike or use political muscle to win days of fewer than twelve hours: this became a major focus of the labor movement throughout Europe and the United States. By 1900, however, ten-hour days were becoming more common, and some well-organized groups in scattered areas, such as coal miners, even attained eight-hour legislation. Campaigns to reduce hours won wider success in the early 1920s, again through a combination of legislation and strike demands. An increasing number of employers were also coming to realize that shorter days might produce better, more sustained work—intensity traded for time with no damage to output. Further reductions in hours occurred in the 1930s in response to widespread unemployment during the Depression. In addition to the trend toward an eight-hour day, weekends were gradually extended to include Saturday, or at least Saturday afternoon. Brief annual vacations were granted; as early as the 1880s Lancashire textile workers won an occasional day off to take a train to the beach, where (not knowing how to swim) they sat, presumably contentedly, in their Sunday best.

Simultaneously, standards of living rose. By 1900 most people in the industrial West were predictably earning more than subsistence, though a distressing minority still suffered greatly. Earnings went up further in the 1920s, except for workers in some of the declining sectors, such as coal mining.

These developments set the stage for a redefinition of the relationship between leisure and industrial life. Leisure opportunities, drastically reduced during the initial industrial revolution, began to explode. Popular theater emerged; called "music hall" in Britain and "vaudeville" in the United States, the mixture of song and comedy helped lead directly to the new motion picture industry after 1900. Professional sports teams drew huge crowds to soccer and rugby in Europe, and to baseball and, a bit later, football in the maverick United States. The new leisure had a number of features. It organized masses of people for rather standardized, commercial fare. It provided escape from the daily routine, but in some versions (notably sports) it also replicated features of industrial work, such as rules, speed consciousness, and specialization. Not surprisingly, the new leisure also depended on industrial technology, from the tram lines that took the urban masses to large concrete and metal stadiums, to the vulcanized rubber balls that were mass-produced from the 1840s onward, to the newly invented stop watches that kept track of athletes' speeds. Much of the new leisure, finally, was rather passive, watching other people perform in various ways. Clearly, a revolution in leisure was under way, but it came a bit later than the industrial revolution itself and it inevitably provoked ongoing debate about whether it really replaced the qualities that more traditional, community leisure forms had provided.

Mass consumer values were not new; they had surfaced in the eighteenth century around the new interests in stylish clothing that had helped trigger the industrial revolution. By the late nineteenth century, however, consumerism could be more widely indulged throughout the West. New products such as bicycles—an 1880s fad—and the automobile represented more expensive consumer items than had ever before been sold widely. Interests in soaps and cosmetics reflected new compulsions surrounding personal hygiene and appearance. For some people, consumerism involved more than money to spend. It came to express deep personal impulses and identities in a society where work conveyed less meaning than had traditionally been the case. A growing advertising industry—another service-sector outcropping—worked to encourage and channel impulse, to make people care deeply about the things they could acquire—or hope to acquire.

Class Warfare

Along with the rise of the service sector and the new leisure and consumerism in Western society, levels of popular protest increased greatly from the late nineteenth century into the 1950s. There were fits and starts in this development, but the trend was obvious. More and more workers gained the ability to protest through strikes, unions, and political parties. U.S. workers showed less interest in socialism than did their European counterparts, but they participated strongly in the same kinds of industrial campaigns. These were peak decades of factory conflict, and a number of bitter and bloody clashes were part of the process (see Photo 10.2).

Strike rates rose almost every decade until the late 1950s, interrupted only by wars and depression. Increasing numbers of factory workers went on strike periodically. Unskilled workers, like dockers in Britain,

Photo 10.2 The Memorial Day Massacre Near the Republic Steel Corporation Plant, South Chicago, May 30, 1937 (Granger Historical Picture Archive/Alamy Stock Photo).

gained the capacity to strike powerfully for the first time in the 1880s. Many strikes focused on improving wages and hours, no small goals; workers showed an increasing ability to phrase progressive demands, asking for conditions—such as a shorter working day—that they were convinced they deserved but that had not existed before. More sweeping objectives were voiced in some major strike movements that disputed employers' rights to set the conditions of work unilaterally. A rash of these strikes over workers' control occurred in western Europe and the United States right after World War I. Most failed.

New levels of unionization matched the surge of strikes and involved ever larger numbers of workers. Craft workers continued to organize, and as factory labor joined the trend, new industrial unions emerged that stressed the power of numbers rather than special skills. Large national confederations grouped the unions, making them more politically potent and counterbalancing, to an extent, the growth of big-business power. The French General Labor Confederation was formed in 1895. The American Federation of Labor started a bit earlier, and the more aggressive, industrially based Congress of Industrial Organizations was launched in the 1930s. Finally, in most European countries, massive votes, largely though not exclusively from the working class, propelled socialist (and, after 1918, communist) parties to great prominence.

For many workers, a new commitment to socialism meant far more than a passing political preference. A German worker, not a fanatic, put it this way shortly before 1900:

> You know, I never read a social democratic book and rarely a newspaper ... All that does not amount to much. We really do not want to become like the rich and refined people. There will always have to be rich and poor ... But we want a better and more just organization at the factory and in the state. I openly express what I think about that, even though it might not be legal.

Others could be more intense: "We are driven like dumb cattle in our folly until the flesh is off our bones, and the marrow out of them." Deep-seated resentment was heard, too: "The consciousness of dependence on the employer embitters me. A gesture of the director is enough to make my blood boil."

The surge of working-class protest reflected new capabilities. Most Western governments had introduced some level of democracy by the 1880s and reduced the legal limitations on strikes and unions. These changes, plus growing experience of industrial life, made more protest feasible. Workers were not necessarily angrier than they had been during the industrial revolution proper—indeed, they may now have accepted more aspects of industrial life—but at last they could do something about their discontent, and they had plenty of discontent left. Furthermore, additional work changes by 1900 triggered unrest that found an outlet in the unions and protest votes. More impersonal employers, new pressures on the pace of work, loss of accustomed skills (even factory skills), and technological threats to job security—all these fueled an unprecedented outburst.

To be sure, there was no outright revolution. The contrast with the pressures that early industrialization generated in Russia remained important. A number of sectors in Western society were content or, if not content, at least hostile to the workers' cause. Workers themselves were more typically bent on shorter hours or higher pay than on fundamental restructuring. Many seemed more intent on bettering their position within industrial society than on challenging the industrial structures themselves. Nevertheless, during the maturing of the West's industrialization, the class warfare implicit in the industrial revolution emerged to color not only factory life but the political process itself.

Redefining the Scope of Industrialization

The extension of the industrial economy in the West, plus some of the specific changes that took shape after the 1880s, linked industrialization to a variety of other developments. During this period the implications of the industrial revolution for war were fully realized. World War I broke out in part because of the social tensions building in industrial life. It cannot be said that leaders in countries such as Britain and Germany saw war as desirable, but they at least viewed it as a potential distraction for the aggressive working class. Military buildups and, particularly, the naval arms race that engulfed Britain, Germany, and France were related to the growing capacity in heavy industry and the power of big businesses to induce governments to buy their wares. Germany's Navy League consisted of a mixture of aristocrats, who saw military glory as a compensation for the decline in their economic status, and armaments manufacturers—both bent on a big spending program. The war was partly caused, then, by stresses in the industrial economy. The conflict itself showed the power of industrial technology in gruesome starkness: poison gas, long-range artillery, submarines, and aerial bombardments showed the hideous side of technological wizardry. They killed far more troops than had ever before died in combat in such a short period of time, and they blurred the distinction between soldiers and civilians in many areas. Industrial organization helped governments devise plans to ration goods and labor and to propagandize the citizenry. Total war—the deployment of newly destructive technology and mass mobilization, a twentieth-century creation—was industrial war, and World War II later documented its further advance.

Spreading industrialization in the West also began to create new kinds of environmental issues. Early factories spewed out smoke and were often condemned for their ugliness. Railroad lines and steamships had provoked realistic fears of fires and noise. Many disputes had developed over the damming of streams for waterpower. The industrial revolution proper, however, had not generated any explicit environmental concern. Even after 1900 most reformist attention focused on worker and consumer safety. New regulations, common in the West's industrial states, called for more protective devices around machines and in the mines, curtailed unhygienic practices in food processing, and introduced some oversight over the production of medicinal drugs.

Water quality drew attention as well. The sheer growth of cities, which often had unprocessed sewage running into local rivers, and the growth of the chemical industry, with its cost-saving impulse to dump industrial waste products into the same rivers, produced noticeable health hazards by the end of the nineteenth century. Government regulations gradually worked against this tide, though the effort to keep pace with industrial and urban growth often seemed hopeless. Pollution rates increased perhaps more slowly in the second quarter of the twentieth century, but the basic problems remained. Air quality was another obvious concern. Heavy industrial centers such as Pittsburgh, Pennsylvania, generated such intense smoke by the 1920s that midday could look the same as dusk. Realization of the health hazards came slowly to a public that depended on this same industry for jobs; a Pittsburgh myth lasting into the 1930s held that smoke was beneficial for keeping down germs. Any industrial setback, like the 1930s Depression, retarded pollution-control efforts, for employment was paramount. "We like to see smoke," said one politico in 1939 as the city eliminated its Bureau of Smoke Regulation. "It means prosperity." Nevertheless, concern did grow in Pittsburgh and other industrial areas during the first half of the twentieth century, though the environmental problems generated by expanding industry grew faster (see Photo 10.2).

The West as New Model

The aftermath of the West's initial industrial revolution had revolutionary qualities of its own. Some basic early industrial trends were reversed, as in the expansion of leisure time and activities. A fierce concentration on production gave way to new interest in consumption and to a new need to provide a growing output that frequently seemed to outstrip demand. Other trends magnified developments inherent in the industrial revolution itself. Class conflict was a case in point, and environmental problems and renewed organizational innovation directly extended industrial revolution themes and increased their visibility.

Recurrent upheaval in the industrial West enhanced the industrial revolution's impact on the course of modern history. Although it would be wrong to argue that the two world wars followed solely from the industrial revolution, it would be folly to ignore industrialization's vast influence. The same ongoing dynamism and disruption obviously affected

Photo 10.3 A View of the Jones & Laughlin Steel Company along the Monongahela River in Pittsburgh, Pennsylvania, Mid- to Late Twentieth Century (Granger Historical Picture Archive/Alamy Stock Photo).

the wider effects of the industrial revolution on the world. The West continued to innovate sufficiently to maintain its industrial lead over the rest of the world. That lead diminished in relationship to Japan and Russia, but it persisted despite two devastating world wars. New productive capacity and problems of generating adequate internal demand, even with the rise of consumerism, increased the pressure to find markets and supplies elsewhere. Part of the industrial revolution's impact continued to involve responses to the West's economic power.

Finally, the West's new features—its consumerism and mass leisure, its industrial unrest, its further innovations in technology and organization—obviously set potential models for other societies making some effort to industrialize. Many Russians, for example, ultimately wondered how successful their industrial society would be if it did not match the consumer standards the West had generated by the mid-twentieth century. The Japanese began to convert to greater consumerism, complete with department stores, soon after 1900. Ongoing changes in established industrial societies, in sum, despite their many limitations and drawbacks, continued to affect the definition of what the industrial revolution was all about. This was as true in the rest of the world as in the West.

11 The Industrial Revolution in International Context

Even in 1950 most people in the world lived in societies that were not yet engaged in a full industrial revolution. The industrial economies were still geographically concentrated in Europe (now including east-central regions such as Poland and Czechoslovakia plus parts of Spain and Italy), Russia, Japan, and much of North America. Most of Asia and virtually all of Africa and Latin America were not yet industrialized. However, the spread and intensification of the industrial revolution inevitably had a far greater world impact than during the revolution's earlier decades. Shipping increased in volume as international trade climbed—the construction of the Suez and then the Panama canals had a huge impact on this growth—and the airplane and radio speeded communication worldwide.

Within this context, several regional reactions to the industrial revolution took shape in the decades right before and after 1900. First, there was a heightened exploitation of nonindustrial areas by the grasping industrial economies. Africa was more fully drawn into the process of supplying foods and raw materials to slake the seemingly unquenchable appetite of industrial Europe. Japan began exploiting raw-materials areas in Southeast Asia. Europe, but and even more the United States, increased reliance on Latin America as a source of cheap supplies. Indeed, North-South trading began to gain ground with great rapidity as larger sections of the Northern Hemisphere industrialized and used areas in the Southern Hemisphere for supplies and materials. To put it simply, western Europe used Africa as its primary reserve, the United States used Latin America, and, more tentatively, Japan began carving out a zone in eastern Asia. Russia pressed its holdings in central Asia to supply various raw materials, often at the expense of the environment.

Second, concomitant with the growing industrial reliance on raw-materials suppliers (and the dependence of the latter on investments and manufactured goods from the industrialized states) was an important extension of manufacturing, including factory production, in centers that were not yet industrialized in any full sense. Many of these centers produced relatively cheap factory goods for sale to the industrial West. These areas experienced considerable economic change, including shifts in work patterns and in technology, but they remained inferior to the industrialized states. Unlike Japan, they did not gain ground in relative terms. Parts of the Middle East, port regions in China, and some Latin American countries such as Mexico experienced this kind of manufacturing expansion, tied to world trade in unfavorable terms.

A third development involved the emergence of significant but discrete industrial sectors within a still largely agricultural economy, after producing goods mainly for internal use. Elements of this evolution had occurred before, but industrial sectors now became more important. India, for example, developed its impressive metallurgical industry, though this did not affect the bulk of the economy or generate a full industrial revolution. By the 1920s several societies had introduced a policy of *import substitution* to limit their dependence on industrial imports. High tariffs encouraged growth of factory production in sectors like textiles and automobiles in places like Iran and Turkey. This was a vital modification of earlier patterns.

Finally, several societies within the British Commonwealth developed extensive industry along with the sophisticated commercial production of food or minerals for sale to the West and Japan. Canada, in particular, became a significant industrial power. Canada, Australia, and New Zealand were industrialized in a distinctive fashion because of the continued importance of the nonmanufacturing sector, but their populations enjoyed essentially industrial living standards and experienced essentially industrial work habits. Even the United States, an industrial giant also dependent on significant exports from commercial agriculture, belonged to this distinctive category to some extent.

Thus, along with the growing international impact of the industrial revolution, different regional responses generated an increasingly complex world economic map. A simple division into those involved and those not involved in an industrial revolution was inadequate to describe the variety of reactions that industrialization now spawned.

The Expansion of Commercial Exploitation

Industrialized areas needed growing amounts of food and raw materials from other parts of the world. Expanding transportation and new technologies in mining and other kinds of resource extractions encouraged growing incursions into otherwise nonindustrial economies. Labor was rearranged to generate the necessary output. In crucial cases such as Africa, new and increasingly effective colonial administrations provided a political framework for economic change. Even in the independent nations of Latin America, Western businesses often acquired direct ownership and management of essential enterprises, no longer relying on local leadership to manage laborers and produce the necessary export goods. For example, U.S. firms owned and operated copper mines in

Chile, and another U.S. concern, the United Fruit Company, ran plantations in many Central American nations. The fundamental spur was the spiraling volume of output required. Although recessions frequently cut into this international economy, the industrial markets of Europe and the United States consumed more and more tropical products, such as bananas, coffee, and raw materials. Their need stimulated their increasingly direct role in nonindustrial economies.

Several tactics were devised to respond to new export opportunities, including outright compulsion. In the European colonies, peasants were subject to taxes that could be paid only in export goods or through wages earned by working on European estates. Forced labor occurred, particularly in the Belgian Congo in Africa, where villagers were flogged, mutilated, or even killed if they failed to meet production quotas. Other devices included company stores—used, for example, in the hemp-producing areas of eastern Mexico, where rope was made for export; workers could be tied to a company by their debts and forced to work long hours for low pay in consequence. In this case, Mexican employers imposed on a largely Indian labor force, supplementing their debt control with cheating—cooking the books so that debts could never be paid off—and flogging. As one English observer noted in 1909, the Indian hemp worker "will never escape the cruel master who under law as at present administered in the Yucatan has as complete a disposal of his body as of one of the pigs which root around in the hacienda yard." Finally, in some parts of the Caribbean and Southeast Asia, plus Pacific islands such as Hawaii, which were rapidly being converted to cash-crop production, additional workers were imported from other areas (such as India, China, and the Philippines) to help keep wages low.

The search for cheap, easily controlled labor was not the only goal. Western managers and many local landlords tried also to compel workers in the export sectors to labor harder and more efficiently. They taught them new farming techniques designed to increase crop yields. And of course they prodded them to specialize in market crops rather than to produce the traditional array of subsistence foods. Cotton, cocoa, peanuts, palm oil, tropical fruits, rubber, and hemp, along with increased amounts of already popular items such as coffee, tea, and sugar—these were the agricultural growth sectors in Africa, Latin America, and Southeast Asia, and they consumed a steadily increasing amount of land (most of it previously devoted to food products for local use) and a growing percentage of rural labor.

Along with cash-crop agriculture, mining sectors grew rapidly in much of the nonindustrial world during the late nineteenth and early twentieth centuries. Roads and railways were built primarily to facilitate the movement of minerals and farm produce from the interior of the nonindustrial areas to ports, where they were then shipped to Europe and the United States (see Photo 11.1). In the mines themselves,

Photo 11.1 Hundreds of Miles of Railtrack Are Used at This Gold Mine in Johannesburg to Bring the Ore from Outlying Shafts to the Processing Plant (Photo by Three Lions/Getty Images).

advanced technology was introduced—for example, dynamite to loosen rock and, of course, rails to transport ore to the surface. Like the rails and modern port equipment, mining technology was imported from the Western industrial nations, so there was little stimulus to local manufacturing. At the extreme, the dependent economies clearly reaped little advantage. They produced cheap goods for foreign companies, traded largely through foreign firms that took a healthy profit for their services; imported expensive modern equipment that yielded another set of profits for the industrial West; and had to borrow from industrial areas to fund the whole arrangement—thus paying interest to the West on top of everything else.

These patterns of export expansion applied to many parts of the world in the second phase of the industrial revolution. Increasing use of rubber spurred the development of the export economy and Western-owned plantations in Vietnam and Malaysia. Other parts of Southeast Asia were pulled into the production of a variety of cash crops. American and British estates grew sugar and pineapples in Hawaii.

Some of the smaller, newly independent nations of eastern Europe were also drawn into a pattern of increasing commercial production based on exports to the industrial West. Romania, for example, steadily expanded its agricultural exports to western Europe during the late nineteenth century. Initially, this expansion depended on the labor obligations of serfdom. Then, when serfdom was abolished in 1864, landlords pressed peasant laborers to step up their export production. To maintain this export agriculture, new techniques had to be introduced by about 1900. Landlords began to adopt steam-driven tractors and other machines, which boosted crop yields but also displaced many traditional rural workers. This process led to a fierce peasant revolt in 1907. At this point, Romania's agricultural exports, supplemented by some wood and petroleum sales, exceeded total imports. Both exports and imports had sextupled since 1865 as Romania became fully engaged in the international market. Imports, however, became increasingly vital, for the mechanization needed to sustain modern agriculture depended on products made in Britain, France, and in particular Germany. After World War I, land reform gave greater voice to the peasants, who reduced export production by returning to more traditional farming methods. But standards of living also fell, and Romania's dependence on German industrial exports actually increased. The country seemed trapped in an economy subordinate to western Europe.

The most dramatic economic change occurred in Africa, which now became Europe's southern economic backyard, just as Latin America increasingly served that role for the United States. European-owned mining firms produced gold, diamonds, copper, and other vital minerals in various parts of southern and central Africa, pulling in huge labor contingents in the process. African work and family patterns were disrupted as men were coerced or cajoled into long stints in mining areas, occasionally bringing back some cash earnings to their native villages and the families they had left behind. European bosses pressed these workers to adapt to a Western sense of time, a process that created resentment on both sides. Both South Africa and the Congo drew workers not only from the immediate vicinity of the mining centers but also from adjoining colonies within a wide radius. Earnings from migratory workers employed in South African mines formed one of the foundations of the economy of southern Mozambique, a Portuguese colony, from about 1900 well into the late twentieth century.

European pressure also generated the familiar pattern of cash-crop dominance. Several areas in western Africa saw the advent or expansion of plantations producing coffee and sugar. The most widespread European interest, however, lay in developing African cotton exports that would reduce European dependence on the more expensive exports from the southern United States. Some African farmers voluntarily shifted to cotton production, realizing that it could earn them enough money to buy food and some cheap imported manufactured products such as bicycles as well. Where self-interest did not work, however, European colonial administrators frequently used compulsion.

This pattern emerged clearly in colonial Mozambique, particularly after 1926. Portugal, desperately trying to increase its own industrialization because it lagged behind most of western Europe, pressed peasant farmers to shift to cotton production. For a time officials relied on market incentives, hoping that peasants would seek to make money by specializing in cash-crop production. With a new authoritarian government in 1926, this policy changed to outright compulsion. A Colonial Cotton Board was established with powers to require peasants to plant a certain number of fields in cotton and to work a certain number of weeks each month to generate the targeted output. Loyal chiefs and police were used to back up these directives, and Christian missionaries preached a dual message of hard, efficient work and acceptance of cash-crop agriculture. Nearly 80,000 peasants in northern Mozambique had been forced into this system by 1937, and 645,000 were involved by 1941. A large number were women, particularly in portions of the colony where the able-bodied men worked in South African mines. Peasants who refused to participate were whipped or imprisoned; terror cemented this system.

The peasants had every reason to prefer their older agriculture. Growing cotton paid little. It was a difficult crop in Mozambique's conditions, and it took both land and time away from producing food for survival. Peasants were also required to hand-carry their cotton to market, another burden on physical strength and time. One woman recalled the system from the peasant perspective when talking with an interviewer:

> Cotton cultivation was very demanding on us. They [overseers or police] decided our fields were not sufficiently clean, they grabbed us when we were eating lunch and forced us to go back to weed. We planted, weeded, harvested and carried our cotton to market even when our husbands were gone. And when we were ill we were still forced to go to our cotton fields.

The index of peasant hardship in this system was the standard of living. Although a few loyal chiefs and overseers earned good money, sometimes buying bicycles or cars and indulging in purchases of art, most of the farmers were impoverished. Diets deteriorated because of meager earnings combined with lack of time to grow traditional foods. Reliance on manioc increased, for the plant required little care; in some regions it came to constitute up to 80 percent of all food intake, even though it offered limited nutritional value and exacerbated health problems. It was small wonder that many peasants fled and others sought ways to circumvent the cotton-production system.

The Mozambique case was particularly dire; not all cash-crop and mining systems produced such hardship. Nevertheless, the Western-induced imposition of new agricultural patterns, plus the growth of mining, invariably distorted standard work routines, spreading many aspects of the industrial labor system literally around the world. But these aspects were not accompanied by some of the compensations (reduced hours and higher earnings) that advanced industrialization brought to factory workers.

Although Latin America, Africa, and Southeast Asia were the principal scenes of evolving commercial dependency, other locations opened up in the twentieth century. Oil was discovered in the Middle East early in the century. In 1912 the Turkish Petroleum Company was founded by German, Dutch, and British capitalists to exploit oil reserves in Iraq. This company underwent several subsequent transformations, merging with other entities and becoming the Iraqi Petroleum Company in 1939 that unified oil explorations and production in several parts of the region. The bulk of the profits went to Western investors until 1952. Oil was discovered in the Persian Gulf in 1932, again by Western companies. In Saudi Arabia the American Standard Oil Company won exploration concessions during the 1930s; massive production developed after World War II.

In all these instances, Western companies provided the technology and technicians for oil production, including, of course, rail lines, roads, ports, and pipelines. They drew thousands of local Arab workers into the process as unskilled labor, in some cases importing workers from other areas where, as in the desert kingdoms, the local population was sparse. The bulk of the profits redounded to the Western owners, though the local officials who granted the concessions were able to earn handsome rewards. Finally, the system kept oil prices low because it inhibited any major buildup of capital in the oil-rich regions and prevented widespread improvement in standards of living. With petroleum an increasingly valuable product to the West and to Japan as they converted to internal-combustion engines and transformers, much of the Middle East was drawn into an essentially Western-dominated economy. Not until the 1970s did Middle Eastern governments gain sufficient control over oil production to dictate substantial price increases; with this power came some larger prospects of economic development.

The final regional expansion of the dependent-economy system revolved around Japan. The industrial West led in the exploitation and transformation of Africa, Latin America, the Middle East, and much of southern Asia. Russia's industrialization did not depend on extensive raw-materials imports from other regions, since the Russians essentially converted territories within the Soviet Union, particularly in central Asia, to some of these same functions—producing oil, cotton, and other products. Japan, however, began to feel the need for an economic hinterland by the twentieth century, and this theme guided its exploitation of Korea after it took over the peninsula in 1910. Korean peasants were compelled to concentrate on rice production for export to Japan, an emphasis that forced them to eat an inferior grain, millet, in order to generate the required cash-crop levels in rice. Other Korean resources were harnessed to the Japanese industrial economy, and railroads and mines were built in what was by now a familiar pattern. There is some debate about whether some Korean factory industry expanded under Japanese occupation—a forerunner of later Korean industrialization—but there is no question about extensive exploitation. As Japanese conquests expanded in eastern Asia during the 1930s, the nation's leaders trumpeted a larger "Asian co-prosperity" scheme that involved Japanese use of crops and minerals from other Asian regions (including rubber from Malaysia and oil from Indonesia) in return for infrastructure development by and factory imports from Japan.

DEBATE #11: *THE FUTURE OF THE NEW DEPENDENT ECONOMIES*

Was the growing inclusion of nonindustrial regions into the global industrial economy good or bad for the areas involved?

Historians and economists have debated the impact of the growing range of commercial expansion throughout most of the nonindustrial world. Some have argued that the results of increasing export specialization, despite some important initial hardships, provided a constructive opportunity for nonindustrial regions to develop comparative advantages—that the introduction of new work skills and habits, railroads and ports, modern communication systems, and other technology created a foundation for later and more independent development. In this view, then, the 1880–1950 period was a stage in a larger global process, serving as a sort of "industrious revolution" for many parts of the world.

Other scholars, however, have insisted that the expansion of the cash-crop and mining thrust served simply to increase the dependency of key regions, to impoverish many of the workers involved, and to leave the profits and the key technical knowledge resident in the West or Japan. Outright foreign ownership increased, and all essential industrial goods—including modern ships and rails—continued to come from the outside world. Clearly, some individuals in Africa, Latin America, and the Middle East profited hugely. Even individual farmers, as in parts of Mozambique, learned to take advantage of market specializations, organizing larger farms with paid labor. At the same time, many people suffered from the change, and many of the regions involved have never, to date, made a smooth transition from this phase of expansion, characterized by outside industrial dominance, to an industrialization process.

(*Continued*)

The variety of ways in which different regions experienced the export-driven commercial phase further complicates any generalization. From the vantage point of 2020, what previously dependent regions seem to have benefited in the long run, and which are still trapped? And what are the main causes of the differential results?

Further Reading: David Jaffee, "Export Dependence and Economic Growth: A Reformulation and Respecification," *Social Forces* 64 (1985), 102–118; Immanuel Wallerstein, *World Systems Analysis: An Introduction* (Durham, NC, 2004).

Environmental Change

The impact of industrially induced economic change on the environment increased notably in this second industrial period not only in the factory centers but also in some of the export-producing regions. This was another result of the intensification of international dependency.

The promotion of new export crops, often not native to the area—such as coffee in Brazil—caused deforestation and often promoted soil erosion. New use of railroads intensified the production in the interior and further destroyed previous forests. The need to export was so great that no voices were raised against this change in Brazil until the 1930s, and there was no government policy response until the 1970s. Similar patterns developed in West Africa with the massive pressure to produce vegetable and palm oils. The drive for cheap exports further limited environmental concerns, launching problems that would persist beyond the twentieth century.

Factory Expansion

Several regions experienced significant factory development from the late nineteenth century onward, often with a strong orientation to the export sector. Factory growth occurred, in other words, but in highly selected branches of production and without bringing full industrialization. The results were in some ways more promising than in the cash-crop and mining sectors, in that a wider array of technologies was brought to bear, but considerable dependency on the industrialized regions persisted.

The Turkish portion of the Ottoman Empire was one region that generated increasing factory production for export in the late nineteenth century. Growing prosperity in western Europe and the United States meant a rising demand for Turkish carpets—no middle-class home seemed to be without these beautiful craft products. Western merchants, along with some Turks, organized expanded hand production from the 1870s onward, drawing in thousands of new workers. This expansion helped provide some employment for workers displaced from the traditional textile industries by imports of machine-made Western cloth. Carpet exports approximately doubled between the 1870s and the 1890s. Given the growing demand, the methods of production began to change somewhat. Chemical dyes, developed in the West, began to replace the customary root and berry dyes used for the rich colors of Turkish carpets. U.S. consumers, in particular, liked the new bright colors better than the traditional ones. But the transition gave Western merchant houses more control over the carpet industry because many Turkish workers were unfamiliar with the new dyeing procedures. In the 1890s export opportunities and Western commercial pressures led to further change: the introduction of factories to make carpets, alongside the more traditional domestic manufacturing system. Several of the factories were set up by Turkish entrepreneurs. With the new system came increased work specialization and pressure to step up the work pace, not only in the new factories but also in home production because home workers had to compete with machines in order to survive. Steam-powered wool-spinning machines (imported from western Europe) were established in a number of towns in western and central Turkey. Factory workers, mostly women, were paid low wages, but they could produce more than the hand workers. The development of rug factories was also stimulated by the establishment of railroads into the Turkish interior; these were sponsored by the Ottoman government and built with Western investment and technical assistance. Rails made it easier to supply the rug-making towns and to transport their expanding product to seaports for shipment to the West.

Rug workers, even those new to the trade, were profoundly upset by the changes in their conditions, including their loss of control over artistic design and the growing separation between work and home. Like Western workers before them, they sometimes responded by acts of Luddism. In 1908, for example, a crowd of women and children attacked three spinning factories in one rug-making center, Usak, carrying off great quantities of stored wool and destroying the engine rooms. But the factories were quickly rebuilt, operating full tilt within three years.

The industrialization of Turkish carpet manufacturing shared features both with early industrialization in the West or Japan and with the growth of commercial production in dependent economies like those of Africa or southeastern Europe. As a result, it did not quite follow either of these patterns. In contrast to Africa, the growth of some factory industry in Turkey brought experience with machines other than those used in railroading and the more modern mines. The rugs produced, although by cheap labor, had considerable value; indeed, their price tended to go up because of Western demand. Turkish merchants and workers gained genuine industrial experience, though (like their Western counterparts many decades before) they often resisted the process. Nevertheless, the establishment of carpet factories did not generate a larger industrial revolution in Turkey at this point. The industry was dominated by Western demand and Western commercial control; it did not feed a broad expansion of the internal economy. Because key technology remained a Western specialty, the necessity of importing the machinery created a new dependency. Finally, the factory sector was isolated in a much larger, traditional peasant and artisan economy. Even after Turkey gained independence and had a vigorously reform-minded government eager to promote wider industrialization in the 1920s and 1930s, the overall Turkish economy lagged.

The experience of China at the end of the nineteenth century and in the early decades of the twentieth century was somewhat similar. A growing factory sector developed, providing important new work and commercial experience, but Western interests controlled the process extensively. As in Turkey, this sector was not large enough or autonomous enough at this point to trigger a wider industrial revolution. Political chaos and foreign attacks (problems Turkey faced also, in the early 1920s) further limited China's industrial potential through the 1940s. After about 1860, Western merchants operated freely throughout China. They even ran the government's custom service, which regulated foreign trade. Several major Chinese ports were acquired by treaty and run directly by Western states. In these places Western merchants established new banks and stores as well as factories, and local Chinese began to copy the economic practices of the dominant European commercial group.

Shanghai became the model of this new China, developing modern industry but under substantial Western control. British, French, and U.S. interests were paramount in the city, setting up businesses, hotels, and social clubs. They ran the local government and began to stimulate rapid economic change. Major banks were established. Modern printing presses made Shanghai the national center of book publishing. Western nations also established shipyards for repair purposes—not only for the oceangoing fleet but for river steamers that foreign companies operated within China. After 1895, other manufacturing was permitted. Foreign textile factories and flour mills competed with those of Chinese industrialists. Large numbers of poor workers were recruited as Shanghai came to symbolize, for many Chinese, both the enormous economic potential and the great social cost of Western capitalism.

At the end of the 1890s other Chinese treaty ports developed in somewhat similar fashion, and Western companies set up additional railroads. (In a similar pattern, Russia sponsored railroads in Manchuria.) The result was considerable commercial and industrial growth, and many Chinese businesses gained experience in new technology. By no means was this an entirely Western show, but Western influence predominated, and the basic equipment for the new factories largely came from the West. The new Chinese factories either were in light industries producing processed food and clothing for sale in China or were designed to manufacture export items (such as silk cloth or decorative items) for the West. The overall result constituted major change, but not full industrialization—partly because the massive Chinese interior did not participate, and partly because foreign capital and technical expertise remained so essential.

China's 1911 revolution brought a new regime eager both to spur further economic advance and to limit Western influence, but the government's weakness limited any real change of direction. Resentments grew. Between 1925 and 1927, Chinese consumers and workers staged a massive boycott of British goods and businesses, severely damaging Britain's role in China even in the treaty port of Hong Kong. Britain prudently withdrew from several areas (though it retained Hong Kong), and the tension subsided. Continued unrest in China, government instability, and then Japanese invasion in the 1930s prevented any major new strides in industrial development. China's role in the world economy became slightly less subordinate, but internal industrialization receded, if anything, amid massive disruption.

A final case of important new industrial development was Mexico, but it, too, experienced extensive foreign control and faced limitations that prevented easy movement into an industrial revolution. Mexico had lagged economically through most of the nineteenth century. Public services were poorly organized, and few railroads were built. On some of the rail lines that did exist, mules rather than locomotives pulled the cars. A new dictator, Porfirio Diaz, took power in 1876, and the Mexican economy began a significant spurt. Per capita income rose by 30 percent between 1877 and 1910, even as the population expanded by 75 percent.

Industrial production increased by an average of 3 percent per year under the Porfirian regime. The number of manufacturing companies rose sevenfold. They included the nation's first major steel producer and a massive new brewery, Cerveceria Cuauhtemoc, named after the last Aztec ruler. The brewery was established by a Mexican of German descent, José Schneider, and its production grew so rapidly that it had to set up a bottle factory as well. The new steel company, in Monterrey, expanded its production of steel rails and beams during the first decade of the twentieth century. Other factories produced chemicals, construction supplies, tobacco, and textiles.

Mexico's industrial economy depended heavily on exports. The government sponsored rapid railroad development, taking over much land from Indian villages and recruiting thousands of impoverished laborers. Foreigners, particularly from the United States, invested heavily and provided much of the necessary technical expertise. The growth of the railroads, combined with government sponsorship of new commercial codes and other organizational measures, encouraged growing foreign investment in mines and estate agriculture, both designed to produce goods for export. Silver continued to be a major export, but it was now joined by cotton, wool, canned foods, cigars, and a variety of raw materials, including petroleum. Many factories, in turn, like the food-processing and rope-making operations, primarily served the Western-dominated export economy. Reliance on foreign capital pervaded virtually all sectors, from many of the cattle and sheep ranches to some of the leading mines, oil wells, and factories. Imports, correspondingly, focused increasingly on vital machinery. Mexico supplied a growing amount of its consumer needs—in this sense, some freedom from foreign industry was achieved—but it did not generate an advanced technology sector. By 1910 expensive equipment accounted for 57 percent of all imports.

The government, staffed by a number of economic experts, was quite conscious of the nation's economic patterns. It looked to foreigners not only for capital but for the business spirit that, in its judgment, Mexicans lacked. It assumed that this stage of development would yield to a wider-ranging, Mexican-dominated process. The policies in the short run did yield a favorable balance of payments: Mexican exports exceeded imports, and the overall growth rates were the highest in Mexican history—and for many decades afterward. A large urban working class developed, many discontented not only by poor working conditions but also by their inferior position to foreign technicians. Several violent outbreaks occurred, many producing army attacks on unarmed workers. In 1907, for example, textile workers struck against a twelve-hour workday, low wages, and a dominant company store that workers were required to patronize. The strikers burned the company store, but troops responded by firing point-blank into the crowd, killing hundreds.

Worker discontent combined with nationalist resentment and grievances by smaller businesses that feared industrial growth and, particularly, increasing foreign business dominance. As Diaz aged, a revolution broke out that unseated the regime and ushered in over a decade of political disorder. Political stability returned in the 1920s under one-party rule, and with it came renewed attempts to develop the Mexican economy, though some limitations were applied to foreign investment and ownership. The earlier momentum was not regained, however, and Mexico's industrial position slipped during the middle decades of the twentieth century.

The cases of Turkey, China, and Mexico were broadly similar. They all involved significant factory development that occurred under extensive foreign control, and the results in each were insufficient to bring about a full industrial revolution. In all three cases the changes that did occur helped generate new kinds of unrest, including labor protest, that in combination with other developments (such as Turkey's loss in World War I) generated major political upheaval. This disruption delayed further industrialization. In contrast to the Soviet Union, where earlier industrialization had proceeded more rapidly and was revived soon after the 1917 revolution, industrial development in postrevolutionary Mexico and China actually declined for a while as political disputes seized center stage and foreign investors backed off. New leadership in several instances reduced foreign economic interference, but this reduction undermined part of the foundation for the industrial development that had occurred. The result, at least for a time, was a new level of uncertainty in societies where traditional economic forms had been modified but a fully industrial economy remained out of reach.

Industrial Sectors: Change amid Tradition

Several societies were able to develop particular industrial sectors, primarily for domestic use, that introduced substantial economic change though again without full industrialization. In several cases the result also reduced dependence on Western imports. Mexico's establishment of a significant steel industry was a case in point, though the larger contours of the Mexican economy diluted the impact of this step by involving the nation so extensively in foreign ownership.

Iran, under a new government in the 1920s, constituted a clearer example of import substitution through sectoral industrialization. The government did more than organize a larger railroad network, though this was an important step in developing internal markets. It also sponsored several manufacturing projects because local business leadership was lacking. It set up factories to produce cotton and woolen goods, refined sugar, and processed foods, as well as plants to manufacture glass, paper, matches, and cigarettes. All these products were for domestic consumption only and were deliberately designed to replace imports from the West; high tariffs were explicitly designed to promote this kind of import substitution. Oil was discovered in 1908 and was exploited by a British-controlled company; refineries were built in 1915. The Iranian government did not win extensive profits from this arrangement, but, unlike its Arab neighbors, Iran did not develop extensive dependence on oil revenues. The regime's principal focus was to construct a small but vigorous modern industrial sector in an otherwise backward economy. The government used advisers from Britain, Russia, and particularly Germany, seeking to balance these nations in order to avoid subordination to anyone. The goals were more political than economic. The Iranian regime was determined to maintain independence and also to extend its control over the population at home; hence, railroads were built more for security purposes—the movement of troops—than for industrial development. Little attention was given to peasant agriculture.

Iran emerged with an elite urban economy complete with merchants and professionals who adopted many Western consumer styles. It did avoid submersion in the larger world economy, but it did not industrialize in any general sense.

India constituted another case of sectoral development, though one entailing a more complex series of circumstances. British-sponsored railroad development proceeded rapidly in India from the 1850s onward. Designed mainly for military and export purposes, rails stimulated the internal economy as well. Some textile factories were established in the late nineteenth century, even in cotton; the machinery was imported from Britain. Most of the textile products were cheap goods, and many were exported to other parts of Asia; ironically, the bulk of India's internal cotton textiles market continued to be supplied by British factories. Growing nationalism, however, stimulated a boycott of British-made goods in 1905. Imported saris and other kinds cloth were ritually burned. Overall import levels fell more than 25 percent by 1908, and many merchants replaced "made in Britain" with "made in Germany" labels to elude the boycott. Indian machine-made textiles boomed in this environment, and other factory industries started up in consumer goods such as sugar, matches, glass, and shoes. As in Iran and several other areas, limited industrialization reduced dependence on imports, even though the bulk of the economy remained in the hands of traditionalist peasants.

India also developed an important steel sector in West Bengal. A Bombay industrialist, Jamshed N. Tata, had begun his career in cotton mills, including some extensive factories. His sons, without government backing but with funding from well-placed Indian nationalists, moved into metallurgy, creating a major center of production during World War I. By 1939 the Tata Iron and Steel Company was the largest single steel complex in the British Empire. Tragically, India's economy overall not only failed to industrialize but deteriorated. Massive population growth in the 1920s and 1930s was not matched by increases in food production, and thus living standards worsened. Cities grew, but less because of factory gains than because of a torrent of unemployed people from the countryside. Yet a significant industrial change occurred, giving India some hold in modern manufacturing and some breathing room vis-à-vis Britain's 200-year-old commercial dominance.

Brazil was a final major nation to develop an important modern industrial sector, building on the initial changes of the mid-nineteenth century. The country had long been a center of cash-crop production, and this continued well into the twentieth century. Although the government was not yet involved in actively sponsoring industrialization, it did change the law to facilitate the formation of business corporations. By the early part of the twentieth century, local industrialists were beginning to establish factories capable of satisfying domestic consumer demand in the area of light industry: processed foods, textiles, and the like. (This was also true in Argentina and Chile.) The import thralldom to Western industrial economies was correspondingly reduced. Brazilian factories featured the characteristic low-wage labor, including many women and children. Half of all workers in the industrial center of São Paulo in 1920 were under eighteen. Safety and housing conditions were miserable, and workers were punished with fines and beatings for mistakes. Many strikes and unions surged against employer control. Industrialization remained limited, however, and Brazil, like other Latin nations, continued to depend on Western imports for heavy machinery. The Great Depression severely damaged Brazil's economy by cutting coffee exports. In this context a new military regime launched a more aggressive industrialization policy designed to reduce reliance on cash crops. The national coffee board used surplus beans to fuel railroad locomotives, and the government supported Brazilian manufacturers with high tariffs, generous loans, and police-enforced labor peace. Early in World War II the government granted the United States military bases in Brazil in return for U.S. construction of Brazil's first giant steelmaking complex. By 1945 Brazil's industrial economy, centered particularly around São Paulo, was booming. Here, as in West Bengal, a genuine industrial center had taken shape in an economy in which the earlier patterns of agriculture and cash-crop exports also maintained important strength.

Under the spur of the Great Depression after 1929, which vastly lowered export earnings for regions producing raw materials, several other Latin American governments adopted aggressive policies of import substitution. Argentina, which already had a significant factory sector, expanded its industrial output mainly for domestic consumption; so did Mexico and several other countries by the later 1930s and into the following decade. As in Iran earlier, these developments carved out a bit more local control in a harsh global economic climate.

Economies of the British Dominions

Between 1880 and 1950 a distinct pattern appeared in four nations that had particular attachments to Great Britain: Canada, Australia, New Zealand, and South Africa. The first three of these countries had been settled largely by Europeans, who displaced the earlier native inhabitants. South Africa had an important white minority. All four countries interacted extensively with Great Britain and received substantial investments and commercial preferences. All four developed significant factory industry in major cities, such as Toronto, Sydney, and Johannesburg. Large factories grew up during the early twentieth century. What marked the four as a special category among industrial nations was their continued reliance on an extensive production of foods and minerals sold at relatively favorable rates—well above the cash-crop levels earned by West Africa or Brazil—that ensured an essentially industrial standard of living for the bulk of the population (or, in South Africa's case, the bulk of the white population). By the same token, all four nations became major players in the world's industrial economy, particularly in relationship to western Europe and the United States.

Like the United States and Russia, Canada depended heavily in its industrial development on the expansion of its railroad system. It also relied substantially on outside investment, initially primarily from Britain. Major railroad building began in the 1850s, and the completion of the Canadian Pacific Railway in 1885 opened the rich western prairie provinces to the international economy. Abundant wheat production and the exploitation of mineral and forest resources were major factors for world trade. Canada exported food widely to Europe. It also exported wood products, including paper pulp, particularly to the United States. Blessed with abundant mineral deposits, including the world's largest holdings of nickel and asbestos, Canadian mines yielded a growing output. Foreign investors offered extensive capital, installing the most up-to-date mining equipment, which, in turn, ensured rising production levels even with a relatively small labor force. Canadian development around 1900 was also marked by rapid immigration, particularly from eastern Europe; 2.7 million immigrants entered Canada between 1903 and 1914.

Canada's initial industrialization focused on processing mineral and agricultural wealth. Canadian paper manufacturing and food processing were booming in the late nineteenth century, undergirding substantial annual growth rates. After World War I, U.S. investments in Canada increased. Concentrated initially in the mines and transportation system, U.S. capital expanded into manufacturing in the 1920s. Canadian automobile production, for example, became an extension of U.S. corporations. These developments produced a genuine industrial economy, but one that had particularly close ties to the larger industrial operations of western Europe and especially the United States. By the 1950s Canadians were exporting approximately a third of their annual economic product in all fields and importing a third of all consumption needs (mainly manufactured goods). Foreign trade levels were three times as high per capita as those of the United States. The economy suffered massively during the 1930s Depression: exports fell by over 65 percent but then boomed again during World War II, when Canadian farms and factories helped supply the war effort against Nazi Germany.

Industrialization in Australia and New Zealand displayed similar combinations of extensive factory industry but a pronounced reliance on agricultural and mineral exports, all leavened by massive foreign investment. In the late nineteenth century New Zealand began to serve as Britain's garden, providing massive agricultural exports, in particular mutton and wool, to the erstwhile mother country. Factory industries developed mainly for national needs in consumer goods, such as clothing and processed foods. By the 1950s a quarter of the New Zealand population worked in factories. Only a seventh worked in agriculture, but the value of agricultural products considerably exceeded that of manufactured goods, and 80 percent of the nation's exports were agricultural. Australia generated some larger-scale industry. A major steel mill was established in 1915 and still constituted Australia's largest single company in the 1950s, by which time 28 percent of the labor force worked in manufacturing. Nevertheless, the Australian economy continued to depend heavily on mining, farming, and ranching. These activities produced over half the nation's income in the first half of the twentieth century; sheep grazing alone yielded 35 percent of the total. British investment spurred mining and factory industry, and investment from the United States increased during and after World War II. Australia boasted substantial factory production in textiles, steel, and automobiles, though these were almost entirely for domestic consumption.

South Africa entered the Western industrial economy on the basis of its unparalleled diamond and gold reserves, as well as other minerals and some export agriculture. It utilized masses of African workers, in that sense fitting the more general colonial African economy. But huge South African companies that developed the diamond and gold trade were important players in the international economy, and in their wake substantial local factory industry sprang up during the first half of the twentieth century, producing both consumer goods and some heavy industrial products.

The industrialization of the major British dominions depended on unusual agricultural and/or mineral wealth, which provided investment opportunities for Western capital and which generated earnings to support a wider-ranging industrialization for national needs in the manufacturing area. Relatively small populations (or in South Africa, the relatively small white minority) won high living standards, as both mining and agriculture were conducted with up-to-date machinery that made productivity high. (South Africa, of course, supplemented this machinery with large numbers of low-paid Black workers.) Iron and coal mines in Australia, nickel mines in Canada, and the vast, mechanized wheat fields of Saskatchewan all integrated agriculture and mineral extraction into the larger industrialization process. By the same token, the value of the export products enabled the dominions to be incorporated as roughly equal participants in international industrial trade, in contrast to most raw-materials producers in other parts of the world.

At the Brink of Global Change

Even aside from the substantial industrial development of Canada, Australia, New Zealand, and South Africa, the world impact of the industrial revolution transformed the international economy between 1880 and 1950. Habits of work were radically altered for millions of workers, male and female, in Asia, Latin America, and Africa. A significant working class and working-class movements developed in port cities and export industries in many centers.

At the same time, outside Japan, Russia, and the British dominions, no full industrial revolutions emerged. Western competition and exploitation impeded full conversion to an industrial economy. So, often, did internal divisions and political disputes. In many areas Western demand for goods significantly reduced economic independence. Even many factory centers were established under substantial Western control. Dependence on sales to the West (and in a few cases to Japan) and on Western capital and entrepreneurship limited the possibilities for autonomous economic growth.

For many regions the Great Depression served as a tragic measurement of world reliance on Western markets, because as opportunities for raw-materials exports plummeted, starker misery resulted than in the West itself. Indeed, several cash-crop areas had entered a depression even before 1929 because of falling export prices and a persistent tendency to overproduce. Even areas that had launched some factory industry proved highly vulnerable if they depended on Western businesses or Western markets—in contrast to Japan, which managed, because of its wider-ranging industrial growth, to overcome the loss of its silk markets during the 1920s and 1930s. Significant industrial growth actually increased dependence on the West if the essential heavy equipment had to be imported—as was true in Mexico. Change, in sum, was almost universal, but it did not all point to a standard direction of industrialization.

Yet the emergence of active industrial sectors in several areas—those designed mainly for internal consumption rather than export—did reduce Western industrial dominance in consumer goods and, in certain instances, metallurgy. Political policies were a means of supporting this process—Iran and Brazil took this course—but they did not necessarily generate a full industrial revolution. Diversity, then, as well as change, dominated the international economic scene outside the industrialized centers. A common industrial world was nowhere in sight, yet the industrialization of the world was proceeding inexorably.

Part 3

The Third Phase, 1950s–2020s

The Industrialization of the World

12 The Industrial Revolution in the Past Seventy Years

The advance of industrialization was not high on the world's agenda after World War II compared to the challenge of restoring war-torn economies and preventing another depression. Both Europe and Japan had suffered huge losses. The Soviet Union seized experts and material from its new satellites in Eastern Europe in its efforts to rebuild. U.S. aid assisted the recovery process in western Europe, and U.S. occupation forces oversaw political and economic reforms in Japan. For a brief time, however, only the economy of the United States seemed poised for further industrial growth. Many experts believed that western Europe would become permanently dependent on U.S. economic leadership. Outside the industrial world, political, not directly economic, issues predominated as a surge of independence movements led to rapid decolonization. Economic inequalities formed a backdrop to these struggles, and newly independent states quickly turned to hopes for economic development. But the initial priorities lay elsewhere.

Yet, in fairly short order, the postwar world ushered in a third phase of international history—a phase societies are still grappling in the third decade of the twenty-first century. By this point, industrialization was directly involving far more peoples than ever before, with huge implications for world power balance, the environment, and the nature of daily life. Key political events helped trigger important new developments. Decolonization did not magically generate industrial revolutions in the new states, and vast economic inequalities persisted, even deepened, among various regions of the world. Several major new governments, however, free from direct colonial control, launched new economic programs that expanded their manufacturing sectors.

Both in Europe and in Japan, it turned out that societies that were already industrial could rebuild surprisingly quickly. Western Europe reacted to the shock of World War II and the ensuing Cold War by seeking to reduce economic and political nationalism and by committing its governments to industrial planning, creating a framework for the surprising economic resurgence of the region, which regained its position as one of the most advanced industrial areas of the world. Japan forged ahead even more rapidly.

The world's third phase of the industrial revolution had several primary facets. First, there were a number of major new industrial revolutions. Expansion started slowly, with particular focus on the Pacific Rim. But by the 1990s a number of huge economies, including India and China, pulled into the process. The revolution that had begun 200 years earlier in Britain had not played itself out yet. By the twenty-first century over half the world was effectively industrial for the first time. Regional inequality remained an agonizing problem, but its dimensions were redefined. Second, at the same time, established industrial societies moved toward a new set of technologies that had substantial social implications. Some observers talked of a third, or postindustrial, revolution in trying to convey the magnitude of these new developments. Continued change in advanced industrial societies, plus the surge of newcomers, raised vital questions about mutual relationships, including how old and new industrial economies could best interrelate. Industrialization had a more decisive impact on the international framework than ever before. Communications accelerated, commercial contacts moved to new levels, and industrial units operated worldwide in a process that came to be called "globalization." The industrial revolution, which had already changed the nature and extent of international contacts, now burst beyond the bounds of nations and even whole civilizations. Finally, global industrial growth helped to generate a new level of social and environmental change, altering many aspects of the human experience in most of the world's regions.

New Members of the Industrial Club: The 1960s

The most dramatic new industrial revolutions took shape starting in the 1960s and occurred in medium-sized nations and city-states on the Pacific Rim. The industrialization of South Korea propelled this nation to unprecedented economic levels, making it a growing force in industrial exports of such goods as automobiles, electrical appliances, and ships; by 2006 the nation had the tenth-largest economy in the world. Taiwan (called the Republic of China after Nationalist forces established their government there in 1948, following their loss to communist forces on the mainland) was a second site of Pacific Rim industrialization. The city-states of Hong Kong and Singapore rounded out the membership of the Pacific Rim's industrial club—along with Japan, of course, as senior member, soon the world's second-largest economy. In another part of the world, the new state of Israel established an industrial economy, which included a strong commercial agricultural sector. And South Africa emerged further as the only substantially industrial economy on the vast African continent.

These centers of new industrialization were not large. They combined some distinctive features in their growing industrial success that were lacking in most other nonindustrial areas of the world. All the new industrial revolutions depended on careful government backing. The Pacific Rim states, most of them initially operating under authoritarian strongman governments, meticulously planned industrial development, implicitly imitating many of the policies that had developed previously in Japan. These governments also limited political dissent. None of the economies was state-run; these countries encouraged free enterprise, but the government's planning role was crucial. Most of the newcomers also operated within a cultural legacy of Confucianism, that may have proved relevant to industrialization as well. All of the new industrial economies also benefited from strong contacts with the West. South Korea emerged from a war with communist North Korea early in the 1950s with massive U.S. support. American economic aid and military spending did not alone account for South Korea's industrialization, but it provided an important initial spur. Taiwan was another Asian Cold War center, as the United States long opposed the new communist regime of mainland China. Again, substantial economic aid and military spending—a U.S. fleet operated from Taiwan—helped launch an industrialization process. By the time the United States recognized the mainland People's Republic of China in the 1970s and reduced its commitment to Taiwan, the island's industrial revolution was self-sustaining. Singapore and Hong Kong gained advantages into the 1960s from heavy British military and economic investment. Israel drew hundreds of thousands of European Jews, who brought with them devastating memories of the Holocaust but also established industrial skills. Israel also won extensive foreign aid and investment, particularly from the United States. South Africa, where significant industrialization had occurred even before 1950, used its holdings of key resources, such as diamonds and gold, to win substantial earnings and considerable investments by Western economies.

The New Wave: The 1980s and 1990s and Beyond

The measure of an industrial revolution in this period, as earlier in the twentieth century, was an ability to begin to catch up rapidly with the economic levels of the established industrial areas. This was the stage Japan and the Soviet Union had reached by the 1930s. After 1960, South Korea fulfilled this criterion admirably.

By the 1990s, China, Brazil, Turkey, and a host of other major countries met the same test, growing far more rapidly than the established industrial centers.

Paths varied, and there were observers aplenty who remained unsure that some of the new entrants would retain their fledgling industrial status. Obviously, big gaps remained in income levels between the newcomers and the mature economies, which complicated judgments. But a prediction that, by 2050, the world's top economies would include

China, India, and Brazil, with places like the United States, the European Union and Japan struggling to match their success, was no longer far-fetched.

Beyond the explosion of outright, though still early, industrializations, a number of other countries gained greater control over their economies after 1945, partly through greater government planning and partly through a noticeable expansion of their manufacturing sectors. The economies of Iran and parts of the Arab Middle East benefited from extensive oil revenues, but they also developed an industrialized manufacturing sector without full industrialization.

A few societies, to be sure, were still simply exploited for raw materials. Far more combined some sectors of this sort with foreign-owned factories seeking cheap labor, a growth in manufacturing that produced key items for domestic consumption, and, finally, a few manufacturing branches capable of significant export. This was not a brand-new combination. Japan and Russia had shown similarly diverse features around 1900, when growing factories coexisted with cheap export operations. Whether all of the complex semi-industrial or early industrial economies would make a turn into a definable industrial revolution could not be predicted by the early twenty-first century. At the same time certain social patterns associated with industrialization became increasingly global, from consumerism to the decline of child labor. And a few new—also global—issues emerged, like a pattern of obesity that had a lot to do with industrial supplies and industrial habits. The industrial revolution still pressed on the economies of every nation in the world. A huge range of conditions, from dire poverty to steadily rising per capita wealth, glaringly revealed the continued inequalities that industrialization had furthered. But the array of adaptations had expanded, and this expansion was one of the most striking characteristics of industrialization's third phase in world history.

The Postindustrial Concept

Established industrial areas clearly built substantially on previous accomplishments. The postwar revival demonstrated that countries that had industrialized had also acquired great resiliency. The German economy was back on its feet, for example, by the 1950s, in what was proudly labeled the nation's *Wirtschaftswunder*, or "economic miracle." World War II bombing had not destroyed nearly as much industrial capacity as intended—only 22 percent was hit—and the damage, after a few painful recovery years, helped trigger investment in new, up-to-date plants. Further, the knowledge of how to run an industrial economy—the human capital in management and labor—persisted strongly. Having this prior knowledge was another reason Germany and Japan bounced back surprisingly fast, as did war-torn France and Great Britain.

The story of the established industrial economies was not simply a resumption of business as usual, however. Although the initial industrial revolution was long past, fundamental change continued to be the hallmark of longer-run developments. Older industrial sectors began to fade. Not only textiles and coal mines but metallurgy declined as a result of expanding production elsewhere in the world and a slowing of demand. New industries surged forward: computers, electronics, biological products. Higher levels of automation reduced the need for manufacturing labor; in the 1970s the growing use of robots in manufacturing accelerated this automation process. Numerous other industrial characteristics were modified. In western Europe and the United States women began reentering the labor force in massive numbers, creating a watershed in women's lives and another set of profound changes in family functions.

To many observers it seemed that another revolution was taking shape in nations that had already been revolutionized. Experts as well as popularizers tried to define a postindustrial revolution that would prove as sweeping as the industrial revolution less than two centuries before. The computer became the established symbol in this postrevolutionary imagery, as the steam engine had been before.

Each phase of industrialization had introduced new technologies; this issues around the idea of a "second" industrial revolution had already raised the tension between a major industrial revolution and subsequent change. The idea of a postindustrial economy, or as some put it a "third" industrial revolution, involved many of the same problems, but in yet another technological context. Headed by computerization—and also robotics and genetic engineering—massive new industries arose in the West and Japan. Some commentators predicted unprecedented change that would redirect industrialization itself. Others noted that, in speeding up office work and permitting greater monitoring of worker activities, computers actually extended, rather than defied, industrial trends. The new technology created great excitement, new job categories, and huge profits for some firms, and also rising anxieties in older industrial sectors; but the jury was out at the beginning of the twenty-first century on the question of how sweeping this technology's impact would be.

Furthermore, new technology was not the only challenge for the industrial leaders. Growing competition from industries in new regions, including evolving areas like Brazil, India, and China, put new pressure on established firms and labor forces, where relatively high wages often made competition difficult. Combined with the costs of aging populations, as the elderly increased in numbers, many established industrial regions faced unfamiliar uncertainties, particularly by the 1980s and 1990s. and into the new century. It was not clear that ongoing technological leadership could fully compensate.

Finally, participation in change was not uniform across the established industrial economies. Japan moved quickly into a leading role; its earlier lag, based on a later industrial start, disappeared. Western Europe also participated strongly, displaying economic growth rates far higher than it had managed during the first half of the twentieth century and, in some cases, higher than during the initial industrial revolution itself. Germany's strength persisted, but France and then Italy were added to the ranks of advanced industrial leaders. The United States helped develop many of the new technologies, but in the 1970s it seemed to falter slightly; its relative economic standing slipped until a new surge in the 1990s. The Soviet Union and its satellite economies in Eastern Europe failed to reach the most advanced economic levels for a variety of reasons, including deliberate state policy that blocked the development of a strong consumer-goods sector, unintended clumsiness due to excessive government planning and control, and the burdens of military expenditure in the Cold War. After 1980, for the first time in industrial history, a major industrial economy seemed to be slipping—not just losing ground relatively but actually shrinking, jeopardizing some previously acquired technical capacity. Shifts in the economic balance were an important part of the latest phase of the ongoing history of industrialized societies, and societies that could not rapidly move forward risked falling back.

Globalization

The international implications of the industrial revolution emerged ever more strongly from the 1950s onward. New industrial revolutions combined with the steady expansion of the industrialized economies added up to more industrialization around the world. Increased international contact was unavoidable. Revealingly, economies that attempted to isolate themselves from world currents paid the price in lagging technologies; by the 1980s both the Soviet Union and China were deciding to reenter the international economy for this reason. Only North Korea clearly held back, with a lagging economy as a result.

The new round of technological innovations associated with industrialization had an obvious worldwide impact. Satellite communications and computer linkages increased the volume and speed of information flow. High-speed air travel made international business meetings and expert conferences commonplace.

The greatest organizational innovation associated with the contemporary phase of the world's industrial revolution centered on the development of multinational corporations. As in many other aspects of ongoing industrial change, the multinationals built directly on earlier patterns. The true multinational, however, did more than establish subsidiaries in various countries. It set up specialized manufacturing operations around the world for the assembly of completed products from parts manufactured in a host of separate countries. The ability of multinationals to find cheap factory labor in societies not fully industrialized testified to the spread of industrial work habits and technical capacities well beyond the industrial societies themselves; this same ability obviously extended industrial conditions ever more widely. The operations of multinationals did not equalize conditions around the world, but they increasingly brought equivalent contacts with industrial operations.

The third phase of world industrialization also saw a new movement of labor from less-developed societies to the highly industrialized nations. Immigration levels in the United States reached higher absolute rates than ever before in the nation's history. Western Europe also had high rates, and even Japan began to depend on a significant number of immigrant workers, especially from other parts of Asia. The immigrant experience offered yet another example of the world's economic inequalities, since many immigrants initially focused on lower-skilled jobs. But the experience also showed the international outreach of industrialization, as some societies came to depend substantially on the earnings that their emigrant workers sent home. Here again, the latest phase of the industrial revolution forged a new international context. The industrialization of the world's labor, like that of the world's technology and the world's business, became one of the most prominent features of contemporary world history. What had begun as a series of important effects radiating from the industrialized centers turned into a global experience.

Environmental and social globalization completed the mix. Factories in one area might now produce smoke that affected forests hundreds of miles away. Industrial accidents and oil spills might similarly pour across regional boundaries. Fossil-fuel use began to generate alarming levels of global warming. Climate change seemed to sum up the most ominous side of industrialization's latest phase.

Interlocking Trends

Not surprisingly, the most recent phase of industrial history embraces a number of key developments. From the standpoint of the industrial revolution itself, the addition of new players in the 1950s, 1960s, and 1990s offers the most straightforward change. It was also in these decades that contemporary forms of globalization coalesced, building on but also altering global industrial patterns. The transformations of advanced industrial economies, in the West and Japan, took increasingly clear shape, though references to a "postindustrial" phase began to command attention main from the 1980s onward. The real "industrialization of the world" surfaced primarily in the final decades of the twentieth century and on into the twenty-first, most obviously with the rapid surge of Chinese manufacturing but with important advances in other nations. All of these developments—from globalization to the rise of new industrial giants—must be assessed in terms of their impact on regional economic balance: the old notion of a few industrial leaders, mainly in the West, and a sea of impoverished feeder economies became increasingly outdated, but important regional disparities remained. A major global recession, beginning in 2008, contributed to new kinds of regional complexity as well. Finally, environmental problems became an inescapable part of global industrial history, raising obvious questions for the future.

13 New Industrial Revolutions

Transforming the International Balance Sheet

The expansion of industrial economies after the mid-twentieth century embraced several developments, though dramatic new industrial revolutions were at the forefront. The integration of parts of southern Europe and Eastern Europe (for example, Romania) with the industrial economies of western Europe and the Soviet Union, respectively, extended the industrial orbit. The process of dispersion showed clearly in Spain. Two Spanish centers—Catalonia in light industry and Bilbao in metallurgy—had industrialized earlier. After 1950 Spain received substantial investment from both the United States and western Europe and ultimately became a European Union member. This investment set the framework for industrialization from the 1970s onward, though Spanish industrial levels continued to lag somewhat. The same pattern emerged in parts of the American South. Before 1900 this region was largely a raw-materials supplier to Europe and the industrial northern United States. Then some light industry began to locate in mill towns, drawing on cheap labor and resistance to unionization. General U.S. industrial expansion during and after World War II created a genuine industrial boom in some southern states, which acquired an appropriate new label: the "New South." Developments of this sort were vitally important, but although they expanded the industrial geography, they created no major new themes. Rather, they extended the process of industrial integration of what had initially been fringe areas of existing industrial regions.

Far more novel and important was the surge of industrial development in Israel and outright industrial revolutions in what became known as the Pacific Rim.

Israel: Development in the Desert

The establishment in 1948 of the state of Israel involved significant industrialization. During the first half of the twentieth century, Jewish settlers in Palestine had brought with them assumptions about commerce and technology drawn from their European background. As Zionists they had a deep commitment to Israel and also to a wider range of economic activities than had been common among European Jews.

In particular, they worked to extend commercial agriculture in an area where centuries of excessive farming had reduced the fertility of the soil. They drained swamps, established new irrigation systems, and sank new wells. A major transformation of agriculture had occurred before the formation of the Israeli state. Extensive commercial production, some of it destined for export sale, was based not only on hard work and cooperation among the settlers but also on advanced agricultural technology and construction. The state of Israel extended commercial agriculture, concentrating on products such as fruits, eggs, and cotton that could be sold abroad.

Commercial agriculture laid the groundwork for the development of new industry, which was also furthered by massive Jewish immigration, initially mainly from war-torn Europe, which doubled the Jewish population between 1948 and 1953. Many of the new settlers, though ravaged by the Holocaust, brought established craft and commercial skills and moved relatively easily into the task of establishing an industrial economy.

Israeli industrialization focused on the production of consumer goods that would both supply needs within Israel and be suitable for export. By the 1960s a quarter of the population worked in manufacturing, and although agriculture remained important, Israel by this point was an industrial leader in the Middle East. The nation depended heavily on imports, particularly of advanced machinery and raw materials for industry. Despite its export energy, it tended to suffer from an adverse balance of payments, which was offset by earnings from tourism and by continued foreign aid.

The Pacific Rim

Led by South Korea, the Pacific Rim began to industrialize rapidly during the 1960s. The achievement of these countries was in many ways unexpected. Many of the new centers, including South Korea and the island nation of Taiwan, had little apparent industrial background and few particular advantages in launching an industrial revolution. Many had been devastated by World War II and subsequent events. Japanese occupation had been brutal and costly. In Taiwan a new, Nationalist Chinese government, committed to continuing the struggle with its giant communist neighbor, took control of the island. Tensions and some outright hostilities with the mainland peppered the 1950s. Korea, divided between communist- and Western-controlled zones after 1945, faced recovery not only from the long period of Japanese control but also from the costly war between North and South that broke out in 1949. Few observers in 1950 could have predicted South Korea and Taiwan as locations of the world's next decisive set of industrial revolutions. Indeed, most assumed that industrialization would come next in one of the more stable newly independent nations, such as India.

South Korea, Taiwan, and other parts of the Pacific Rim certainly matched the classic latecomer industrial model, much as Japan had before them. They faced immense industrial competition from established areas, including a rapidly rebuilding Japan. They needed to develop special advantages to catapult them into the ranks of the industrializing powers. Again like Japan and Russia, the previous leaders in latecomer industrial revolutions, the Pacific Rim nations relied heavily on state planning and state guidance—in societies governed by authoritarian leaders who actively supported the process of economic transformation and who were eager to prevent political instability. Government direction was supplemented by low-wage labor, which provided opportunities for developing relatively inexpensive factory production in certain sectors despite an initial lack of technological leadership.

Some parts of the Pacific Rim were also able to build on previous if limited experiences with factory industry. Hong Kong, for example, was one of the centers in which British and Chinese business interests had developed extensive commercial institutions and some modern manufacturing from the late nineteenth century onward. Scholars have found unexpected signs of significant development in the case of South Korea as well. Japanese occupation after 1910 had been exploitative, and many observers have assumed that the results held down Korean economic development. However, some recent research has suggested that although Japan unquestionably used Korean resources and labor as supplements to its industrial economy, it also provided some significant industrial experience on the peninsula. The Japanese government built railroads and Japanese businesses invested in some Korean factories with an eye to sales back home.

Explicit government support and some prior factory development do not, however, account for the extraordinary surge of the Pacific Rim after 1960. Many other regions of the world had governments that backed industrialization, and many had gained at least as much experience in modern manufacturing during the 1880–1950 decades. Many, certainly, could and did offer low-wage labor. Two other factors seem to have prompted Pacific Rim industrialization, differentiating this region from the many other areas where the next industrial revolutions might instead have occurred.

First, most of the areas initially involved enjoyed some special contacts with the West after World War II. Singapore, for example, had been founded by Great Britain in the nineteenth century and had long served as a major military base in Southeast Asia; this encouraged business investments even after independence in 1959. Hong Kong was another British enclave from the imperialist period; even as it gained growing autonomy in the 1960s, it was able to use commercial and technical contacts with Britain and the United States as part of its economic development. Taiwan became a major Cold War partner of the United States, particularly during the 1950s and 1960s, when the United States refused to recognize the communist regime on the mainland. Partnership meant military support, but it also meant considerable economic aid until the late 1960s. By the time U.S. aid ended, Taiwan was developing rapidly on its own and indeed generating some manufacturing competition against the United States. The same pattern applied in South Korea. During and after the Korean War, the United States poured substantial economic aid into the nation, hoping to rebuild it as a staunch Cold War ally against the communist regime in North Korea. Again, this provided not only investment but technological exchange. Many Koreans, like many Taiwanese, studied in the United States, particularly engineering, management, and agriculture.

The second factor distinguishing Pacific Rim industrialization had to do with important features that these societies shared with Japan. The fact of Japanese industrial success, including the nation's striking recovery after World War II, served as inspiration in the Asian Pacific, even in the nations that had cordially detested Japanese occupation. Commitment to reform through the agency of strong government also revived a pattern from Japan's early industrial decades. Most important, the initial Pacific Rim industrializers maintained a substantial Confucian cultural tradition. Like Japan, they had to modify Confucianism substantially in order to industrialize, providing more attention to scientific and technical training and more defiance of purely traditional learning than strict Confucianism entailed. But Confucianism also provided special habits of deference and cooperation conducive to forming industrial management strategies, building on group loyalty, and engaging in collective decision making. The same habits encouraged a bond between workers and managers, promoting a willingness to work hard and sacrifice for the good of the firm or the nation. Confucian culture provided a different context for the industrial revolution from that of Western or Russian culture, and it promoted different patterns of management and labor; but it was demonstrably successful. This cultural factor was critical to the region's ability after 1960 to steal a march on the rest of the nonindustrial world and to gain on the established industrial giants themselves.

Industrial Growth in the Pacific Rim

South Korea, the most obvious exemplar of Pacific Rim industrial revolutions, emerged in the 1980s as the most important industrial economy in the region after that of Japan. Government support combined with active business entrepreneurship to create huge industrial firms from about 1960 onward. Exports were actively encouraged, for Korea needed to earn foreign exchange to buy the most modern equipment and some raw materials. By the 1970s, when Korean industrial growth rates began to match those of Japan, Korea was competing successfully in cheap consumer goods, such as plastics, and also in steel and automobiles, and was serving a variety of international markets. Korea based its surge in steel on the most up-to-date technology, a skilled engineering sector, and low wages, soon pushing past the Japanese steel industry. The same held true in textiles, where Korean growth (along with that of Taiwan) erased almost one-third of the jobs in the same industry in Japan.

Huge industrial groups like Daewoo and Hyundai resembled the great Japanese holding companies before and after World War II, wielding great political influence. Hyundai, created by Chung Ju Yung, had 135,000 employees by the 1980s and offices around the world. The company virtually governed Korea's southeastern coast. It built ships and automobiles. It constructed thousands of housing units for its low-wage labor force, promoting worker stability at a relatively modest cost. Its sponsorship of technical schools provided a steady supply of skilled workers and technicians, for South Korea did not import labor from other areas. Hyundai, like other major Korean companies, also built a framework for workers' social life and a series of rituals that helped tie workers to each other and to the company. The similarities to the kinds of labor policies installed in Japan, particularly after 1920, were striking. Company sports facilities included an arena for the practice of the traditional Korean martial art, taekwondo. Workdays began with group exercises and other expressions of solidarity. With their lives carefully organized, Hyundai workers seemed to respond in kind, putting in six-day weeks with three vacation days per year and participating in reverential ceremonies when a fleet of cars was shipped abroad or a new tanker was launched.

Korea's steady economic gains resulted in a per capita income that rose almost tenfold between 1950 and 1990 despite massive population growth, though Korean living standards still lagged well behind those of Japan. Leading Korean businessmen amassed considerable fortunes. Korean industry competed not only in Japan but also in the United States, where Korean cars made noticeable inroads alongside more massive imports from Japan. The nation was in the world's top industrial ranks by the twenty-first century, by which point the nation had also become a political democracy.

Industrialization in Taiwan was slightly less impressive than that in Korea, but many basic trends were similar. An authoritarian government, led by Nationalist Chinese, generated some discontent but also provided considerable political stability; this pattern, too, paralleled that of Korea. Elaborate economic planning mechanisms were designed to make the most of limited capital and resources, though as in Korea government action was compatible with considerable latitude for private business. Increased government funding of education produced rising literacy rates and rapid improvement in levels of technical training.

Taiwanese manufactured products sold widely around the world. Inexpensive consumer items, including plastic products and textiles, became a Taiwanese hallmark. Japan served as the nation's most important trading partner, purchasing foodstuffs, manufactured textiles, chemicals, and other industrial goods. Japan's own explosive growth by the 1980s clearly facilitated the further development of Pacific Rim industrialization, as Japan concentrated increasingly on high-technology production, depending on other areas not only for raw materials but also for the less expensive categories of factory goods—some of which had once been Japanese staples when the nation launched its surge into world industrial markets.

The two other centers of Pacific Rim commerce and industry were the city-states of Hong Kong and Singapore. Manufacturing and banking services came to surpass shipping as sources of revenue. Oil refineries and textile and electronics factories joined shipbuilding as major sectors. Hong Kong also built on its status as a major world port. Its banking sector expanded because the city served as a commercial bridge to communist China. Export production in industry, particularly in textiles, combined high-speed technology with low wages and long hours for the labor force, yielding highly competitive results.

DEBATE # 12: *WHAT KIND OF GOVERNMENT INDUSTRIALIZES BEST?*

Political structure is a vital component of industrial revolutions. A certain degree of stability, a reasonably clear legal structure, a capacity to restrain worker protest, and some active encouragement—as in building new infrastructure—are common components. Political disarray in some regions certainly helps explain why industrialization fails to take strong root.

But is there a best political form? During the Cold War and beyond, many Western nations urged liberal democracy as the most suitable framework. What advantages might a democracy offer for a solid industrial revolution?

In fact, however, the linkage can be questioned. Where, after all, have industrial revolutions occurred in societies that were already democratic (there are one or two important cases, but not necessarily very many)? Why might democracy be a drawback?

The rise of the Pacific Rim certainly suggested the relevance of authoritarian structures, if appropriately motivated toward economic change. Later, China's impressive example of industrialization under strict government control pushed the linkage even further, and by the twenty-first century ambitious Chinese leaders were explicitly arguing that theirs was the most appropriate political model for aspiring economies. Why might authoritarianism, whatever its other drawbacks, provide a useful framework?

Of course debate does not have to end with the beginning of industrialization. Most Pacific Rim countries, like Japan after World War II, also provided vivid examples of the possibility of converting to active democracy once the industrial process was actively under way. Indeed, while granting regional diversity, a good argument can be made, both historically and in principle, that democracy may be the best form over the long haul, in consolidating and maintaining industrial change. How might this linkage be defended and explained?

Further Reading: Richard Robison, "Authoritarian States, Capital-Owning Classes, and the Politics of Newly-Industrializing Countries: The Case of Indonesia," *World Politics* 41 (1988), 52–74; Roegnvaldur Hannesson, "Democracy and Enlightened Authoritarianism," ch. 5 of his book, *Debt, Democracy and the Welfare State* (London, 2015).

Expanding the Rim?

By the 1980s the steady industrial development of the Pacific Rim—led, of course, by Japan as the oldest and largest industrial power in the region—was beginning to draw in other parts of eastern and southeastern Asia plus Australia. An eastern Pacific economic zone was taking shape, with the most advanced sectors stimulating factory development in outlying areas; the Asian countries involved gained the label, "Little Tigers." During the early 1960s, for example, the Malaysian government began to fund expansion of the manufacturing sector (then responsible for only about 15 percent of total national income). No full industrial revolution occurred, but the range of manufactured products climbed, and standards of living improved as well. Thailand was another entrant into the region's rapid-growth sectors. A significant stream of Thai workers labored in Japan (along with migrant workers from the Philippines and Korea, since Japan's labor force no longer sufficed for all the nation's needs). Exports from Thailand expanded, mainly in the category of foods and raw materials, but Japanese demand helped extend the manufacturing sector as well. The expansion of the Pacific Rim economy embraced Indonesia, where economic growth accelerated, though without as much manufacturing as in Thailand or Malaysia. Australia participated actively, expanding its industrial exports but, particularly, serving as Japan's major supplier of foods and raw materials aside from petroleum.

The Pacific Rim encountered serious setbacks in the 1990s, and Japanese growth slowed decisively. By the early twenty-first century, however, growth in countries such as South Korea had resumed vigorously, providing renewed evidence that a durable industrial revolution had occurred throughout the region.

Brazil, Mexico, and Turkey: Toward the Next Wave

The emergence of growing industrial economies in Mexico, Turkey, and Brazil did not initially rival the industrialization of the Pacific Rim in importance or drama. All three countries—particularly Brazil—entered the ranks of significant industrial exporters by the 1980s. Factory textiles in Turkey, for example, became competitive in world trade, with significant exports to advanced industrial nations such as Germany. Brazil's steel industry exported successfully to the United States, and Brazilian and Korean steel combined to dent American production by the late 1970s. Brazil also became the world's fourth-largest exporter of computers, deliberately tapping markets below the level of the most sophisticated technology and developing a substantial manufacturing sector in the process.

Governments in Mexico, Turkey, and Brazil eagerly backed industrial development, beginning their support in the 1920s (Turkey) and the 1930s (Brazil and Mexico). Government sponsorship of industry included carefully negotiated trade arrangements with other regions, active solicitation of foreign aid and investment, and support for technical training and infrastructure. Finally, all three nations had developed sectors of factory industry in the previous period in world industrial history, based in part on explicit policies of import substitution, and these served as the basis for subsequent industrial expansion. In short, none of the three was a newcomer to the industrial game.

At the same time, however, Mexico, Turkey, and Brazil continued to experience rapid population growth, though the birth rate began a rapid decline as industrialization took greater hold. A substantial proportion of the labor force remained rural, and the production of agricultural goods for export—including Brazil's traditional cash crops such as coffee and Turkey's newer success in growing fruits and nuts for sale in Europe—served as clear reminders that industrialization had not yet displaced earlier commercial patterns. All three countries contained large and expanding numbers of urban poor, as factory growth could not keep pace with the movement of impoverished people to the cities. Brazil and Mexico, in addition, had a substantial foreign debt, which hampered independent economic growth, and Turkey continued to depend on earnings from Turkish workers in western Europe. All three countries thus showed intriguing symptoms of serious but incomplete industrialization, as older economic patterns and dependencies vied with genuine factory growth. Yet there was change: Mexico, Turkey, and Brazil deliberately expanded modern industry to meet internal needs and produce export earnings.

Brazil's computer industry was a striking case in point. A nation well behind the world's industrial leaders deliberately fostered an industry capable of serving the nation's computer needs and so avoided yet another dependence on expensive imports. Governmental regulations protected this new Brazilian industry, and heavily subsidized computer engineers at the technical university in São Paulo constructed independent computer prototypes. Although the industry itself developed only in the 1970s, it clearly built on Brazil's earlier commitment to industrial growth and technological progress. The engineering group at São Paulo thus stemmed from earlier advances in university-based science and technology, including nuclear physics; Brazil by the 1970s was producing 3 percent of the scientific articles in international physics journals. Beginning in 1959 the government had supported computer research directly, in connection with the Brazilian navy. Training in advanced electronics expanded steadily. Imports of advanced Western military equipment spurred a growing interest in computers, and collaborative programs were developed with U.S. universities. By 1971 Brazil was ready to develop its own computer model, in partial imitation of European prototypes. A variety of small companies linked to the university center in São Paulo then sprang up to produce computers. Brazilian computer production depended on imports of microchips from other areas, including Japan; hence, this was not an isolated national industry. But the Brazilian computer industry did demonstrate that prior technical progress, careful government sponsorship, and a growing awareness of production and export opportunities could cause a genuine industrial breakthrough even in an economy that was, in terms of overall standards, still struggling to industrialize.

A new focus on production sectors such as computers added to Brazil's earlier manufacturing developments in steel, chemicals, construction products, textiles, and a host of other industries, as the nation generated a wide range of factory products for internal consumption and for an impressive array of industrial as well as materials exports. Although some factory sectors, such as textiles, continued to depend on low wages (as in earlier textile industrialization elsewhere), the technologically advanced branches like electronics, chemicals, and heavy industries offered reasonably good pay. Not surprisingly, this industrial surge provided Brazil with the highest annual economic growth rates in Latin America—over 6 percent per year by the 1960s and 1970s. Standards of living improved accordingly. By 1990, 22 percent of all Brazilians owned cars, 56 percent had television sets, and 63 percent had refrigerators. These levels were well below those in the advanced industrial nations, to be sure, but they were actually higher than rates in Eastern Europe and South Korea.

Brazil by this point was moving away from the patterns of the earlier twentieth century, when most industrial production had been for local needs and a surprising number of companies were run by immigrants from Europe or Japan. Now, government support for industrial growth moved front and center, and a growing number of technically trained Brazilians moved the industrialization process to a new level. Growth in sectors like metallurgy was particularly striking, often a key index of movement toward a more decisive industrial age.

For several decades, even Brazil's industrialization remained tentative. Although manufacturing generated 26 percent of Brazilian economic output by 1990, manufacturing and mining workers constituted only 22 percent of the labor force. Over a quarter of all Brazilians still worked in agriculture, and an amorphous service sector—including large numbers of domestic servants and other poorly paid, low-tech urban employees—loomed large. Brazil's economic problems, furthermore, often overshadowed its industrial development. Astronomical inflation rates—running between 600 and 900 percent per year in the early 1990s—reflected excessive government spending, which included the heavy state investments that were spurring the industrial sector. Foreign debt was also high, necessitating crippling interest payments to Western and Japanese banks and frequent efforts to negotiate some modification of the financial strictures from abroad. Nevertheless, Brazil had triumphantly demonstrated that an economy once effectively controlled by European commercial interests could gain a real margin of independence and generate an internal transformation. By the early twenty-first century, growth rates were accelerating, placing Brazil among the so-called BRIC nations (Brazil, Russia, India, China) that seemed to be the next wave of industrial success.

Mexico also experienced an impressive industrial surge after 1950, with growth rates of over 6 percent per year. Mexican president Miguel Alemán Valdés, whose administration began in 1946, fostered a policy of import substitution, deliberately promoting the growth of factory production in steel, chemicals, and other industries in order to reduce the need to buy manufactured goods from abroad. Inexpensive government loans were offered to entrepreneurs in these sectors. This policy was combined with stiff tariffs on foreign goods, excepting only the advanced machinery and tools needed to get the modern industries started. Significant factory sectors developed in metallurgy, construction goods, and chemicals, boosting mining and manufacturing to 26 percent of Mexico's total production value.

Problems remained, however. Industrial jobs did not keep pace with population growth or with factory output; by 1990 only 11 percent of the labor force worked in factories, compared with 24 percent still in agriculture and a massive floating population in the growing cities. Mexico's government also borrowed heavily, partly to finance new industry. Major Mexican-run factories still did not export widely enough to cover import needs, and debt remained intractable. The presence of many U.S. subsidiaries, openly exploiting low labor costs, signaled a mixed industrial picture despite rapid change.

Turkey had long been studied as a case in which conscious government policy, unusually open to innovation, bumped against massive poverty and cultural resistance. Expansion of education, laws promoting a more secular lifestyle than strict Muslim practice, and a host of other measures changed Turkish life, but they did not set the stage for much modern industry. Foreign investors were wary of a Muslim society, and periodic political instability also warned them off.

Nevertheless, a government focus on industrialization took clearer shape by the 1930s. State investments expanded the road and railway systems, creating the best internal transportation network in the Middle East. A central bank was set up in 1931 to control the monetary system and manage large state investments in factory sectors such as textiles and chemicals. Government mining companies also expanded. Foreign investments increased, and a state planning agency emerged in 1960 to regulate these investments while also coordinating national planning. Only from about 1970 onward did private-sector industries receive much attention. By this point extensive factory industry that used advanced technology had been established not only in textiles but also in automobiles (Turkey assembled some foreign makes and also established a domestic line for internal consumption), metallurgy, and chemicals. By 1980 Turkey had become the second most industrialized nation in the Middle East, after Israel. A mixture of enterprises was now operating; multinationals, which employed a labor force with both men and women, existed alongside more traditional, smaller units that produced for more local markets, often relying primarily on female workers. Export activity increased in sectors such as textiles. As in Brazil, economic growth accelerated further after 2000, based on industrial growth as well as agricultural exports. Overall, industrialization in Mexico, Brazil, and Turkey showed a steady buildup during the later twentieth century, followed by even more solid success for several years after 2000. By this point, their industrial expansion seemed to be self-sustaining, much like that of the Pacific Rim a few decades earlier. Slowing rates of population growth facilitated improvements in living standards as well. The result formed part of a picture of substantial global industrialization during this most recent phase of industrial history.

China and India

In broad outline, developments in these two great nations of Asia were similar, with clear industrial breakthroughs by the 1990s. The result was an even more massive rebalancing of the world economy. At the same time, each nation carved out its own particular path.

China became one of the world's great industrial producers, replacing Japan as number two overall in earnings behind the United States—but after several decades of experimentation and recovery. After some consolidation following the communist victory on the mainland, China's leader, Mao Zedong, had launched a period of intense industrialization in the 1950s based on earlier Stalinist models in the Soviet Union. Heavy industry was emphasized in a rapid-growth program backed by Soviet advisers and limited economic aid. Then in 1958 Mao shifted gears, touting a "Great Leap Forward" that emphasized the formation of rural communes that combined farming with some small-scale industry. The idea was to generate a distinctively Chinese version of communist industrialization—to rely on masses of people rather than high technology. Technical universities were dismantled. Backyard steel furnaces sprang up all over the countryside. Mao boasted that his Great Leap Forward would enable China to overtake Britain in industrial output by way of the united efforts of a galvanized people organized for mass labor, but in largely nonfactory settings.

The experiment was a disaster, at least in the short run, and China's industrialization was actually set back by as much as 30 percent. The ideal was noble: to avoid the huge, exploitative factories of the rest of the industrialized world and to limit pollution and strain on transportation facilities. But the industrial output, in fact, proved unpredictable and expensive, for advanced technology and economies of scale were deliberately absent. Politics and a heroic vision of an alternative to standard industrialization held China back for almost fifteen years. Some scholars now contend that Mao's efforts did familiarize a growing number of rural Chinese with industrial processes and products—in contrast to earlier decades when the modern industrial sector was mainly a coastal phenomenon, with traditional crafts protected in the interior (see Photo 13.1). This new familiarization may have provided the foundation for the more obviously successful industrialization from the 1970s onward. Here, some argue, was the Chinese version of the kind of "industrious revolution" that many societies need before turning to industrialization outright.

Strategy shifted after Mao's death, in what amounted to a policy revolution. In 1978 China began to adopt a more flexible and conventional industrialization strategy. Exports were promoted, and foreign technical advice was eagerly sought. Despite China's commitment to communism, including considerable state planning and a fiercely authoritarian government, private business sectors were encouraged in agriculture and industry. Some rural industry persisted, but urban production was emphasized as China worked to recover familiarity with advanced technology. Economic growth rates boomed in the 1980s, and China, thanks to its size, became a massive industrial force. Not only factories but also roads and railroads expanded rapidly. By the 1990s the nation's

Photo 13.1 A Man Drives an Early Chinese Tractor. Even Today, Much Farm Work Is Done without the Aid of Machinery (Photo by Keystone-France/Gamma-Keystone via Getty Images).

economic output was growing by 10 percent per year. In 2003 China used a full half of the world's production of concrete for factories, housing, and infrastructure expansion.

Industrial growth in China, as in other evolving economies, brought new wealth to many people. A select group of rich entrepreneurs surfaced in China, complete with symbols of high consumer standards, including television sets, tape recorders and travel abroad. Even many villagers enjoyed bicycles and other new products. Other industrial fruits were less palatable. Pollution levels in many countries surpassed those of the West and Japan. Chinese cities were choked with industrial smog, called the "Yellow Dragon," and the chemical pollution of water sources was considerable. Industrial revolution had more than local pollution effects. By 2000 China's industrial advance, combined with its huge population, placed China in second position as a world contributor to the chemical emissions causing climate change. The growing use of coal for fuel (as China became the world's largest coal-mining nation) promised a further Chinese advance on this negative achievement scale, as Chinese policy long placed economic growth ahead of environmental concerns.

China's growth remained mixed. It depended heavily on cheap labor and continued pressure on the large peasant class. Hundreds of thousands of workers from the countryside took up industrial jobs without fully abandoning village ties. Multinational companies set up low-cost factory operations in China, as in Mexico. Chinese exports were impressive, but they involved primarily inexpensive factory products such as toys (China was filling almost half of the U.S. toy market by the 1990s), as well as growing inroads in high technology. At the same time, however, China's rapid surge, combined with the growth of the Pacific Rim, caused some observers to wonder whether a vast new East Asian industrial complex was emerging, following Japan's initial lead. They noted that the area continued to emphasize modified Confucian values—which include hard work, discipline, loyalty, and education—along with forceful governments.

India's industrial growth was steadier than China's after World War II, but it took a new turn slightly later, in the 1990s. Again a government decision to loosen economic regulation in favor of more open competition was involved, though India had always had considerable private business. As in the other major cases of later twentieth-century industrialization, India's economy continued to display mixed signals.

Substantial metallurgy and mechanized textile sectors, developed earlier, continued to expand. Notwithstanding the fascinating anti-industrial sentiments of Mohandas Gandhi—India's great nationalist leader, who opposed the squalor and exploitation of modern industry and looked forward to an India of crafts and agriculture—most leaders of the new nation judged industrial growth a precondition of economic independence after political independence was achieved in 1947. The government did provide some support for handicrafts and small rural industries, including hand weaving, but the major attention went to urban industrial growth. Five-year plans focused on factory development above all. India was generating industrial growth rates of as much as 5 percent per year by the 1950s, though massive poverty remained amid crushing population growth. Advanced technology spread in metallurgy, chemicals, and computer chips, creating islands of very productive factory industries with well-trained engineering staffs in a still agricultural nation.

During the 1960s population growth briefly outstripped agriculture, but new agricultural technology and improved seeds—the Green Revolution, backed by Western expertise—restored self-sufficiency in food. Economic growth in the 1970s resumed and then managed a respectable 3 percent annual pace in the 1980s—ahead of U.S. growth but well behind that of the Pacific Rim. Government regulation, including the allocation of scarce foreign exchange, dominated the Indian economy, seeking to restrict imports to oil and advanced technology. India managed to export manufactured goods to other parts of the Indian Ocean basin, but not more widely. Import restrictions created some consumer discontent; Indian automobile production focused on two compact models, designed for fuel efficiency, and did not keep pace with demand. But dependence on other countries, such as Britain, for basic manufactured goods was a thing of the past.

With the liberalization of the economy after 1992, however, India increasingly added high-technology products, particularly software, exporting both to the industrial countries and to Southeast Asia. Using English-language as well as high-technology skills, India also entered the global service sector, with both Indian and multinational firms organizing operations that provided sales and telephone services to the entire English-speaking world. By the early twenty-first century, the country boasted a large middle class (80 million or more), complete with extensive consumer interests. Economic growth reached 9 percent per year.

Both India and China had clearly broken earlier patterns of economic lag, in many ways regaining, on dramatically new industrial bases, their more traditional manufacturing role in the world economy. Both relied on policy change, on cheap labor, and also on extensive education as ingredients for success, though their precise patterns varied. Chinese leaders proclaimed a fully industrial society as a goal for 2020, though they acknowledged that theirs was still a developing economy in many ways.

Waves of Change

The most recent period in industrial history initially highlighted rapid change in several small or midsized societies. Their innovations were striking. The internal transformation of the Pacific Rim was every bit as substantial as those of earlier industrial revolutions elsewhere. And the international impact of these new industrializations was also considerable. The industrial newcomers on the Pacific Rim not only realigned economic patterns in eastern Asia and Australia but also participated strongly in the world economy, independent of Japan's even greater voice.

The larger wave of global industrialization did not take full shape until near the end of the twentieth century, and even then there were complexities. Some of the world's largest societies, such as Brazil or India, long continued to combine four industrial features. First, they exported cheap goods, based on low-paid labor, as dependent economies had for several centuries. Mexican oil and vegetables and Turkish farm produce were examples. They also sent many workers to more industrialized regions, depending on payments sent back to their families. Second, their manufacturing growth provided import substitution, reducing their reliance on manufactured imports. Third, multinational companies, such as the Nike shoe company in China or Union Carbide chemicals in India, exploited low-paid labor and weak environmental regulations. Fourth, several industrial strong export sectors emerged, such as Brazilian computers and Chinese housewares. This fourfold combination generated growth, change, and massive new international economic competition, and at least in several key cases it was leading directly to a fully industrial economy.

Specific patterns varied: India's service-sector strengths were different from China's more single-minded focus on manufacturing, while Brazil continued to mix factory and raw materials exports. The overall change, however, forced revisions of standard historical interpretations, even as it fundamentally altered the world's list of leading industrial powers. It turned out that more modest changes earlier—such as the emergence of small industrial sectors in India and Brazil, or Mao's experiments in China—while limited in initial impact, helped set the stage for the kind of rapid growth that became possible in the decades around the year 2000. Pilot projects, in these instances, were more significant than had been clear at the time.

To be sure, there were skeptics that doubted whether full-scale, durable industrialization processes were under way. They pointed to the continued importance of more traditional, and impoverished, economic sectors. They highlighted problems that might still reverse the process of change. Thus they noted China's huge, undeniable environmental problems and the growing gap between rich and poor, along with an authoritarian government that might limit continued economic flexibility. Some of the criticisms ignored the extent to which most industrial revolutions had generated some similar issues and doubts, though it was always possible that the historical record—of ultimate industrial success—would prove to be a poor guide.

Yet most observers expected that solid initial industrializations would continue to mature, as they had in other cases early on. Already, the sheer size of the Chinese or Brazilian economies was generating massive shifts in the global economic balance, raising vexing questions in some of the older industrial centers.

14 Advanced Industrial Economies

A New Revolution?

The established industrial societies in the 1950s were centered in North America, western Europe, Australia/New Zealand, Eastern Europe, and Japan. All began to generate explosive further industrial growth during the 1950s. The results followed many of the lines set by the previous industrial revolution: extensions of new technologies, the introduction of new products, more sophisticated organizational forms. But sheer expansion created some novel results. Further, it became increasingly apparent—by the 1960s and 1970s—that more fundamental changes were occurring in many of the advanced industrial societies—though Eastern Europe lagged—as a new generation of industrial technologies seized center stage. These, too, had widespread social effects, altering yet again the definition of industrialization's wider impact.

These developments, then enhanced after 1990 by the rapid growth of the Internet and whole economic sectors based on information technology, raised a new set of questions about whether another—possibly a third, or even a fourth—industrial revolution was taking shape. It also complicated the relationships between the technology leaders and new industrial entrants like South Korea, China, and India.

Growth Rates

Between 1960 and 1990, manufacturing output in the United States more than doubled, growing by 134 percent—the lowest growth rate of any major industrial nation outside the communist bloc. Manufacturing in Canada expanded 137 percent, in Britain 195 percent, in Sweden 200 percent, in Germany 226 percent. Other European countries tripled or quadrupled their output—France by 323 percent, Italy by 375 percent. Japan, in its own league, posted an almost sevenfold increase: 666 percent.

These were astonishing rates by any historical standard. Population increased also, but because output more than outstripped this growth, per capita productivity soared, even in the United States. Several European countries during the 1950s and 1960s saw their gross national product increase by 8–10 percent annually; France and Italy, in particular, easily outstripped their performance during the earlier industrial revolution phase. Growth slowed somewhat during the 1970s as a result of two sharp crises induced by a shortage of petroleum from the Middle East, but output continued to improve overall, and there were no catastrophic depressions like those of the 1870s and 1930s.

Eastern Europe participated strongly in the industrial boom of the 1950s and 1960s. Growth rates in the Soviet Union were reported at 8–10 percent per year, about on a par with the most rapidly expanding areas of western Europe and ahead of the United States. Indeed, a Soviet leader in the 1950s stated to an American audience, "We will bury you"—claiming that the Soviet economy was on the verge of beating the United States at its own industrial game. This boast turned out to be greatly exaggerated, but the industrial surge was impressive even so. Major technological gains included the world's first and most successful space program. By the late 1970s Soviet industrial output was about seven times greater than it had been in the late 1940s. Throughout Eastern Europe employment in agriculture dropped as a result of further agricultural modernization, freeing additional workers for industry. Strong state investment focused on spurring heavy industry. Some East European regions that had long lagged behind began now to catch up, completing their industrial revolutions and seeming to move forward beyond the minimal industrialization level. In Bulgaria, for example, per capita manufacturing production increased fivefold between 1950 and 1970. Industrial output in Romania rose 120 percent from 1963 to 1970. These gains did not generate the same levels of prosperity that prevailed in most of western Europe, and they did not match the Japanese explosion, but they were significant nevertheless.

In western Europe and the United States, rapid industrial expansion often occurred in regions different from the previous centers of factory industry. Coal mining and textiles continued to decline, leaving troubling industrial backwaters in places like northern England and Appalachia. Even in Japan some previous metallurgical centers suffered. But the decline of older centers was more than balanced by the advance of petrochemicals, electronics, and heavy consumer goods such as automobiles and appliances. Regions that were particularly appropriate for some of the newer industries, such as the Silicon Valley computer cluster near San Francisco and the London region in England, surged forward.

There were several causes of this new round of rapid industrial growth, though of course they varied somewhat from one society to the next. Rising military spending played a role in stimulating armaments industries and aeronautics in the United States and the Soviet Union. In general, further improvements in agricultural methods freed labor for industry while creating new consumer spending in the countryside. Greater use of mechanical equipment, particularly notable in western Europe, brought a rapid reduction in the size of the rural labor force, along with lower food costs. France's rural population, for example, declined from 16 percent of the nation's total in 1950 to 6 percent by the 1980s. French sociologists wrote of a "vanishing peasantry" not only because of its falling numbers but because of its new fascination with maximizing market production and with mechanical efficiency. Although European agriculture remained somewhat more costly than that of North America, the industrial revolution had definitely come to Europe's countryside.

New government policies stimulated economic growth. The Japanese government resumed its careful planning and coordination, operating in close harmony with business leaders. The state set production and investment goals while directing public revenues to encourage research and capital development projects. The government also reduced the population pressures that had afflicted prewar Japan by actively promoting birth control and abortion; Japan's population growth slowed to essentially the same levels as in Western society and the Soviet Union. The government also sponsored technological research in state laboratories and carefully developed foreign trade policies designed to spur exports. By the 1970s Japan was turning out more engineers than many larger nations such as the United States. Overall, Japan's orchestration of cooperation between government entities and leading business giants prompted the half-mocking, half-envious label from the West, "Japan, Incorporated" (see Photo 14.1).

Photo 14.1 Workers in a Japanese Automobile Plant in the 1980s, as Japan Became One of the World's Leading Industrial Nations. Goods Manufactured There Include Steel, Motor Vehicles, Chemicals, and Electronic Products (Photo by The Asahi Shimbun via Getty Images).

Government policies shifted rapidly in western Europe, though they fell short of Japanese coordination. West European governments late in the 1940s made a fuller turn toward the welfare state, providing state-sponsored health or health insurance programs, payments to families with numerous children, and a host of other benefits such as the construction of low-cost housing. Canada, Australia, and New Zealand also expanded their welfare provisions. Many programs were financed in part from tax revenues, which offered some cushion for those most poorly paid. Not all welfare programs worked well, and some drew protests from various groups. On balance, however, the European welfare state won great popularity. It helped integrate certain groups, notably from the working class, more firmly into the national political structure. It reduced the worst material misery as well, and, by providing some income floors for the poorest groups, stimulated consumer demand. At the same time, many European governments complemented the welfare state with an active planning effort. Various sectors were nationalized outright; most states, for example, took over the railroad system and improved its efficiency. More generally, planning mechanisms aimed to stimulate industrial growth in backward regions and spur more rapid technological development. France went furthest here, establishing a national planning office, the Commissariat du Plan, in 1946 to steer capital toward economic sectors deemed significant for long-term growth. Private enterprises remained free to run their firms as they saw fit, but the French government used its powers to guide investment and credit. Not all European governments moved quite so far. Germany, for example, emphasized market competition as an alternative to its statist experience under Nazism. All governments undertook planning, however, and the impressive economic growth rates suggested that the initiatives were paying off.

Government planning in Eastern Europe was by far the most extensive because the Soviet system of a command economy, directed by the central government, was spread to the new communist regimes in the region. State planning committees allocated resources, set prices and wages, and determined production goals. After 1968, certain governments, as in Hungary, modified this rigid planning by providing some autonomy to individual enterprises. By this point some suspicion was developing that rigid state planning—effective in mobilizing resources for early industrialization—might not be best suited to further development. Major changes in direction, however, occurred only after the industrial collapse of the region in 1985.

Only the United States did not extend new government measures in any systematic way, though increased military spending involved the government more heavily in economic issues than ever before. Welfare programs did not greatly expand, though there was some growth in the late 1960s. The United States was also unique in having no economic planning office, though the Federal Reserve Board coordinated fiscal policy in the interest of economic growth. The lack of major U.S. policy initiatives seemed irrelevant in the 1950s and 1960s, when economic demand was fueled by rising wages and high consumer expectations. As growth eased in the 1970s, many experts began to urge a shift in the American policy framework, but without major results into the 1990s.

Diplomatic shifts contributed to the industrial surge. The active foreign policy of the United States, including various international gifts and loans, helped stimulate U.S. exports, particularly in the 1950s and 1960s. The United States also participated in a number of international efforts to lower tariff barriers, and trade among the industrial nations increased in part as a result of these initiatives. The Soviet Union built a separate economic bloc with its East European satellites, which helped coordinate exports and resource allocation within the bloc. In the long run the isolation of the communist economic grouping reduced the flow of technical information necessary for a vigorous economy, but in the short run certain industries were aided by easier access to resources such as the Soviet Union's vast petroleum supplies. The greatest shift in market policies occurred in western Europe with the formation, from 1956 onward, of the European Economic Community, or Common Market. This group, ultimately embracing most of the European nations, progressively reduced trade barriers internally—gradually creating the world's wealthiest total market. Full economic unity was proclaimed in 1992, but well before then the Common Market (now called the European Union) had helped stimulate internal economic growth.

Rapid industrial growth in the established industrial areas had several major consequences. First, it greatly increased the standard-of-living gap with most of the rest of the world. Even regions that improved their economic performance, such as India, saw themselves falling further behind the material levels of the industrial zones. Only an outright industrial revolution, as in South Korea, enabled a nation to catch up at all. For several decades after 1950, many people worried about the growing gap between the minority of advanced industrial economies and the rest of the world—though of course this division began to change by the 1980s.

Within the advanced industrial societies, rapid economic growth paid off in improvements in living standards. Consumer goods remained scarce in Eastern Europe; there were long lines for many items and products were often shoddy. Nevertheless, growth had some impact. Eastern-bloc countries such as Hungary fared particularly well; by the 1980s one family in three had a private car in Hungary, well below Western levels but a thirtyfold increase in the nation since 1960. Many people in the communist nations also enjoyed improved vacation possibilities because of state-organized resorts in such areas as the Black Sea coast.

Japan made a clearer turn toward a vigorous consumer economy, though the Japanese maintained a distinctive commitment to high rates of personal saving along with unusually long hours of work. Japan's standard of living grew close to Western levels by the 1980s. Purchases of a variety of consumer goods, including appliances and automobiles, increased steadily. By the 1980s over half of all families had cars, and 95 percent had washing machines and refrigerators. A joke as early as 1970 described the "three sacred objects" in Japanese society as a color television, a car, and an air conditioner. Huge department stores were by this point providing an immense variety of standardized goods, including cameras, audio equipment, and other delights of a high-tech consumerism in whose production Japanese factories participated strongly.

Western Europe became a consumerist paradise as living standards in some countries, such as Germany and Switzerland, pushed beyond those in the United States. Ownership of automobiles, televisions, and a variety of household appliances became commonplace. At the same time, vacation time increased, reaching an average of five weeks a year for many groups. Europeans swarmed to the sunny beaches of Spain and Italy from the 1960s onward, ventured widely into Eastern Europe and parts of the Middle East, and began to visit the United States and Latin America in increasing numbers, as a memorable vacation became one of the hallmarks of the European version of mass culture in an affluent age.

Structural Changes: The Postindustrial Thesis

Sheer growth had an obvious impact, but the advanced industrial economies also introduced some important new features. As always, a series of technological changes lay at the heart of the new economy. The development of automatic circuitry helped reduce the hands-on labor necessary on certain kinds of assembly lines. New materials, such as plastics, could be automatically poured into molds. Supervising automatic processes, workers in many petrochemical plants became more like technicians than workers in the traditional style of factory industry. The rise of the computer soon added an even more powerful innovation. A German engineer, Konrad Zuse, had devised an electromagnetic computer before World War II, but American firms, headed by IBM (International Business Machines), led in further development during the 1940s and 1950s. Huge computers began to be installed for information processing. The transistor, a major advance by Bell Laboratories in 1948, greatly improved the reliability of computers and cut their size. Accounting, inventory control, and other procedures began to be computerized. The technology was applied to manufacturing processes as well. The development of robotics, from the 1960s onward, replaced many assembly-line workers with machines that could perform repetitious processes like drilling and assembly. By the 1980s, 20 percent of French industry and about 10 percent of American manufacturing depended on robots; Japan would surpass these levels by the early twenty-first century. Finally, genetic engineering began to affect manufacturing in the 1960s; the emphasis was less on new manufacturing methods than on new products, including new medicinal drugs, but some genetic technology also operated under the supervision of technicians rather than machine-aided manual laborers.

The new technologies lay behind a host of new products, including sophisticated sound equipment and, soon, personal computers and iPhones. More importantly, they spurred greatly increased productivity that reduced the need for blue-collar labor. The manufacturing labor force reached its peak size in the 1950s in the United States and western Europe and then began to shrink—a reversal of one of the staple trends of the industrial revolution. Many hardships resulted from the displacement of workers in industries like steel and automobiles; they were the victims of increasingly automated technology as well as heightened foreign competition. But employment in the service sector grew rapidly, and these jobs by the 1950s commanded a full half of the labor force in the West. This trend had begun in the late nineteenth century, but it now reached new proportions. The typical worker was an employee in insurance, government, a hospital, a school, an office, or a hotel or restaurant, or even a management consultant firm. Some of these service jobs were attractive and gave people upward mobility from the working class. A fourth of the traditional French working class moved up to white-collar work during the 1950s. Canada's labor force included a 46 percent share for service workers by the late 1950s, many of whom had come from farm or working-class backgrounds. But low-level service jobs also were created in fast-food restaurants, custodial services, and security jobs.

Many service industries, like health care, catered mainly to a local population, but the surge of service industries also generated new export possibilities. Japan began to export a variety of entertainment products, including anime and then computer games. The United States and Europe exported banking services and consulting operations. The value of these service products might outstrip manufacturing exports by the twenty-first century, another dramatic symptom of basic economic change.

Associated with the new technologies were some changes in management. Corporations continued to grow. In 1940, for example, the top 100 companies accounted for 30 percent of all manufacturing in the United States; by the 1950s the figure was nearly 70 percent, as a host of new mergers swallowed smaller competitors and as government purchasers during the war had favored big business. In western Europe many old-line manufacturing families died out or were displaced because of dubious activities during the Nazi years. The giant Krupp firm, for example, shifted away from tight family control. A new breed of managers from middle-class backgrounds and with substantial technical training came to the fore. These people were friendlier to business–government cooperation and to long-range planning than their predecessors had been, and they worked also to stabilize labor relations. New technologies supported a growing emphasis on abilities to master information and use specialized knowledge; some observers argued that the control of knowledge was replacing the control of property as the cornerstone of the industrial elite. Japanese management changed less than its West European counterpart, but it worked more consistently to foster careful relations with labor than had been the case before the war. Efforts to ensure about 50 percent of the labor force lifetime job security and to consult workers about potential improvements in methods showed a more effective use of Japan's tradition of group spirit than in the prewar years.

Some authorities contended that new technologies and management forms added up to a decisively new economy; they heralded a postindustrial revolution and argued that it was as sweeping in its implications as the industrial revolution before it. They pointed, of course, to the shift away from manufacturing jobs and from traditional management styles. They also predicted that with robotics and computers the nature of work would shift. Products would become more individualized. Work would be decentralized, even located in the home, and supervision would accordingly lighten. Time constraints would decrease because workers could log on to their computers whenever they desired. These were interesting visions, but they did not fully accord with reality. Most service jobs became more, not less, routinized. New equipment enabled management to speed up the work of secretaries and bank personnel; work tensions increased in many cases. Supervision could be enhanced by computer checks. And although jobs did move away from some city centers and the traditional factory declined in importance, group work settings continued to predominate. New management did not necessarily mean a new freedom from regimen. An American oil company's recruiting pamphlet noted that "personal views can cause a lot of trouble" and suggested that moderate or conservative ideas were preferred. Airlines trained flight attendants to smile courteously at all times, suppressing their emotions; annoyance, their personnel authorities urged, was bad not only business but also for one's health. Growing conformity and coordination at work increased for many people, and this new age in many respects constituted an intensification, although in new forms, of work trends that had been associated with the industrial revolution from the outset. The question of whether this was a new revolution, or a major change that maintained many crucial industrial themes, was not easy to resolve.

Two additional shifts accompanied the larger changes in industrial structure, occurring particularly in Western society, though there were some echoes in Japan. First, women began to reenter the labor force in large numbers. Working-class women started taking jobs during the

1950s, and a middle-class surge followed a decade later. Young women actually reduced their employment levels, instead staying in school longer. But the typical woman now expected to work not only after marriage but after childbearing. By the 1970s over 40 percent of the labor force in western Europe, Canada, and the United States was female. At the root of this historic shift in Western industrial trends—the reversal of women's initial removal from the labor force—were several factors. A key ingredient was the rise in the number of service jobs, to which women seemed particularly suited and for which their lower wages were often preferred. Women's hold on key occupational sectors intensified; whereas about 60 percent of all American secretaries were women before 1960, over 90 percent were female by the 1980s. Women's employment, in other words, was not spread evenly over industrial jobs but was concentrated in the service sector. Women provided a vital increase in the number of available workers at a time when growing economies were crying out for new help and when older workers were increasingly choosing (or being forced to choose) formal retirement over remaining active. The result was a major shift not only in women's lives but also in the larger relationship of family to the economy. During the first century or more of industrialization in the West, the focus had been on relying mainly on men to provide industrial labor, while keeping many families somewhat separate, under women's tutelage. In the new setting the family was diluted; the rise of day-care facilities for children, particularly rapid in western Europe, was an obvious result of the new evaluation of the work-family equation. Japan lagged somewhat in this trend, with a smaller percentage of married women at work and more emphasis on mother-intensive child rearing. But women's work roles shifted somewhat in Japan as well by the 1970s, and after about 2000 the continued growth of the service sector and Japan's acute labor needs, heighted by a rapidly falling birth rate, brought growing numbers of women into the labor force.

Finally, and in many ways surprisingly, the class warfare so characteristic of the initial industrial revolution and the ensuing decades declined after a peak in the 1950s. It did not disappear, and a surge of protest around 1968 included a series of intense labor strikes. On the whole, however, agitation directly associated with workplace issues dropped off. This was particularly true in the United States and western Europe; in Japan labor agitation also remained low. Trade union membership in the United States and western Europe began to plummet after the late 1950s, and many union members reduced their effective commitment. French unions found many workers too busy with their new motorcycle or car—or with overtime work to pay for such items—to attend meetings. Strikes trailed off as well. Average annual strike rates in the United States during the 1960s were down approximately 15 percent from their 1950s rate, and although levels rose again in the 1970s, they still barely approximated those in the 1950s—despite a massive growth in the size of the labor force. German workers, who had maintained an active political and trade-union current of protest before the triumph of Nazism, now acquiesced to a very cooperative labor movement. Specifics varied, and employers in the United States and Britain were particularly active in attacking the union movement, but the overall trend was the same: the class-based protest that had risen with the initial industrial revolution was fading.

Prosperity and welfare programs helped explain the change. But some puzzles remained. U.S. workers began to experience a drop in real wages starting in 1973 and continuing into the twenty-first century, as prices rose faster than wages. Furthermore, hours of work increased, partly to compensate for falling standards of living. By 1992, American workers put in 140 hours a year more than their counterparts had in the early 1970s. Yet protest did not arise from these growing pressures, or at least not the kind of labor protest typical of the second phase of industrialization. Changes in the industrial structure helped explain the relative silence. Many blue-collar workers feared for their jobs as their numbers shrank. Service-sector employees, including women, had never been very active in formal protest, and now they predominated. Families with wives as well as husbands working often lacked the time to devote to organizational efforts. It seems likely however that the novel conditions of advanced industrialization help explain new forms of protest in the twenty-first century, particularly populist political attacks on elites and immigrants. Furthermore, the new industrial economy helped promote other innovations in protest, associated for example with feminism or the environmental movements.

The New Industrial Balance

The changing nature of the advanced industrial economies obviously affected the balance among major regions in the world, though the results were complex. As we have seen, Japan, the United States, and western Europe led the way, though with different specifics. Germany, for example, maintained a larger stake in high-tech manufacturing than did the United States or Britain; the United States generated the new giants of the information technology industry. Many observers contrasted Japan's organizational approach to industry with American corporate policies that emphasized less careful collaboration with the government and a particular emphasis on short-term profits over longer-term gains.

The surge of new technologies and organizational forms left much of Eastern Europe at a disadvantage. By the mid-1970s the Soviet Union and most of the East European nations had completed the basic construction of an industrial economy. They had reached a situation where, earlier, Western nations had begun to make a turn toward greater consumer affluence, basing further industrial growth and workplace motivation on a growing proliferation of goods. The communist economies did not make that turn. The shortage of consumer goods forced many East European workers to use massive amounts of time shopping, and it reduced incentives for strong work performance. Along with growing health and environmental problems, the result was a measurable reversal of the region's industrial progress. Industrial production began to stagnate, and after about 1980 it actually dropped. Worker productivity declined in part because of poor morale and related alcoholism. Falling production forced the Soviet regime to commit so much to the military program to keep up in the Cold War by matching U.S. spending that other initiatives were starved for resources. By the mid-1980s up to a third of all Soviet gross national product was spent on military outlays.

Soviet leaders began to acknowledge these problems under Mikhail Gorbachev, from 1985 onward. Efforts to introduce greater flexibility into the system ran into entrenched bureaucratic opposition and widespread popular anxiety about potential price increases on basic staples once government control was removed. Movement toward a more market-oriented economy was widely hailed, but practical implementation lagged. Meanwhile, in 1989, most East European countries broke away from the communist orbit, installing varying versions of looser planning; Poland established a market economy outright.

The short-term results of the attempt to convert to a market economy were chaotic. By the late 1990s Poland had made the turn toward renewed industrial growth, though it remained far poorer than western Europe. Russia saw a great deal of freewheeling capitalism as state businesses were sold off. Food supplies improved and a new wealthy class emerged, along with greater income inequality. Limitations on Soviet industrialization even earlier, plus the recent collapse, made it impossible to forecast a speedy recovery. The Russian government hesitated to convert to a full market economy, retaining extensive state controls; after 2000, new investment in the military also complicated the picture. Internationally, the Russian economy depended far more on oil and gas sales than on industrial exports. A pronounced gap with the advanced industrial economies remained.

The development of advanced industrial economies posed an obvious challenge for many of the new industrializers—just as, around 1900, changes in the industrial world created at least a temporary gap with newcomers like Japan. By the twenty-first century, however, it was becoming obvious that the divide between "advanced" and "developing" was extremely porous. South Korea, though a relatively new arrival, became actively concerned about overreliance on industrial staples like automobiles and metals; aided by the government, it became the most "wired" society in the world, and began to develop a range of information-age products and services. India, though not yet fully industrialized, participated strongly in information technology. China, still bent on completing its industrial revolution, also jumped squarely into the new economy. Chinese leaders were acutely aware that their nation's future depended on going beyond mass-producing items largely designed by others—though this activity continued. By the twenty-first century China led the world in developing mobile payment methods and products, rapidly reducing the role of cash in its urban centers. Production of electric cars and solar energy panels surged forward. A government–industry collaboration also generated the earliest and most sophisticated 5G wireless network, not only for domestic use but for export, putting tremendous pressure on Western societies either to accept the Chinese lead or figure out how to catch up.

Obviously, the new industrial economy that had developed by the early twenty-first century challenged most regions of the world. Established sectors in Japan and the West faced major dislocations, as manufacturing declined and new centers developed. Newer industrializers had to figure out how to combine basic industrialization with participation in the newest technologies. The overall result blurred some of the lines between established players and newcomers, further complicating global relationships in this newest industrial phase.

15 Globalization and Exploitation

A New World Economy

The industrial revolution effectively caused the modern version of globalization. In turn, globalization, particularly since the mid-twentieth century, has reshaped the industrial experience in many ways.

The connection first became clear in the late nineteenth century, when international trade grew at an unprecedented rate. New transportation and communication technologies—steamships, the telegraph, and transcontinental railways—set the framework for intensifying global contacts. New international agreements worked to coordinate time zones, facilitate international telegraphy, protect patents around the world, extend agreements on commercial law.

We have seen that big business reached out to establish production branches in other countries and also assure access to needed resources. New migrations facilitated the international flow of labor, in a period before passport regulations complicated the process. This was genuine globalization, but it was almost entirely Western-dominated, capped of course by the surge of imperialism in many parts of Asia and Africa. During the first half of the twentieth century several societies sought to pull away from globalization, to have a better opportunity to control their own economic development—most obviously in the case of the Soviet Union.

After 1945, however, globalization began to gain ground once more, in direct interaction with the changes in advanced industrialization and, soon, the expansion of industrial development. The results extended global relationships well beyond their previous level. They also, gradually, began to cut into Western dominance of the process. But many observers argued that globalization also still facilitated the exploitation of many parts of the world, and most particularly the several regions where significant industrialization had yet to take hold.

The New Sinews of Globalization

The two basic features of the industrial revolution—technology and organization—extended their worldwide impact after 1945. International technology included routine air travel that enabled business leaders and technical experts to meet regularly and thus form something of an international community in their fields, across political and ideological boundaries. With advances in computer linkages and satellite communication, which greatly speeded the flow and volume of messages, came instant access, literally, to developments on the other side of the world. The organizational revolution showed most clearly in the emergence of multinational corporations (stemming mainly from western Europe, the United States, and the Pacific Rim, including Japan and South Korea, but soon adding China as well) that maintained complicated manufacturing operations around the globe. Some authorities argued that multinationals were replacing established governments as the most influential organizations in contemporary life.

Globalization also gained ground thanks to new policies explicitly designed to facilitate international trade. Leading capitalist nations set up several institutions right after World War II, including the International Monetary Fund, to help support postwar industrial recovery and to prevent the narrow nationalist responses that had greeted the Depression. A new level of tariff coordination was launched in 1948, and in 1995 this became the World Trade Organization. Here too, the goal was to promote exchange of goods and to encourage stability in the world economy. The assumption was that this approach would yield lower prices for consumers around the world and enhance opportunities for peace. The measures were not aimed at industrialization alone, but they both encouraged and reflected global connections relevant to industrial growth. All the major economic powers, including newcomers like China, ultimately sought membership in the World Trade Organization, seeing this as an important facet of their overall international economic position.

International organization and technology were complemented by new flows of labor from Latin America, Africa, and Asia into the industrialized regions, resulting in the creation of an almost unprecedented mixture of cultures around a common industrial base. New competition for resources also emerged as China and India joined the West and Japan in seeking access to oil and other vital goods.

Finally, the pervasiveness of international economic links showed in an increasing realization that no economy could successfully isolate itself from global industrial contacts. This would reverse earlier isolationist efforts, not only in Soviet Russia but in communist China under Mao. The cost of isolation, through lagging behind technological developments elsewhere and failing to take advantage of organizational innovations, was simply too great. Hence, post-Mao China orchestrated an unprecedented economic openness to the world after 1978, and the Soviet Union built extensive international contacts into its reform movement in the late 1980s. Even India and Latin America, never closed, developed wider global connections. Going it alone had, seemingly, become impossible.

The Multinationals

Corporations that developed massive stakes in economic operations outside their home country—the multinationals—expanded the previous international interests of industrial firms. There was no magic dividing line between the internationally minded corporations of the 1920s and the multinationals that spread from 1950 onward; the difference lay in sheer scale and overall international impact. Multinational corporations fanned out from the United States and Canada, from western Europe, and from Japan, with others from areas of the Pacific Rim and China increasingly joining in. They were the consequences, in other words, of the general advancement of industrial economies in the three major geographic centers of industrialization.

U.S. firms had $7.2 billion invested abroad in 1946; this figure rose to $78.18 billion in 1970 and to $133 billion in 1976. U.S. corporations invested and operated in other industrial countries, exhibiting particular interest in western Europe. They also expanded their operations in nonindustrial countries, particularly in mining and transportation but also, increasingly, in factory industry. By the 1980s the foreign operations of U.S.-based firms were generating between 25 and 40 percent of total corporate profits. Major oil companies, computer companies, and some consumer products firms regularly earned over 50 percent of their totals from foreign operations, and some U.S. commercial banks reaped over 60 percent of their annual profits from activities abroad. The foreign stake of U.S. companies expanded steadily, as did their impact on various regions of the world.

Multinational operations from western Europe and Japan increased more rapidly than those from the United States. Between 1965 and 1971 German and Japanese foreign investment rose at triple the rate of the growth in American overseas commitments. Japan held over $4.5 billion in foreign investment by 1973, a fifteenfold increase in a decade. Initial Japanese investments focused on mining and other raw-materials sources in countries such as Brazil and Australia—logical targets given Japan's import needs. Germany long emphasized manufacturing and high-technology branches, setting up automobile and chemical factories in several countries. In the 1980s Japan also began to expand its foreign manufacturing interests, opening a number of automobile manufacturing branches in parts of the United States and elsewhere. European and Japanese investment in the United States, correspondingly, increased rapidly: even by 1975 direct foreign investment (with Britain in the lead, followed by other parts of western Europe, Japan, and the oil-rich Arab states) had almost quintupled over that of 1960. German cars, Japanese and Korean cars, French tires, German chemicals and pharmaceuticals, and Dutch petroleum all had substantial American operations.

The advantages of the multinational activities of big firms—such as Mitsubishi, Royal Dutch Shell, Bayer Chemicals, General Motors, and IBM—were numerous. Many companies, of course, established foreign operations to obtain vital raw materials, such as uranium, iron, and, inevitably, oil. This interest was one of the oldest inducements for international expansion. The collapse of the Soviet Union gave multinationals opportunities to penetrate the new, resource-rich republics of central Asia. In time-tested fashion, many multinationals were able to take the bulk of their profits on resource production out of the countries of extraction, making the rich nations richer and the gap between the industrial and the nonindustrial countries ever wider.

Branch factories also offered a way to save on transportation costs. Japanese automobile assembly plants in Kentucky and California boosted their earnings because delivering the cars did not entail heavy shipping charges or import duties. Branch operations in Latin America, the Middle East, and various parts of Asia carried the same benefits for multinationals based in all of the major industrial centers. Not only cars but also medicinal drugs, household appliances, processed foods, and a host of other products spread through many parts of the world by virtue of multinational operations.

A third motivation involved a worldwide search for capital and for high returns on investments. Multinational corporations drew investments from many different countries, so they could attract capital from regions with temporary overabundance and apply it to opportunities in other areas. One reason for extensive European and Japanese investment in the United States during the 1970s and 1980s was relatively high U.S. interest rates, which meant that many U.S. firms, in turn, were drawing capital from places where it was easier and cheaper to find than if they had had to compete for investment funds in the high-interest U.S. market.

An increasing search for cheap labor provided a fourth reason for the expansion of multinational corporations. Setting up plants in low-wage areas like the Caribbean or Indonesia allowed the multinationals to farm out some of the simpler manufacturing operations, such as producing computer chips or assembling household appliances. Most of these products were then reimported to the home country or to other industrial markets.

This global exploitation of labor was not uncomplicated, however. In the first place, multinationals often offered better conditions than local firms—though the multinational competition put pressure on local production that could generate deteriorating wages and safety standards and an even greater use of child workers. Second, by the 1990s global world opinion was paying serious attention to multinationals—and their subcontractors, which were particularly abusive. Both in western Europe and in the United States, organizations sprang up to oppose global sweatshops, using the Internet and other publicity devices to name names. The Clean Clothes Campaign, based in the Netherlands, and American-centered groups such as Students Against Sweatshops maintained active links with local organizations that provided the actual data on conditions in places like Vietnam and Indonesia; electronic petitions against specific perpetrators of abuse could garner hundreds of thousands of signatures from Japan, South Korea, India, and Latin America as well as western Europe and the United States. Many firms—such as Nike, which was accused of exploitation in its Vietnamese factories—did make important gestures, pledging better minimal standards and, sometimes, a certain amount of worker representation. Whether these two sides of globalization—the exploitation and the human rights standards—would balance out remained to be seen.

Finally, multinational operations depended on literally global specialization. This was the newest facet of the multinationals after 1950 or 1960, aside from the sheer expansion in scale and number. Finished products were assembled from components made in several different countries, each with specialist factories capable of benefiting from massive economies of scale in turning out far more parts than the home economy required. Cars sold in Japan and in the United States, for example, whether officially "made" in one country or the other, were routinely composed of parts originally produced in Japan and the United States, possibly Korea and Mexico, and sometimes other places besides. Japanese cars imported into the United States sometimes had fewer Japanese-made parts than did cars made in Detroit.

What the multinationals were doing, clearly, was creating a world economic system through which the coordination of various business functions—production, finance, and distribution—could take place without regard to the conditions or policies of any individual nation-state. The globe was treated as a single industrial unit, a factory that could achieve maximum efficiencies through the international coordination of all aspects of manufacturing operations. Specialization, in particular, became a worldwide operation. Only a few carefully controlled economies were partially exempt, but even in these the future seemed to lie with the multinationals. Indeed, substantial multinational penetration followed the opening of China after 1978 and the collapse of the Soviet system in the 1980s.

Multinational corporations raised a host of new problems. Because they found it relatively easy to move operations in response to unfavorable labor conditions or government policies, the power of a given nation to regulate, or of a particular trade union to bargain, was newly constrained. Multinationals' management policies varied, and some granted considerable autonomy to local branch operations. Some multinationals, however, insisted on tighter controls from the center, distrusting local managers and trying to install labor practices and other procedures imported intact from the home country. Obviously, the power of multinationals frequently exceeded that of the governments in many of their host societies, particularly, of course, in smaller and less industrialized nations. The largest multinationals, like General Motors or Toyota or Google, had annual revenues far greater than the total tax intake of many of the countries in which they operated, and their bargaining power was commensurately high. The scale of economic organization, thanks to the international expansion of industrialization, exceeded that of political authority. This disparity, in turn, created abundant possibilities for quarrels over responsibility and for clashes over appropriate taxation, labor, and environmental policies.

Labor Migration

The explosion of multinationals and their increasing ability to operate a variety of economic activities, from resource extraction to capital transfers, in almost every part of the world constituted the clearest sign that the industrial revolution had entered a new, global phase after 1950. Other industrially based contacts occurred as well, and like the multinationals they demonstrated the increased ability of industrial development to pull people from widely different cultural backgrounds into contact that defied not only purely national boundaries but the often more deeply rooted distinctions among major civilizations as well. Unprecedented movements of people constituted a second major international force operating under the umbrella of industrialization.

Movements of labor were a constant feature of all phases of the industrial revolution. Immigration into the United States and Canada fed the factory and mining labor force taking shape around 1900, providing relatively cheap workers willing to accept not only modest wages but also novel working conditions in hopes of earning enough to return home or simply because they saw little alternative. West European, Japanese, and Russian industrial growth depended on similar movements of displaced rural inhabitants into the factory centers. Most of them came from within the nation—unlike the immigration into North America—but a minority spilled over from neighboring areas in which population pressure limited local options. Thus, French industrialization was aided by Belgian immigrants, and around 1900 numerous Poles and Italians sought work in French and German factories. The British industrial labor force was supplemented by migration from Ireland, particularly of the unskilled.

Industry's need for new workers and its success in recruiting immigrants—some of them drawn to new opportunities but more of them pressured to migrate by changes in rural life—were basic to the industrialization process. Before 1950, however, much industrial migration had drawn workers from a background somewhat similar to that of the host society. Poles in France faced some discrimination and culture shock, but they were partially cushioned by common Catholic religious traditions. Eastern and southern European immigrants to industrializing North America faced greater barriers because they moved into countries whose dominant culture was Protestant. This religious difference helped account for the harsh measures U.S. employers adopted to police immigrant workers and for the patronizing "Americanization" campaigns designed to convert "inferior" peoples into good American workers. One industrial immigrant group—the Chinese workers recruited to the American West by railroad companies seeking cheap construction labor—faced unusual barriers of cultural unfamiliarity and the massive racism of both their employers and other workers.

After 1950 the experience of immigrant laborers shifted, as the recruitment of industrial labor internationalized still further. Major industrial regions continued to need additional workers, particularly for lower-paid, unskilled jobs deemed unsatisfactory by the native-born working class (including sons and daughters of previous immigrants). Declining rates of population growth and the rising expectations of the native-born combined to create new labor needs in a context of considerable economic expansion. At the same time, population pressures in various nonindustrial parts of the world, improved transportation and growing information about industrial life, and in some instances prior experience with commercial work settings in the home country produced a growing potential immigrant pool.

Japan was least affected by labor migration from outside its boundaries. Nevertheless, Japanese expansion, plus its falling birthrate, had created an unprecedented interest in foreign workers by the 1970s. Immigrants were recruited from Korea, the Philippines, and Thailand to work primarily on construction crews and on the docks. By the early 1990s approximately 600,000 foreigners were laboring in Japan, a country with a considerable cultural suspicion of outsiders.

The United States began to receive substantial new immigration from several nonindustrial areas. By the 1970s, in fact, the nation was experiencing the highest absolute rate of immigration in its history. Immigrant groups included some trained professionals from parts of Europe and Asia, but the largest numbers were unskilled workers from Korea, the Philippines, Mexico, and the Caribbean. A significant flow of illegal immigrants, particularly from Mexico and Central America, added to the official total. Over 6 million Mexican workers, both legal and illegal, provided agricultural, construction, and factory labor in the Southwest and in major midwestern centers such as Chicago.

A new immigrant underclass also took shape in western Europe, as industrial prosperity and growing opportunities for the native-born working class created new needs in the unskilled ranks. Initial post-World War II migration came from relatively established sources, particularly southern Italy and Spain, but the industrialization of these countries quickly reduced this flow. The major migration sources then shifted to include Yugoslavia, Turkey, North and West Africa, Pakistan, and the West Indies. Immigrants from these areas, euphemistically labeled "guest workers" in West Germany, typically were residentially segregated and poorly paid and were victims of prejudice, racial violence, and job discrimination. They formed something of a separate labor force, confined for the most part to unskilled factory and construction jobs and transportation slots like bus conducting. By 1990, legal and illegal immigration had brought more than 12 million immigrants into the economy of the European Union. Islam became the second religion of countries such as France. Migration flows increased still further in the twenty-first century thanks to turmoil in the Middle East and Africa.

The inclusion of racial and cultural minorities in the industrial labor force increased immensely through the internationalization of the industrial experience after 1950. Pressures to seek work continued in many nonindustrial regions as economic growth failed to provide fully for an expanding population. Industrialized societies, though hardly welcoming the new immigrants, also benefited from their cheap labor. In the short run, something like a dual labor force resulted, with native-born people competing for the better-paying jobs and the racial minorities for the stubborn residuum of low-paid work. Service-sector jobs, particularly, were hard to come by for groups that looked distinctive and seemed to behave distinctively as well—yet service-sector jobs were the most rapidly growing category in these same economies. Racial tensions with other workers added new political issues to the agenda of western Europe and complicated politics in the United States as well. Anti-immigrant movements began to flourish in Europe by the 1980s, combining concerns about job security with long-standing racial fears and prejudices; these increased still further after 2000, with fears of terrorism adding to resentment of the sheer number of newcomers. At the same time, immigrant workers themselves became increasingly restive. Between 1980 and 1985 a series of race riots involving mainly workers of West Indian origin occurred in British cities. Immigrant rioting burst forth again in French cities in 2005.

Clearly, international industrialization had introduced a new component into the ongoing formation of the urban labor force. Equally clearly, the expansion of the sources of labor, as it drew in diverse, often hostile, cultures, posed new problems of identity and tolerance in the most established industrial centers. Finally, the industrial centers were not alone in being affected. Many societies, such as in Turkey, Algeria, and Central America, depended considerably on the earnings sent back by workers who had emigrated to Europe. They benefited also from the industrial experience of those who ultimately returned. Thus, international economic links, though generating suspicion and inequality, also increasingly bound a number of parts of the world together.

Globalization and Convergence

The process of globalization combined with the spread of industrial revolutions to new areas created growing similarities among many economies and societies—sometimes, despite very different political systems. In some cases the process also involved new kinds of regional but transnational arrangements.

Postwar Europe showed led the way in attempting new coordination, with what came to be known as the European Union (EU), creating a single zone for exchanges of goods, workers, and investments. At least until 2010, from formation in the 1950s, the EU seemed to spur industrial growth and to encourage additional industrial development in member states like Spain or Ireland. Other linkages took shape. Many former Soviet leaders hoped that economic ties could be preserved within most of the dissolved state even as formal political institutions were carved up regionally, though the durability of the first makeshift coordinating device, awkwardly named the Commonwealth of Independent States, was not at all assured. By the 1990s Pacific Rim states were holding various coordination discussions concerning tariff and development policies. They included not only the Asian industrial leaders but also governments like those of Mongolia and China that were newly open to international economic contacts. Some discussions also embraced Australia, New Zealand, Canada, the United States, and the Latin American nations bordering the Pacific, and in 2018 a new trade agreement united most of these countries except China and the United States. Even earlier, tariff coordination between the United States and Canada increased trade freedom, and leaders of both countries joined Latin American nations in discussing a more effective trading zone composed of North and South America. The North American Free Trade Agreement (NAFTA) linked Canada, Mexico, and the United States in 1993; it was revised and slightly modified in 2019. Most data suggested that it aided economic growth, at least modestly, in all three of the countries involved. Brazil also coordinated a trade zone in Latin America.

For its part, and reflecting its growing industrial muscle, China began to reach out internationally in new ways, particularly through its great Belt and Road Initiative, announced in 2013. This massive investment and loan program promoted infrastructure development through much of central and south Asia, and into East Europe; East Africa was also heavily involved. Chinese leadership and, often Chinese labor, prompted expansion of rails, roads, and ports, plus many public works projects, obviously extending opportunities for Chinese business but potentially promoting development in other areas as well. Here, as in the other regional arrangements, the industrial economy was spilling beyond national borders.

Global Societies

The spread of industrialization in the later twentieth century, along with more intense global contacts and influences, furthered a host of common developments in regions at various stages of industrialization.

Urbanization was a crucial case in point. Cities grew wherever industrialization began to occur. To be sure, by the later twentieth century, urbanization occurred in some places even without full industrialization, as in parts of the Middle East and Latin America. But industrial development and city growth were still closely linked overall. Chinese cities, large before, now swelled to embrace millions of factory workers, business people, and service employees; one manufacturing city reached 35 million inhabitants. Whole new cities sprang up in India. Globally, half the world's population became urban in 2008, obviously a first in human history and a clear sign of the general movement away from the patterns of older, agricultural economies.

Demographics also transformed as industrialization became global. Both new and old industrializers, for example, continued to reduce birth rates, often quite rapidly. Too many children were a burden to industrial families, and many governments tried to cut birth rates to promote industrial growth in the first place, seeking to free up capital and move away from mere subsistence toward technological change. Housing costs in many cities contributed to change as well. China led the way, with its one-child policy after 1978. By 2010, countries such as Italy and South Korea featured the lowest birth rates in the world, well below maintenance levels. A key result, again in old and new industrial societies, was an aging of the population, as a smaller number of children combined with longevity gains for adults. Here was another major trend throughout the industrial zone.

Global industrial patterns also affected children themselves. More and more societies saw rates of child labor drop and rates of education expand. This revolutionary redefinition of childhood seemed to be an inescapable part of the most recent period of industrial history. Young children were simply not very useful in many branches of modern industry, which in turn depended on some levels of formal literacy and numeracy among workers and even more education for technical experts and managers.

Global consumerism was a vital facet of global industrialization in its most recent phase. Japan and the United States developed new toys for children (though they were often made in China by 2000). Consumer celebrations such as birthday parties spread widely, and even the gift-giving associated with "industrial" Christmas expanded to non-Christian regions. Adult fascination with products such as automobiles was another global trend; for example, China became the world's largest market for cars by 2010. More and more people, especially in the expanding middle classes of old and new industrial societies, found pleasure in shopping and in acquiring goods they did not strictly need. Consumerism was widely seen as a reward for successful industrialization, and in turn was propelled by global industrialization's steady expansion of product output.

Individual regions provided their own flavor, of course. Americans were more enthusiastic consumers than Europeans, who emphasized vacations somewhat more than acquisition of things. East Asians showed particularly high rates of saving, which constrained consumerism to a degree. Still, key social changes—and many popular consumer brands—cut across borders, creating important new commonalities through the growing industrial world.

Nothing showed the power of international industrialization to shape social behaviors more than obesity, which the World Health Organization declared to be a "global epidemic" in the early twenty-first century. The problem affected all industrial societies, new and old. Better food supplies, more time spent in sedentary work or schooling, plus the growing attraction of consumer pastimes like watching television and playing video games, created increasing weight gains, especially among children. The problem affected middle-class children in China and India, and wider populations in the advanced industrial societies of the West. Industrialization had always reshaped daily life; now this was occurring on a global basis.

Attacking Globalization

The intensification of globalization drew a host of critics. Street protests against global arrangements began in 1999, in protests against a World Bank meeting in Seattle, and became a common feature of global gatherings.

There were many targets. All sorts of people worried about cultural globalization, that seemed to threaten values national and religious identities. Environmental deterioration was a growing target, to be explored more fully in the next chapter. Exploitation of labor was another major theme: multinational companies, whatever their merits, often sought low wages and benefits, and they or their subcontractors vigorously opposed unions and other forms of protest. More broadly, many globalization opponents continued to attack the huge economic disparities among different parts of the world. Though the cast of characters was different from the earlier phases of the industrial revolution, with new industrial societies like China and India generating their own regional exploitation, the basic problem was not new: industrial societies depended heavily on cheaper resources and other products from parts of the world that remained predominantly nonindustrial.

Inequalities

For several decades after 1950, economic deterioration, low wages and massive unemployment described many parts of Africa, Latin America, and southeast Asia. Economic polarization seemed to be increasing, and observers talked about a distinctive Third World, or a nonindustrial "South," and in some places, such as parts of Africa, deterioration continued for a time into the twenty-first century, along with massive unemployment. The division between industrial and largely nonindustrial regions seemed to be hard to shake, with only a few newcomers like South Korea complicating the picture. By 2000, however, the industrial gains in giant nations such as India and China had reversed the trend: there now seemed to be more winners than losers, in terms of interregional balance. The old specter of a permanent division between mature industrial societies and the rest of the world receded, and once-familiar terms like Third World began to fade from use. In the Middle East, the emergence of a number of oil-rich nations also complicated the global picture, as leading producers gained control over their own resources by the 1970s: here, considerable wealth did not depend on local industrialization, though there were growing efforts to diversify economies in countries like Saudi Arabia. However, a number of large areas had yet to gain active participation in industrial change and remained desperately poor. Many now depended on shipping cheap materials not only to the West and Japan, but also to the voracious industrial appetite of China.

In 1992 the U.S. Department of Labor charged several American clothing manufacturers with major abuses of factory workers on the Mariana Islands, an American protectorate in the western Pacific 1,500 miles from the Philippines. Subcontractors producing men's clothing for some stylish American brands had for years been importing workers from China and the Philippines, putting them to work in sweatshops with sewing machines but few amenities. The workers were compelled to labor eleven hours a day, seven days a week, for a salary of $1.50 an hour. Any hint of discontent or lack of discipline was controlled by the threat of sending the workers home.

Exploitation of this sort, forcing nonindustrial areas to serve needs in the industrialized societies, persisted in the late twentieth century, although its dimensions changed somewhat. On the one hand, exploitation was encouraged by the sheer growth of the industrial sector in western Europe, the United States, Japan, China, and the Pacific Rim. Industries needed more raw materials than ever before. The search for cheap labor was intensified by improving wages at home, by government-enforced welfare programs that increased the cost of domestic labor still further, and by the slowing rate of population growth in most of the industrial world, which inevitably increased competition for workers. At the same time, population growth in parts of Asia, Africa, and Latin America extended the possibility of finding workers whose desperation would drive them to accept abusive conditions. The workers recruited for the Marianas sweatshops resisted being sent home because finding jobs in the Philippines amid rapid population growth was so difficult. It was small wonder that many of the unequal relationships between industrial and nonindustrial economies endured or even expanded after 1950.

A number of parts of Africa and some in Latin America continued to depend so heavily on Western purchases of raw materials that they imposed few effective controls. Even after independence from Belgium, for example, Zaire (the former Belgian Congo) continued to be dominated by Western mining concerns. The most abusive recruitment practices were modified, but considerable child labor persisted and most adult workers still received low pay amid rigorous working conditions. Expanding the exploitation of copper and uranium brought profits to the Western companies and some wealth for local businesses and politicians, but little improvement in living standards or funding for a larger program of industrial development. Several Caribbean and Central American countries continued to find it difficult to shake loose from cash-crop dependency, supplemented in some instances by foreign tourism. Efforts to diversify sugar economies, even in revolutionary Cuba, won scant success. Sugar was overproduced on the world market; overproduction led to declining prices and continued economic marginality for many of the sugar-growing regions. A few dependent areas sought to diversify their exports to the industrial West by growing illicit drugs, in what was, in fact, a variant of the classic cash-crop export. Impoverished Bolivian and Ecuadoran peasants produced opium, which was then handled by a small number of high-living local merchants, whose profits soared without much wider impact on the regional economy. Dependency also showed in the growth of child labor in southern and southeastern Asia, where 6–8 million child workers were added between 1980 and 2005. Even when rates began to drop in this region, many children were still exploited for their low costs in traditional industries facing global competition, or even sold into sex-trafficking networks. Dependency showed, finally, in the rapidly growing rates of unemployment and underemployment, particularly for younger workers, in many parts of Africa and the Middle East, especially the regions that lacked substantial oil reserves.

As the industrial demand for resources and tropical crops continued, expanding the need for low-paid wage labor in many parts of Africa and Latin America, these same regions continued to rely heavily on the import of industrial goods from other areas. Even some oil exporters like Nigeria, once prices stabilized again in the 1980s, found that their need for equipment imports exceeded their capacity to pay—an imbalance that created heavy foreign debts that further constrained the national economy.

Thus, elements of the industrialized world's advantage over many resource-producing areas endured in a pattern that had been sketched in the early decades of Europe's industrial revolution. The greatest innovations in this relationship after 1950 involved the rise of multinational corporations and the increasing role of the new industrial regions. Appliance manufacturers, electronics firms, and other businesses established branch factories in many parts of the world with the primary objective of re-exporting products back to the industrial regions. In a few instances, assembly plants also issued goods for local consumption and thus reduced the transport and tariff costs of shipments from the industrialized world. More commonly, however, the expansion factories looked for cheap labor (much of it female) in regions where population growth had generated endemic underemployment and scant bargaining power. These companies prized inexpensive or nonexistent benefit programs and, in some instances, loose environmental regulations. They thus sought a basket of advantages that would enable them to undercut the costs of production in the United States, Europe, Japan, or even China. They expanded the geographic range of modern technology and the factory system in the process, but not necessarily with any intent to generate a full range of industrialization.

A variety of areas were drawn into factory industry on this basis, including parts of North Africa, the Caribbean, Indonesia, Vietnam, and Pacific Oceania. One of the most striking examples was along Mexico's border with the United States, where a maquiladora industry (the term refers to fees millers charged for processing grain into flour) expanded dramatically from the 1980s onward. Hundreds of foreign firms, mostly from the United States, set up assembly factories in northern Mexico, transforming regions around cities like Juarez (the border town next to El Paso, Texas) in a fashion reminiscent of a true industrial revolution. Thousands of workers were drawn in, 85 percent of them young women between the ages of fifteen and twenty-four. Industrial refuse was in many cases released without precaution and created barren wastelands behind many factories and amid worker housing.

As in earlier interactions between industrial economies and other regions, an exploitative relationship brought some benefits in its wake. A growing number of Mexicans learned factory skills, extending Mexico's own growing industrialization. Wages, though low, brought vital relief to some families amid massive underemployment. At the same time, the spread of industrial operations under foreign control spelled only limited benefits for the host countries. Most of the profits were often exported rather than reinvested locally, and the larger impact of the search for additional labor outside the industrialized world itself was extremely difficult to calculate. As in the early days of industrialization elsewhere, many employers blatantly intimidated workers, encouraging the government to arrest potential union leaders and firing dissidents. Overall, only 15 percent of maquiladora workers were unionized. Observers in

Mexico and elsewhere debated the long-run consequences of this new industrial growth, which some claimed simply institutionalized poverty. What was clear was the transformative impact industrialization could still bring to bear, changing the lives of thousands of families and the physical face of whole regions when it was exported to new locales.

Variety and Inequality

Very few countries failed to generate some growth in factory industry after 1950, even if they remained very poor because of extensive foreign commercial penetration and/or extensive sectors still rooted in a traditional economy. Newly independent African nations such as Ghana and Nigeria embarked on a process that they called "indigenization," in which foreign ownership was discouraged in favor of local business interests. This process had some results similar to those generated by the earlier policy of import substitution in places such as Iran and Brazil, spurring some factory industry to produce consumer goods for the national market and thus replace the import of foreign textiles, metal products, construction goods, and the like (see Photo 15.1). By the early twenty-first century, opportunities to export raw materials and some

Photo 15.1 A Man Uses a Soldering Iron to Work on Central Telex Equipment—A Vital Part of Contemporary Communication Technology—In Abidjan, Ivory Coast, in 1967 (UN Photo. Reprinted by Permission).

factory products to China and India as well as the West spurred encouraging growth, particularly in East Africa. Kenya, Uganda and particularly Ethiopia began to expand at annual rates ranging up to 10 percent, raising the possibility of another genuine industrial turn. Most of Africa, and particularly populous West Africa, remained however in a more dependent position.

Regional patterns were more complicated than before, both because the number of truly dependent regions had shrunk and because many economies, as with Mexico, now combined dependent and industrializing features. By the twenty-first century the overall answer to the question: Was globalization causing greater regional economic inequality? was a resounding no. But major issues persisted, and globalization also encouraged some of the problems. Even new global ventures, like China's Belt and Road initiative, raised the specter of new forms of exploitation, as many local economies became dependent on Chinese overseers and lenders. Further disruptions in the global economy after the Great Recession that began in 2008 added to the complexity, surfacing new tensions in many regional economies.

16 Global Industry and the Environment

The industrial revolution had a marked impact on the environment from the outset. In industrializing societies themselves, factory centers were often blanketed with smoke. Many people came to view smoke as normal, even a sign of health—economic health most obviously, but even personal health. By the twentieth century, when medical research began to suggest the harmful effects of air pollution, business leaders sometimes managed to suppress scientific results or at least to sponsor alternative findings.

Water pollution was another major result, with more widespread impacts than regional smoke. Well into the twentieth century, many factories simply poured waste into the ground or directly into local rivers. One German chemistry giant, founded in the mid-nineteenth century, regularly sent a magnesium–chlorine mixture into the Rhine River without hesitation until a new environmental consciousness emerged in the 1960s. Many rivers in industrial societies saw dramatic reductions in fish. The human health impact of using polluted water or eating chemically altered seafood is not as easy to calculate, but it was surely considerable. Industrialization was not, of course, the only villain in the piece: growing populations, and particularly expanding urban populations and the resulting waste, contributed greatly to water pollution as well.

Less obvious, but just as portentous, were the consequences of industrialization for the environments of many dependent economies, in places such as Africa and Latin America. Pressure to produce foods and raw materials for industrial societies led to the planting of crops not native to the regions in question—for example, rubber trees in Brazil—that often resulted in soil erosion and other local damage. In tropical regions also, pressure to expand production led to substantial deforestation.

The Ivory Coast in West Africa was a case in point. French interest in the region expanded steadily from the 1840s onward. At the same time, African business leaders became increasingly eager to develop an export crop that could replace slaves in sustaining the region's position in world trade. A focus on growing coffee and cocoa crops—not native to the region—was the result, mainly by African planters but with products destined mainly for European markets. A substantial new trade in palm oil also opened up, and cotton cultivation, using plants brought from the Americas, expanded as well. French colonial officials sponsored railway and port development to make products from the interior more widely available. Several urban centers arose. Timber sales of tropical hardwoods followed from new market opportunities and also the need to cut back the forests to make way for more commercial agriculture. All of this activity deprived the region of forest cover, and thus led to rapid erosion. Deforestation also robbed the land of natural organic nutrients, so the soil deteriorated and artificial fertilizers became necessary. Most observers predicted increasing ecological difficulties in the region due to the overexploitation of nonrenewable resources.

Similarly, in southeastern Brazil, the destruction of massive forests began in the eighteenth century, initially to promote gold mining but later to make room for the cultivation of foreign crops, such as sugar and coffee. It became virtually impossible to restore the forests because of the degradation of the soil, and hundreds of plant and animal species were eliminated in the process. Over 20,000 square miles of forest were cleared in the nineteenth century alone, because the wood was essential for fuel in sugar processing and as the source of railway crossties. By the twentieth century, people in the region began noticing apparent regional climate changes, toward drier, hotter seasons, presumably as a result of the ecological transformation.

The Pace Quickens

Clearly, the first two main phases of the industrial revolution profoundly affected local environments. Ironically, the damage around factory centers proved easier to reverse than the environmental degradation of the more dependent economies—mainly because there was more wealth available for addressing the problem. By the 1960s, new regulations and cleanup campaigns were reducing air pollution in some of the oldest industrial centers, and control over chemical wastes helped in the dramatic cleanup of many rivers, even allowing the native fish to return.

On the whole, however, environmental issues intensified in the third, most recent phase of industrialization, and for the first time they became clearly global rather than merely regional. The sheer expansion of industry, as well as its spread to new regions, set a new basis for environmental change, along with the continued impact of earlier trends like tropical deforestation. Industrial environments might improve in places like Pittsburgh, but not because of new regulations so much as the migration of the dirtier industries to other places. Many newly industrial societies—like their earlier counterparts in the West and Japan—were also far more eager for growth than for environmental preservation, and their leaders argued that they could not afford the types of controls that were now available to the mature industrializers.

Overall, on a global basis, larger and more numerous factories meant more potential emissions into air and water. Substantial consumer goods generated their own pollution through the use of electricity, the belching exhausts of automobiles and the accumulation of waste products like plastics. Chemical industries expanded rapidly, building on an earlier trend, with new kinds of artificial fertilizers and pesticides, the huge plastics industry, weaponry, and other branches. Chemical emissions and spills contributed disproportionately to environmental problems. Greater demands on energy and the obvious limits to petroleum production prompted a growing interest in nuclear energy. Nuclear power stations spread across the United States and particularly in Eastern Europe and the energy-short nations of western Europe, where nuclear generation came to account for a substantial portion of all power. Nuclear wastes and accidents—such as the partial meltdown of a reactor in Chernobyl in the Soviet Union in the 1980s, and the earthquake and tsunami damage to Japanese plants in 2011—drew particular attention to the environmental hazards of advanced industrial societies. So did frequent oil spills, which fouled many coastlines and killed a great deal of oceanic life. Ironically, nuclear worries returned emphasis to fossil fuels, which produced far more regular pollution.

New environmental devastation occurred throughout the industrial world. Acid rain from coal-burning factories spread widely. Tall smokestacks, used to control damage locally, dispersed damaging chemicals more widely than ever before. Forests in Scandinavia suffered from the industry in Germany's Ruhr Valley. Forests in Canada and New England dwindled under the pall of chemicals from the American Midwest. Many rivers and lakes effectively died as a result of chemical pollution; some occasionally even caught fire.

Japan suffered heavily from the environmental by-products of its rapid industrial surge and the attendant growth of its cities. By the 1970s traffic policemen in Tokyo often had to wear protective masks simply to breathe safely. Offshore pollution endangered the fishing industry. Several episodes of industrial poisoning occurred; a famous case was a series of illnesses resulting from methyl mercury exposure that became known as "Minimata disease," after the town in which it occurred.

Pollution problems in the West and Japan were partially counterbalanced by increasing legislation, though many activists contended that the regulations fell short of the need. New standards of fuel use aided in the cleanup of grimy factory cities such as Pittsburgh. Japan's worst pollution problems eased after the 1970s as the government was pressed by public opinion to take a stronger stand. A protest against the expansion of Tokyo's airport, for example, proved to be one of the most successful popular movements in recent Japanese history. Awareness of Minimata disease also sparked a successful grassroots movement. In a number of countries public uneasiness and nuclear accidents combined to slow the growth of nuclear power.

The established industrial region with the most agonizing environmental problems proved to be the Soviet Union and Eastern Europe. Industrial growth and the fierce arms race with the United States—in which the Soviet bloc participated successfully, but with great strain given its smaller industrial base—prompted tremendous neglect of the environmental consequences. Safety precautions were ignored because of their cost, and the results were chemical spills and waste dumping. According to Soviet estimates, half of all the rivers in the Soviet Union were severely polluted and over 40 percent of agricultural land was endangered by the late 1980s. Over 20 percent of Soviet citizens lived in regions of "ecological disaster." Huge natural resources, such as the Aral Sea, were rendered unfit for use. The rates and severity of respiratory and other diseases increased, impairing both morale and economic performance; infant mortality figures also began to climb. Problems that existed also in the West but on a much more limited regional basis (in some petrochemical areas in the southern United States, for example, as measured by per capita cancer incidence) occurred in Eastern Europe on a massive scale. Until political changes opened Eastern Europe to freer discussion and political opposition to the governments, no effective countermeasures existed; the governments, bent on maximizing short-term growth, stood idly by.

The first set of environmental changes in contemporary industrialization, then, involved the accumulation of regional impacts. More regions were involved by this point, and the assault on the environment was fiercer than before because of advancing technologies, and because of the pressure of industrial and military competition on societies like those in the communist bloc. After 1978, China's rapid industrial growth and its ascent toward being second in world rank among polluters, behind only the United States, simply added to this overall trend.

But the second set of changes was yet more international. Activities in one region now affected others and, in some cases, the entire planet—the environmental impact of industrialization turning visibly global after 1950. The expansion of industry in the established centers, including new ventures such as nuclear power, and the frenzied growth efforts in other regions contributed to new levels of worldwide concern. Persistent industrial pollution from factory centers regularly carried across national boundaries; acid rain in northern Europe and in Canada came from sources in nations to the south. Accidents spilled over as well. The partial nuclear meltdown at Chernobyl in 1986 not only devastated the immediate region but also increased levels of radioactivity in a wide swath of Eastern and Central Europe. The operations of multinational firms had similarly far-reaching effects. Oil spills knew no clear boundaries. Operations of foreign chemical plants in places such as India, Indonesia, and Mexico, sometimes established specifically in part to take advantage of lax environmental regulation, altered the regional environment. In a few tragic cases, industrial companies from the West successfully won contracts in poor African nations to dump dangerous industrial waste for which no acceptable place could be found at home. Finally, industrial growth in the cities of China and Latin America brought substantial pollution not only to each regional environment but to international waterways. Increasing poisons in many ocean fish, including high mercury levels, resulted from industrial pollution from advanced industrial areas as well as newcomers. Plastic waste in the oceans caused growing death rates among marine animals. The expansion of mining and commercial agriculture in many tropical countries, including Brazil, further decimated the oxygen-producing rain forests. This effect extended the trend toward deforestation and soil change that had begun in the nineteenth century. Mexico City became a major pollution center, with levels often three times those tolerated in the United States—levels that sometimes forced firms to cut back daily activity because of the poisons in the thin mountain air. Worldwide growth in the use of hydrocarbon fuels produced a growing impact on the global climate, including an alarming increase in average temperatures, and the emission of certain chemicals (particularly, in this case, from the leading industrial centers) reduced the ozone layer protecting the earth from damaging rays from the sun.

The list of global environmental hazards expanded steadily. The problem was complicated by the fact that most policy agencies remained resolutely national, inclined to focus only on local environmental issues. Several individual industrial nations demonstrated that environmental protection was consistent with continued industrial growth. Energy conservation and other measures in Japan reduced once-severe pollution levels without dampening the world's most impressive industrial progress. Through new environmental policies, the average Japanese citizen by the early 1990s was contributing over 90 percent less to environmental degradation than his or her U.S. counterpart. But success in one nation was hard to impress on the international arena. Further, some of the most rapidly growing polluters were not the wealthy nations but those, like China and Brazil, just entering the industrial ranks through rapid evolution. Understandably, these nations argued that their struggle to compete was already too difficult, without adding special environmental goals. They further contended, predictably if not necessarily effectively, that it was up to the industrialized nations to contribute disproportionately to an international regulatory operation and thus compensate the newer industrial regions for some of the funds that a sound environment required.

Attempts at Addressing a Large-Scale Problem

Initial international meetings to deal with environmental change began in the 1970s, spurred by Sweden. But it was in the 1990s that a series of international conferences began to vow greater global collaboration to reduce industrial emissions. Measures were agreed upon to cut pollution that affected the earth's ozone layer. The so-called developed countries pressed new industrializers to include environmental constraints in their planning. In 1997 western Europe sought to push back the emissions that had caused global warming, by as much as 15 percent below 1990 levels in the industrial countries themselves. But the United States, which had effectively regulated oil use during the shortages of the 1970s and reduced pollution in the process, now held back, seeking much more modest limits lest economic growth and business profits be curbed.

Even more than with labor exploitation, the internationalization of industrial impact on the environment created issues with which existing governments could not keep pace. The global framework was inescapable. Whether international remediation was possible remained unclear.

As with global labor abuses, world opinion began to target environmental issues by the 1970s. News reports about global warming and the emission of greenhouse gases became increasingly common. Major disasters, like the chemical spill from an American company in Bhopal, India, in 1984, which killed and injured many people, prompted wide protests. By the mid-1980s a number of nongovernmental organizations were developing to call attention to environmental problems. Green movements in several European countries gained substantial votes, forming minority parties large enough to influence national legislation and foreign policy in favor of curbs on growth and greater environmental protection. Here was another basis for wider public opinion.

In the late 1980s, for example, attention focused on the environmental impact of the giant McDonald's food corporation, blasting the company for buying Brazilian beef and so encouraging further encroachment into the rain forests, and for using Styrofoam products that were not biodegradable. Boycott efforts, and later, websites such as McSpotlight.org, had a direct impact on McDonald's sales and reputation; by the mid-1990s the company had changed tactics, renouncing both Styrofoam and tropical beef. Again in the 1980s, a variety of voices attacked Brazilian plans to expand rubber production in the rain forests involving the construction of new roads and dams. Extensive public petitions, plus shock when a local environmentalist was assassinated, led to a change in plans.

Opinion campaigns also focused on Indonesia, again targeting forest destruction but also the spilling of chemical wastes. Local groups often called abuses to the attention of larger international agencies, such as Friends of the Earth or Greenpeace, which could then mount Internet petition drives. Regional governments were often relatively eager to cooperate, seeing less danger in environmental organizations than in labor movements. As in the case of labor programs, multinational companies often felt quite vulnerable when placed in an international spotlight and agreed to abide more fully by local regulations.

Ultimately it was the prospect of further climate change that commanded the greatest attention in the area of industrially based environmental change. Scientists in the nineteenth century had already suggested that gasses in the atmosphere serve as barriers to solar radiation escaping from the earth, causing what is now called the "greenhouse effect." Carbon dioxide, the major gas resulting from burning coal, gas, and other fossil fuels, is the key component, but other gasses, such as hydrofluorocarbons, produced by industrial societies by the twentieth century, are involved as well. Their function in trapping radiation began to be more precisely calculated by the early 1990s; industrial countries such as the United States and Australia were producing, per person, many hundreds of times the amount of the greenhouse gasses produced by the rural societies in Africa or Southeast Asia.

Despite the great debate and some real uncertainty about precise rates of change, most scientists came to agree that climate change was both a reality and a threat. Continued warming was clearly melting polar ice caps at a rapid rate by the early twenty-first century, and alarms were raised about the resulting probability of rising sea levels and the potential flooding of low-lying islands and coastal areas. Climate change also affected established patterns such as the Gulf Stream, making it possible that Europe would begin suffering from cold temperatures. Most authorities also predicted increasingly disruptive and extreme weather patterns—violent storms, heat waves, and the like. By the second decade of the twenty-first century, increased devastation from forest fires added to the list of environmental threats. Finally, these various menaces were already threatening a variety of species, leading to increased rates of disease in many types of frogs and limiting the food supply for Arctic animals. By 2006, many scientists were stating not only that halting climate change would be extremely difficult, but also that only a few years might be left before the process became absolutely irreversible.

Still, the capacity of world opinion and environmental organizations to curb the abuse of natural resources was limited. One corporation might be persuaded to end one set of operations, but other abusers seemed to operate with impunity, a circumstance that reduced the motivation even of the more visible players.

Formal international arrangements also failed to keep pace with the problems. A major conference in 1997, in Kyoto, Japan, resulted in a protocol by which many of the industrial nations agreed to reduce hydrocarbon emissions, particularly from automobiles. This protocol was followed by several other conferences aimed at the same problem. By the early twenty-first century, enough countries had signed the agreement to bring it into play. Most European countries, including Russia, joined in. Several major countries, including Britain, became increasingly serious about environmental controls. But the whole effort was seriously jeopardized because the United States refused to sign the agreement, claiming it would hamper economic growth, but failing to come up with alternatives. Developing countries such as China also held back, and the effect was, of course, to reduce the enthusiasm for regulation among some of the industrial leaders increasingly affected by competition from China and the other nay-sayers.

In 2015 a more ambitious accord was reached in France, with 196 nations participating, and the resulting Paris Agreement sought unprecedentedly ambitious curbs on global warming. Many new industrial powers, headed by China, now participated enthusiastically. The goal was to reduce the production of greenhouse gasses sufficiently to prevent global warming from surpassing two degrees centigrade. Countries particularly threatened by rising sea levels provided an urgent voice, and other societies like China increasingly realized the threats that atmospheric pollution poised for their own populations.

But implementation of the new goals—which some experts found inadequate in the first place—proved difficult. Many countries, sincerely interested in limiting pollution, hesitated in implementation. Germany lagged behind its own goals in reducing the use of coal, though in 2020 a new plan sought to address the problem. China, working hard to reduce internal pollution, continued to expand coal production, building smoke-belching power stations in many less developed countries. Russia and Saudi Arabia pushed for continued use of oil. Compounding the problem was an active segment of public opinion, in several key countries, that refused to acknowledge the problem at all. Australian leaders, despite growing environmental issues, insisted that climate change was a hoax, and pressed to expand their coal mining operations. Brazil in 2019 elected a president hostile to climate regulations, eager to cut further into the Amazon forest to create more ranch land. The United States, heading the list, elected a leader openly scornful of environmental regulation, who pulled the nation out of the Paris accord.

Not surprisingly, environmental change continued to accelerate according to almost all the relevant scientific opinion. Various species were affected, and some, like polar bears, were seriously endangered by the loss of their traditional food sources. The rapid melting of glaciers—as average annual temperatures now shattered all previous records—began to raise ocean levels, jeopardizing many islands and coasts.

The global framework of the industrial-environmental link was inescapable, as was the fact that political remediation now lagged massive behind the pace of change. There was bitter irony here. The industrial revolution had greatly advanced human control over nature, greatly expanding productive capacity, and wealth, in the process. But the pattern of environmental change and its rapid intensification threatened to escape all efforts at control. Nature itself was changing and, with it, the human prospect as well.

17 Industrial Disruptions, 2008–2020

While many people would argue that environmental deterioration constitutes by far the greatest industrial problem facing the world in the twenty-first century, there is no question that other industrial issues gained greater attention in the years after 2008, from a variety of world leaders and a variety of ordinary voters as well. A host of new and growing problems affected most regions, creating political tensions and distracting from the environmental challenge.

Something of a triple whammy was involved. First, a major recession unfolded in 2008, the worst global economic setback since the Depression and one that global institutions were supposed to prevent. Virtually every country was involved to some degree, but the recession hit home particularly hard in some sectors of the advanced industrial economies and also in a number of countries that were combining low-cost exports with a growing industrial base. Second, a number of established industrial countries began to take greater notice of the competition coming from newcomers like China or Mexico. The contrast between slow or stagnant growth rates and the numbers that were being recorded by some of the newcomers became increasingly obvious. Third, clearer gaps began to emerge between groups that were benefiting from the latest forms of industrialization, and those being left behind. This problem, too, was most obvious in some of the advanced industrial countries, but it also affected China, India, and many parts of Latin America. In combination, these issues generated new and often fierce political protest, and also new questions about globalization itself: some countries, and groups in many countries, wanted to redefine the global economic rules.

It is important not to exaggerate. Globally, economic growth persisted, and rates of poverty continued to decline. While there were no new industrial revolutions, rates of change in places like Ethiopia, Kenya, and Ecuador suggested promising economic futures. The problems of these troubled years did not, yet at least, involve some massive redefinition of industrial societies or even of globalization itself.

There were, however, some new issues. It is literally impossible to say how serious they will turn out to be. Writing a history of the most recent decade, even a short sketch focused mainly on the industrial economies, inevitably poses a challenge: there is no way to know how the story ends, or even how significant the changes will turn out to be compared to past patterns. We have noted a few references to a "fourth" industrial revolution, but it is too soon to make that kind of call, certainly on a global basis when so many economies are still striving to make it into the industrial inner circle.

The Great Recession

The recession started with a collapse in U.S. banking, for several years beginning at the end of 2007. Many banks and investment houses had speculated unwisely on American real estate, offering loans to homebuyers and other developers who might not be able to repay. The collapse of the speculative bubble forced a few banks out of business but, more generally, dried up investment funds for a considerable period. Construction activity slowed precipitously, and the crisis reverberated through the whole economy. Over 8 million American workers lost their jobs, and many others suffered from falling wages or shorter hours.

The crisis quickly became global, affecting almost every region. Africa, interestingly, suffered the least. The European economy quickly slid into recession, again on the heels of a banking crisis. Every country, except Poland and Slovakia, saw a drop in production and employment. Nations that had particularly high debt levels, like Greece, were forced to accept drastic levels of austerity, with falling employment, wages, and benefits. South Korea and Japan also took substantial hits.

Several newer industrializers fared better. India and China, most notably, retained substantial growth rates, though well below their previous levels. China saw its vaunted 10 percent annual surge drop back toward 5 percent. India also experienced more sluggish annual gains. But the opportunities in several of the major industrial sectors, combined in China's case with massive government investment, kept the industrialization process going though amid substantial concerns and uncertainties. It was in 2010 that China surpassed Japan as the world's second-largest economy, a sign of the continuing changes in the global economic balance.

Less robust growth in China plus the outright decline of the advanced industrial countries created larger shock waves. Many countries that depended on raw material sales suffered from declining or stagnant markets (though Australia, interestingly, stood apart on the basis of its strong exports to China). Oil producers took a major hit, as lower demand meant lower prices as well. Russia, Venezuela, Mexico, and Nigeria suffered particularly in consequence, and none of them had a sufficiently robust industrial sector to compensate fully. The Brazilian economy also slowed, thanks to lower raw materials orders from China and other parts of the world. An economy that had been touted as a rising industrial star fell into considerable disarray.

The effects of the recession lingered for several years, although for the advanced industrial countries the worst was over by 2011. Employment rebounded in the United States and several European countries; the German economy continued to perform well, relying on its sophisticated manufacturing sector.

However, recovery was complicated by several factors, involving more basic features of the global economy. First, the slower growth rates in China and India were not yet repaired, nor was the larger crisis in places like Russia and Brazil; and this generated ongoing constraints on global opportunities more generally. Second, recovery in the advanced industrial countries was limited. Several countries, like France, suffered from longer-term unemployment, hitting up to 10 percent of the labor force. Japan was held back by a declining and ageing labor force, as population levels fell. In the United States, rising employment was not matched by comparable increases in wages. Many workers who had lost manufacturing jobs had to take service sector positions at lower pay; a number participated in what was called the gig economy, taking work on a day-to-day basis rather than landing full-time employment with benefits. Even by 2020, the global industrial economy had not entirely healed. Few countries projected heady confidence for the future.

The Great Recession has one other impact, which was substantively and symbolically important. It called attention to the changing balance among national economies. For several decades, leaders of the largest advanced industrial economies—the United States, Canada, the major West European countries, and Japan—had met periodically as a "Group of Seven" to discuss global economic trends and also their shared commitment to democratic political forms. With the crisis, however, it became apparent that a larger group needed to meet as well, more representative of the actual distribution of economic power even though not uniformly democratic. So a new "Group of 20" began to meet as well, including China, India, Brazil, Turkey, Mexico, Saudi Arabia, and South Africa, arguably more closely mirroring the world's new industrial map.

Global Competition

The Great Recession highlighted a wider development in the industrial world: the disparity between robust growth rates in several of the newer economies and the sluggish performance of most of the advanced industrial regions. Even in recovery, the United States had trouble generating annual growth rates much above 2 percent, whereas China, though, faced with its own troubling slowdown, more than doubled that. Living standards remained much higher in the advanced industrial societies, thanks to accumulated wealth: this applied to Japan and the Pacific Rim as well as the West. But there was no question that global relationships were changing.

Most obviously, the manufacturing sector was shrinking in virtually all of the advanced economies. More advanced production techniques, including the growing use of robots, allowed countries like the United States or Britain to maintain high output with a rapidly declining number of workers. The growth of the service sector, including the explosion of activities in information technology, took up much of the slack, but sometimes at lower wages and unquestionably in different locations. In the United States, as a result, new contrasts emerged between prosperous corridors along the coasts—Silicon Valley, Seattle, the Boston area—and the declining fortunes of the old industrial Midwest. London surged forward, but the old industrial Midlands suffered. All of this was further complicated by a decline in the rates of population increase, as most advanced industrial countries no longer supported birth rates high enough to maintain population size, depending on immigration for any growth while supporting an ever-expanding old age segment.

Changes in economic and demographic structure were compounded by the relentless competition from some of the newer industrial or industrializing economies like China, India, and Mexico. These societies enjoyed a competitive advantage in lower wages, though their industrial success did begin to push wages up. As newcomers, they may simply have had greater opportunities for innovation. Some authorities argued that they displayed a more adventurous spirit as well, tackling projects that, in the older industrial societies, now seemed risky or debatable. The lead that China established in areas like electric cars or 5G data transmission had far less to do with low wages than with a commitment to industrial leadership.

The challenge to the established industrial economies was obvious. Even earlier, in the 1980s, the rise of Japanese exports had caused something of a crisis, because of direct competition with Western manufacturing but also a symbolic challenge to comfortable notions of Western world leadership. The result had been some discussion of trade barriers and occasional physical attacks on iconic Japanese imports like automobiles. By 2020, the position of China generated even greater uncertainty, as the Chinese steadily pushed their export advantage and sought new world position through projects like the Belt and Road initiative. Leaders in many Western societies began to worry about the Chinese surge, pointing out that the Chinese economy was linked to a very different set of economic and political policies. Competition extended beyond the export challenge: as China became the largest importer of African goods, for example, rivalry for influence on the continent took on new dimensions. But for many people in Western countries, the focus seemed particularly clear: Chinese imports, sometimes compounded by imports from other countries like Mexico, seemed to be taking good jobs away, as well as eroding Western confidence.

Experts in fact debated. Most contended that the loss of manufacturing jobs in places like the United States or France had far more to do with new technologies than with foreign competition, though they granted that the latter did play a role. They noted that some industrial societies, headed by Germany, seemed to do better than others in maintaining a more balanced economic portfolio. But whatever the precise diagnosis, there was little question that advanced industrial societies were undergoing yet another round of fundamental change, that their position in the world economy was shifting—and that the results were troubling to many citizens.

DEBATE #13: *HOW CAN THE UNITED STATES AND CHINA COMPETE?*

Well before 2020, it was clear that the United States, for over a century the undisputed industrial leader of the world, faced a new challenger in China. A few experts continued to argue, or hope, that the Chinese would falter: that pollution problems, or political dissent, or other issues would dent their forward march. But a long period of intense mutual competition seemed the more likely prospect.

The real question was: competition or hostility? Industrial history had already tossed up one example of a change in industrial balance that had fairly directly led to war. While Britain had grumblingly accepted the rise of industry in the United States, by the early twentieth century the German challenge to Britain's industrial lead had become unacceptable in the eyes of many British leaders. The rapid German surge translated directly to military rivalry, most notably in an unresolved dispute over whether the new Germany navy could be allowed to reach levels that competed with Britain's traditional strength—an issue that tied directly to the larger competition in heavy industry, which after all supplied the materials for the big ships. In this case—though amid other diplomatic factors—the British and German leaderships decided that reconciliation was impossible, and the result contributed directly to World War I.

Would this kind of history repeat itself with the United States and China? By the second decade of the twenty-first century a number of American pundits began to argue that war was inevitable—if not a global conflict, at least a regional one. And while tempers were hottest among some Republicans, many Democrats were almost as fervent in their hostility to things Chinese. As a result, new tariffs were levied on Chinese goods after 2016. New limits were

(*Continued*)

placed on Chinese scholars and students, amid a widespread fear that exchanges of this sort simply gave the Chinese a chance to spy on American technologies. An earlier policy, that had assumed that growing economic ties, including the rising level of Chinese imports, would contribute to a peaceful relationship was giving way to increasing tension. "China bashing" became an increasingly popular political strategy in the United States, though less so in other parts of the West.

It takes two to tango, of course, and developments in China contributed to the new atmosphere as well. Chinese leaders, worried about the decline in economic growth rates, often turned to anti-American nationalism to shore up popular support. They refused any basic modification of their commitment to strong government involvement in the economy, which many Westerners—not just Americans—felt gave them unfair advantages in global competition.

The questions were obvious, though there were cultural and military factors involved besides industrial rivalry. What was the best position for the United States to take in response to China's economic surge? Was a new kind of "cold war" now inevitable—or even worse? Might China change as it gained increasing prosperity, with more people insisting on reducing state power in favor of more democratic rights? Did the rise of China to at least a share in world industrial leadership threaten basic Western prosperity?

Most fundamentally: what can industrial history as well as industrial forecasting tell us about what prospects are more likely in the China-U.S. relations, what policies most constructive?

Further reading: Scott Moore, "An Abyss Is Opening under China-U.S. Relations," *Foreign Policy Magazine*, July 17, 2019; Peter Navarro, *Death by China: Confronting the Dragon* (Englewood Cliffs, NJ, 2017).

The Problem of Inequality Revisited

In many countries around the world, the Great Recession also highlighted the increase in economic inequalities during the latest phase of industrial history. Somewhat ironically, even as regional inequalities lessened, and growing numbers of people rose out of poverty, internal disparities increased.

The pattern was widespread. Some sectors of the population, and some regions, were able to take advantage of the newest economic forms, and some were not. Prosperity in China's coastal regions was matched by considerable ongoing poverty in the interior. In Latin America, long victim to particularly pronounced economic disparities, industrial growth seemed to make the problem worse. Regional disparities grew in many parts of western Europe and the United States. The decline of manufacturing jobs and the rise of new high-tech sectors placed a growing premium on educational credentials, creating another opportunity for some, another barrier for others. The results of the Great Recession and the problems of recovery compounded some of these problems, but they were not the basic cause. Industrialization had never created equality, but gaps widened at some points more than others. And developments in the late twentieth and early twenty-first century raised the issue in particularly acute forms.

Worldwide, incomes of the top 20 percent or so of the population unquestionably increased more rapidly than those of the population at large. In the United States the wealth of the fabled top 1 percent surged forward, as they were garnering 20 percent of all income generated by the economy in 2015, with earnings 40 times higher than the bottom 90 percent. This small privileged group had gained 52 percent of all income growth between 1995 and 2015, and disparities continued to grow in the years thereafter. But it was not just the 1 percent: the top 10 percent of American earners earned nine times the incomes of the remaining 90 percent. Again, however, the pattern was global, though degrees varied. Germany also reported a growing wealth gap from 1980 onward, despite social programs noticeably more generous than those in the United States.

The new trends generated some interesting arguments. Critics pointed to the unfairness of the huge rise in the salaries of the top executives, now earning hundreds of times the average of most employees in their corporations. Sympathizers claimed that the growing complexity of industrial leadership, amid globalization and rapid technological change, simply required unprecedented rewards: the very wealthy deserved their growing share of the pie. Were these patterns an inevitable part of the third phase of industrialization?

In some cases, inequality actually reflected not only growing wealth at the top but growing poverty below. In the United States between 2000 and 2006, despite overall, if modest, economic growth, the number of people under the poverty line rose—with a particularly rapid increase among children. In other instances, as in China and India, poverty diminished gradually even as top fortunes soared.

New Uncertainties

By the second decade of the twenty-first century, new economic dislocations, rising global competition, and troubling inequalities directly generated important signs of frustration, particularly but not exclusively in the advanced industrial economies. New voices were raised against globalization, in favor of a revival of nationalism that not only attacked global institutions but also sought new kinds of tariff protection against foreign competition. In Britain, resentments of this sort explained majority support for leaving the European Union; old industrial regions were pitted against more cosmopolitan centers like London, and they won the 2016 referendum on the subject; leaders of the movement called "Brexit" professed commitment to global competition, but they obviously sought a more favorable national position. In the United States the Trump administration after 2016 engaged in an unusual number of tariff battles and in general signaled disdain for the postwar rules of global economic engagement.

Immigrants were a particular target, throughout Europe, in Britain, and in the United States. Immigrant workers, along with foreign competition more generally, were widely blamed for loss of jobs and stagnant wages. New so-called populist movements surged, forcing new limits on immigration in many cases—at some cost, many experts argued, to actual economic growth and entrepreneurial dynamism.

Industrial issues were not the only factor in this new turmoil. Cultural disputes also loomed large, against immigrants but also against the "elites" who were seen as unfairly prospering from industrial globalization and failing to understand the plight of ordinary people.

Some countries reflected industrial tensions in different ways. In Russia and in Turkey, sluggish economic growth propelled leaders who sought to compensate by new diplomatic and military activity, hoping to maintain support despite industrial stagnation. Brazilians elected a populist president bent on reducing environmental regulations and pursuing a conservative cultural agenda. Popular protest in several other Latin American countries and also parts of the Middle East showed new resentments against reigning elites.

It is always dangerous to label a current period as particularly unsettled—for all periods are unsettled at least to some degree, and it is easy to lose perspective. So far, global reactions to the Great Recession have not been as dramatic as those that responded to the Depression of the 1930s. But the most recent phase of the industrial revolution, in its global aspect and in its challenge to previous industrial patterns, clearly raised a number of difficult issues—along with a host of new gains. By 2020 it was impossible to deny that many readjustments were proving to be exceptionally complicated, with a number of outcomes, including the short-term fate of globalization itself, still unclear.

Finally, many of these issues were further exacerbated by the coronavirus pandemic that fanned out globally during 2020. Efforts to limit contagion led to massive declines in production and employment in every region of the world. Chinese growth rates ground to a halt, at least temporarily, for the first time in decades; unemployment rates in the United States and Britain matched those of the 1930s depression; reduced demand for raw materials raised poverty levels in many parts of Africa and Latin America, again reversing trends. International supply chains were disrupted, raising still further questions about the possibility of limiting dependence on the global economy. Would these problems, on top of the other tension in the industrial balance, lead to durable shifts in the structure of the industrial world, or would a quick rebound restore greater calm? The history of contemporary industrialization provided precedents for both possibilities.

18 Conclusions

Since its inception, the industrial revolution has raised vital issues of analysis and many intense debates. Although these issues have changed as the technology and organization associated with the revolution have advanced and as additional societies have been drawn into the process, historical assessment remains essential not simply for understanding the past but for grasping what the industrial economy is now and what its implications are.

Causation remains a fundamental issue. Explaining why Britain or Japan or, more recently, China generated an industrial revolution remains a challenging historical exercise. Interpreting what basic factors were involved, and how they might be replicated even today to produce healthier patterns of economic growth, merges history with contemporary concerns. Asking why some societies continue to face difficulties in making a turn to industrialization (or why some societies may not even really want an industrial revolution because of its threat to their more important values) requires a serious understanding of what causation has entailed for the past 200 years.

Precedent as a Guide to Prediction

Since the industrial revolution spread from Britain to other parts of Europe and then well beyond, a balance between commonality and diversity has been central to comparative analysis. This, too, continues to be true. All industrial revolutions have had some essential common features. They obviously involved not only massive technological and organizational change but also redefinition of family function and alteration of the nature of work and leisure. Cities invariably grew. Agricultural groups were reassessed, their status diminished—though usually amid persistent clamor. Yet industrial revolutions have also varied greatly. They differed according to their geography and their available resources. They differed according to timing; latecomers inevitably emphasized different features from earlier industrializers, and some of these distinctions proved long-lasting. They differed, finally, according to prior culture and institutions. Various cultures proved suitable for industrialization, but they also created different management structures, government involvement, attitudes toward consumerism, and labor relations. It became increasingly clear that concerns about the relationship between industry and environment would vary as well. Juggling the relationship between standard patterns and vital variants is a significant interpretive challenge. It particularly directs attention to the need to avoid equating Western versions of industrial society with some sort of inevitable product. This simplification, one of the weaknesses of the modernization model, has become less common in the last two decades because of the obvious success of East Asia's distinctive industrial enterprise, but it can still intrude into historical judgments.

The theme of variety also extends to the experience within any individual industrial process. One of the great advances in knowledge in recent years has been a fuller appreciation of the immense differences in effects industrial revolutions have had on workers and employers, urbanites and farmers. Gender is now also seen as crucial. In many instances industrialization reduced economic roles for women, at least for a time. This is true not only in many industrializing societies but also in many other areas, such as large parts of Africa, where industrial pressures from the West and now Asia have unseated the balance of traditional agricultural economies. In the West many aspects of contemporary history (including feminism, but also debates over retirement policies, for example) relate directly to the ongoing attempt to assimilate and rearrange the different results that industrial revolutions have brought to various segments of the population.

The range of the effects of industrialization constitutes a compelling analytical category. How exactly will further industrialization replicate the effects that have historically followed from the industrial revolution process, and in what order must developments occur? Demographics is a crucial case in point. Every industrial revolution so far has yielded a dramatic turn toward slower population growth through lower birthrates resulting from the reduced utility of children's work. The precise process has varied according to region and social class—and the methods used have ranged from sexual abstinence to widespread abortion—but the birthrate revolution has been a fairly uniform result. Will this always be true? Can other societies industrialize without birthrate reductions to Japanese or Western or Chinese levels—a question particularly acute for African societies in the coming decades? Or must they (as many Western observers have argued) indeed launch this reduction in order to industrialize in the first place? Will South and Southeast Asia lower the use of child labor to levels common in the West or East Asia, or will a distinctive regional pattern persist? Knowledge of industrialization's historical impacts helps define contemporary analysis of crucial social trends, influencing predictions and policies alike.

Since the 1980s a similar set of issues have arisen concerning political structure. What political systems were compatible with the ongoing development of industrial societies? Before 1980 the answer seemed obvious, if messy: Various systems had worked, depending on the specific conditions and cultures. Western industrial revolutions had arisen under governments that usually recognized some formal limits on their functions and had some openness to parliamentary institutions. The process fairly quickly generated pressures for more political democracy (which in the United States had been established before industrialization). The vote helped give workers an outlet for demands and reduced, or seemed to reduce, radical pressures. Some analysts have argued that the massive growth of industrial cities, filled with workers and potential labor grievances, requires either democracy or a new kind of authoritarian system. For the most part the West opted for democracy, though Nazi Germany briefly demonstrated that a repressive state could function industrially until it self-destructed through the folly of war. The Soviet experience proved that a controlled economy and a strong police state could also promote rapid industrial development. The examples of Meiji Japan and, after World War II, other parts of East Asia suggest that although traditional governments must change in order to industrialize—giving new groups some access to power and developing new functions for the state—authoritarian systems with strong state involvement may be quite compatible with rapid industrialization and perhaps, in some cultures, even very useful.

By the 1980s, however, economic stagnation in several societies prompted a new belief that installing democracies might be essential to keeping industrialization going by opening up to demands for greater progress. Advanced industrial technology, notably the computer, required so much information exchange that maintenance of rigid police controls over ideas might be impossible. As a wave of democratic change developed in Latin America after the mid-1970s, many leaders associated their political reforms with hopes for more rapid industrial growth, though there were other motives as well. The Soviet Union, under Mikael Gorbachev in the 1980s, clearly, if haltingly, moved toward the position that more democracy and political openness (glasnost) were an essential concomitant of economic reform and industrial progress (perestroika). In fact, of course, political change proved easier to achieve in Eastern Europe than did movement toward renewed economic growth and a more advanced industrial economy, but the experiment continued into the 1990s. As we have seen, China and Vietnam, working to industrialize in the first place, have dissented. In their view a command state, free of the distraction and inefficiency of political protest, is still the best context for industrial advance. In turn, contemporary technology can be directly deployed to increase state control over the population. Will these kinds of differences in political approach complicate global economic competition in the future, or can they be reconciled?

History and Changing Contexts

Developments over the past few decades created new opportunities, but also new challenges, in using history to understand ongoing industrialization. Some of the questions raised about newer industrial revolutions, as in China, reflected lack of adequate awareness of historical precedent. Critics pointed out that Chinese economic growth was creating new hardships for many workers and peasants and dangerous divisions among social classes. The claims were worth noting, but they would have been more credible had the critics recognized that, broadly speaking, problems of this sort have been part of any industrialization process in its early phases, and that most industrial countries had managed to survive them. The notion that there was something terribly special and unsettling about this aspect of the Chinese process might well be modified through better grasp of standard historical patterns.

At the same time, recent history also demonstrates that contexts for industrial history themselves change, modifying links to the past without erasing them. For example, industrializations have always caused environmental damage, though sometimes this has been partially corrected later on. By the twenty-first century, however, this process arguably changed in nature because of the larger environmental impacts now possible. We should not be trapped by a purely historical model. The same may apply to globalization. Industrialization has always promoted and reflected new global contacts. Now, however, these may have altered more fundamentally, with such new manifestations as the multinationals, which outstrip global capacities of political control. Demographics may be generating even more striking departures. Industrializations have always linked to birthrate limitations and therefore a decline in the percentage of children in the population, at least after initial decades. Now, however, in the twenty-first century this pattern is changing shape, with many industrial societies faced with unprecedented population aging and birth rates so low that the population itself may shrink. How will this affect these societies in the future?

Analyzing contemporary industrial trends, clearly, requires a lively balance between grasping historical patterns—including their ongoing relevance—and dealing with major shifts in framework.

The Balance Sheet: A Final Debate

Assessment of the industrial revolution in its many manifestations raises vital questions about gains and losses. These questions are not simply historical, since they involve the values of the observer as well as the objective data, but they should not be avoided simply because they must be debated.

Very few people living in an industrial society could or would readily trade places with someone in their society's preindustrial past. Too much would seem strange; too many material comforts would be lacking. A significant handful of Westerners, to be sure, have deliberately sought lives in agricultural or herding societies, finding greater truth and beauty there than in the industrial context. During the 1960s, for example, some American and European youths journeyed to places like Nepal on a quest for a more natural existence. Far more Westerners occasionally use industrial means of transport to take brief visits to nonindustrial locations, and even there they more often than not surround themselves with industrial artifacts, in their luxury hotels, to cushion the shock.

This tendency to prefer the present is understandable, because the benefits of the industrial revolution have been quite real. Industrial societies have curtailed infant death, making it a rare experience for the first time in human history. Until recently, they have reduced the impact of vagaries of nature and thus improved the reliability of food supplies. They have lifted a growing number out of extreme poverty: in 1981 42 percent of the world's population lived in misery, earning at best $12 per day; in 2019 the percentage had dropped to 10, with 245,000 people moving above the lowest poverty line *every day* (though the 2020 pandemic halted this process at least for a time). Massive new access to sanitary toilets, or electricity, or the Internet, shows comparable rates of progress in recent decades. These advantages, though still greatest in fully industrialized societies, are now having significant impact on the world at large. Industrialization has also enabled many societies to support far larger numbers of people than ever before, though economic imbalances have ironically generated the greatest population concentrations in societies where industrialization is, at best, incomplete. Industrialization has been associated with new opportunities, since it has shaken established social hierarchies and created new kinds of work as well as supporting larger educational systems.

At the same time, like any major transformation in the human experience, the industrial revolution has had very real costs, and some of these continue as well. It has led to unprecedented opportunities to damage the environment, and here its impact seems to increase exponentially over time. It has created new sources of social tension and perhaps has narrowed basic life experiences, particularly in work, for many people. It has altered and in many cases weakened the family, another process that may be continuing today. Unquestionably, even where industrialization now seems to bring new ease, the process involved many decades of physical and psychological strain for millions involved: was this anguish worth the result, and are we still suffering from its aftereffects?

There is also a question of values. When the 1830s textile manufacturer decorated the machine that had been most productive the previous week with a garland of flowers, he celebrated not the people who ran the machine, just the machine. Industrialization has brought a steady increase in materialism and time pressure and a growing dominance of technology, plus the use of economic growth as the primary measure of social quality. Other cultural sectors, including art, the humanities, religion, and the people who specialize in them, tend to lose ground. Is this a good thing? Renewed religious interests in several societies in the late twentieth century—especially societies not yet fully industrialized—raise interesting tensions. Islamic revivals in the Middle East, Hindu fundamentalism, and the spread of evangelical Protestantism in the United States and Brazil suggest that many people have doubts about purely industrial cultural values.

Then there is the question of international tension and, at worst, war. From the early decades of industrialization some people have argued that the process should replace the need for violent conflict: industrial populations would be focused on economic achievement and competition, not disruptive aggression. More recently, observers have hoped that, as more societies gain some industrial affluence and interact more extensively, war would become unacceptable. A nice tag line urged that no two societies that have McDonalds—that is, which have growing consumer opportunities—have ever gone to war with each other. The claim was interesting, though by 2020 it was no longer true. There have been long stretches of time—the decades after 1815, the decades after 1945, when at least all-out wars were avoided, and industrial progress may have had something to do with this. On the other hand, industrial competition can add yet another reason for war, as with Britain and Germany in 1914. And it is hard to be sure that the new competitions associated with the most recent phase of industrial expansion will remain peaceful. Further, we also know that when industrial war does occur, it is particularly terrible.

The final tally of the industrial revolution has yet to be reckoned. People have been debating its balance sheet since the process began—not only scholars but also the businesspeople and workers directly involved. The analysis is not simply a historical exercise, for the process is ongoing. The most fearsome toll of the industrial revolution may still await us in the form of greater environmental degradation or new kinds of conflicts between the haves and have-nots at the industrial table. Great opportunities may also beckon as various societies become increasingly able to make adjustments to the industrial world and to the advantages it brings. The industrial revolution, caused by an unusual set of circumstances in world history, unleashed forces that have been hard to control. The one certainty is that the process has not slowed. It continues to shape world history, from the societies seeking higher industrial achievement to societies desperately striving to preserve a newly challenged industrial lead.

The Ongoing Experience

The industrial revolution is too often treated as merely a piece of history. It is that. The phenomenon has played a major role in shaping the experience of most societies in the world, either directly or indirectly, for two centuries. But the industrial revolution is also an ongoing event, a very recent development in terms of its sweeping implications.

Most obviously the industrial revolution continues in places like Brazil and China, where, while building on earlier, more limited precedents, it is really still just taking off. In these societies, and in the growing influence they exercise on the world economy, the industrial revolution remains an active agent of change.

Beyond this, adjustments to the industrial experience continue in other societies as well, even though the period of greatest disruption ended some decades back. People are still getting used to the separation of work from home (or trying to find ways to reunite the sites). They are still dealing with issues associated with the industrial pace of work—as the common use of words such as *stress* and *burnout* so readily suggests. Industrialization, in other words, is still an active force in shaping our lives, which is why its history uniquely combines past and present.

19 Suggestions for Further Reading

The literature on the history of the industrial revolution is considerable. A disproportionate amount focuses on Western Europe and in particular Britain, but there is good reading on most areas. At the same time, many topics are incompletely explored; some, like industrialization and women, are currently being recast, with much analysis still to be fleshed out. Still, a host of topics, including some crucial comparative issues, can be pursued in greater depth. For the idea of using industrial history to stimulate contemporary policy, Patrick Collison and Tyler Cowen, "We Need a New Science of Progress," *The Atlantic*, July 30, 2019.

Europe as Crucible and the Global Context

A wide-ranging recent study is Jeff Horn, Leonard Rosenband, and Merrit Roe Smith, eds., *Reconceptualizing the Industrial Revolution* (Cambridge, MA, 2010). A useful compendium for the European side is Derek Aldcroft, ed., *Bibliography of European Economic and Social History* (Manchester, 1984). Other current works include Colin Crouch, *Capitalist Diversity and Change: Recombinant Governance and Institutional Entrepreneurs* (Oxford, 2005); Frederic L. Pryor, *Economic Systems of Foraging, Agricultural, and Industrial Societies* (New York, 2005); Susanna Delfino and Michele Gillespie, eds., *Global Perspectives on Industrial Transformation in the American South* (Columbia, MO, 2005); Marina V. Rosser and Barkley Rosser Jr., *Comparative Economics in a Transforming World Economy* (Cambridge, MA, 2004). On specific topics, with reading suggestions, see Peter N. Stearns and John Hinshaw, *The ABC-Clio World History Companion to the Industrial Revolution*, rev. ed. (Denver, CO, 2012); Emma Griffin, *Liberty's Dawn: A People's History of the Industrial Revolution* (New Haven, CT, 2013), looks at industrialization through the eyes of working-class participants.

On the global context and globalization, Kenneth Pomeranz, *The Great Divergence: China, Europe and the Making of the Modern World Economy* (Princeton, NJ, 2001); Jürgen Osterhammel and Niels P. Peterson, *Globalization: A Short Story* (Princeton, NJ, 2005); James A.

Piazza, *Going Global: Unions and Globalization in the United States, Sweden, and Germany* (Lanham, MD, 2002); Kenneth Pomeranz and Steven Topik, *The World that Trade Created: Society, Culture, and the World Economy, 1400 to Present* (Armonk, NY, 2006); Jan Luiten van Zanden, *The Long Road to the Industrial Revolution: The European Economy in a Global Perspective, 1000–1800* (Leiden, 2009); Bruce Mazlish and Akira Iriye, eds., *The Global History Reader* (New York, 2005). Other good surveys include Alice H. Amsden, *The Rise of the Rest: Challenges to the West from Late-Industrializing Economies* (New York, 2001); Diane Davis, *Discipline and Development: Middle Classes and Prosperity in East Asia and Latin America* (Cambridge, 2004); Douglas Farnie and David Jeremy, eds., *The Fibre That Changed the World: The Cotton Industry in International Perspective, 1600–1900s* (New York, 2004); Yong-shik Lee, *Reclaiming Development in the World Trading System* (Cambridge, MA, 2006); Harold Kerbo, *World Poverty: Global Inequality and the Modern World System* (Boston, MA, 2006); Jonathan Friedman and Christopher Chase-Dunn, *Hegemonic Decline: Present and Past* (Boulder, CO, 2005); and Peter N. Stearns, *Consumerism in World History: The Global Transformation of Desire*, 2nd ed. (London, 2006).

On protoindustrialization and the origins of the industrial revolution, see P. Kriedte, H. Medick, and J. Schlumbom, eds., *Industrialization before Industrialization* (Cambridge, 1981), in particular Medick's essay, "The Proto-Industrial Family Economy," and Kriedte's contribution, "Proto-Industrialization between Industrialization and De-Industrialization." For a critique, see D. C. Coleman, "Proto-Industrialization: A Concept Too Many," *Economic History Review*, 2nd ser., 36 (1983), 435–448. A fine study using the protoindustrial concept is Gay L. Gullickson, *Spinners and Weavers of Auffray* (Cambridge, 1986). On the "industrious revolution," Jan de Vries, *The Industrious Revolution: Consumer Behaviour and the Household Economy* (New York, 2008); Giovanni Arrighi and others, *The Resurgence of East Asia* (London, 2003).

The term *industrial revolution* was introduced in Arnold Toynbee, *Lectures on the Industrial Revolution* (New York, 1884; reprinted 1979). Older and/or conventional treatments of the industrial revolution, focusing mainly on Britain and western Europe, are legion, and some still serve as a useful introduction to many basic features. See T. S. Ashton, *The Industrial Revolution, 1760–1830* (New York, 1948); Rondo Cameron, *France and the Economic Development of Europe* (Princeton, NJ, 1981); Phyllis Deane, *The First Industrial Revolution* (Cambridge, 1969); David Landes, *The Unbound Prometheus: Technological Change and Industrial Development in Western Europe from 1750 to the Present* (Cambridge, 2003); and Karl Polanyi, *The Great Transformation* (Boston, MA, 1944).

Recent works on Britain and other parts of Europe include Robert C. Allen, *The British Industrial Revolution in Global Perspective* (Cambridge, 2009); Priya Satia, *The Empire of Guns: The Violent Making of the Industrial Revolution* (London, 2018); Michael Stephen Smith, *The Emergence of Modern Business Enterprise in France, 1800–1930* (Cambridge, MA, 2006); Jon Stobart and Neil Raven, *Towns, Regions and Industries: Urban and Industrial Change in the Midlands, c. 1700–1840* (Manchester, 2005); Kenneth Morgan, *The Birth of Industrial Britain: Social Change, 1750–1850* (New York, 2004); Kenneth Pomeranz, "Political Economy and Ecology on the Eve of Industrialization: Europe, China and the Global Econjuncture," *American Historical Review* (2002), http://www.historycooperative.org/journals/ahr/107.2/ah0202000425.html (2006).

A bold effort at historical modeling, now somewhat discredited, is W. W. Rostow, *The Stages of Economic Growth* (Cambridge, 1960). A useful discussion of whether *industrial revolution* is a useful term and whether the debate is worth attention, with citations of other work, is Rondo Cameron, "*La révolution industrielle manquée*," and R. M. Hartwell, "Was There an Industrial Revolution?" *Social Science History* 14 (1990), 559–566 and 567–576. See also Charles Kindleberger, *Economic Growth in France and Britain, 1851–1950* (New York, 1964). For an extremely useful introduction to newer economic history analyses, see Joel Mokyr, ed., *The Economics of the Industrial Revolution* (London, 1985), and the rich bibliography. See J. Mokyr, *Industrialization in the Low Countries* (New Haven, CT, 1976); Robert W. Fogel, *Railroads and American Economic Growth: Essays in Econometric History* (Baltimore, MD, 1970), a classic of the "cliometric" approach; R. M. Hartwell, ed., *The Industrial Revolution and Economic Growth* (London, 1971); J. R. T. Hughes, *Industrialization and Economic History* (New York, 1970); and J. G. Williamson, "Regional Incquality and the Process of National Development: A Description of the Patterns," *Economic Development and Cultural Change* 13 (1964–1965), 1–82.

On the technological component, see H. J. Habbakuk, *American and British Technology in the Nineteenth Century: The Search for Labor-Saving Inventions* (Cambridge, 1962); Daniel Headrick, *The Tentacles of Progress: Technology Transfer in the Age of Imperialism, 1850–1940* (New York, 1988), an important recent work on dissemination; David Hounshell, *From the American System to Mass Production, 1800–1932: The Development of Manufacturing Technology in the United States* (Baltimore, MD, 1985); Melvin Kranzberg, "Prerequisites for Industrialization," in M. Kranzberg and C. W. Pursell Jr., eds., *Technology in Western Civilization*, 2 vols. (New York, 1967); A. E. Musson, ed., *Science, Technology, and Economic Growth* (London, 1972); A. E. Musson and E. Robinson, *Science and Technology in the Industrial Revolution* (Manchester, 1969).

Social Impact: Western Europe and the United States

On overall social impacts, see Peter N. Stearns and Herrick Chapman, *European Society in Upheaval*, 3rd ed. (New York, 1991), and the extensive bibliography. Good introductions to artisanal developments are John M. Merriman, ed., *Consciousness and Class Experience in Nineteenth-Century Europe* (New York, 1979); Joan W. Scott, *The Glassworkers of Carmaux* (Cambridge, MA, 1974); William Sewell, *Work and Revolution in France: The Language of Labor from the Old Regime to 1848* (Cambridge, 1980). On another key traditional urban group, see Philip G. Nord, *Paris Shopkeepers and the Politics of Resentment* (Princeton, NJ, 1986).

On labor relations in European industrialization, see Reinhard Bendix, *Work and Authority in Industry: Ideologies of Management in the Course of Industrialization* (Berkeley, CA, 1974); and Sidney Pollard, *The Genesis of Modern Management: A Study of Industrial Revolution in Great Britain* (Cambridge, MA, 1965). The classic study of management history per se is Alfred Chandler, *The Visible Hand: The Managerial Revolution in American Business* (Cambridge, MA, 1977). See also François Crouzet, *The First Industrialists: The Problem of Origins* (Cambridge, 1985); Katrina Honeyman, *Origins of Enterprise: Business Leadership in the Industrial Revolution* (Manchester, 1983); Anthony Howe, *The Cotton Masters, 1830–1860* (New York, 1984); Hartmut Kaelble, *Social Mobility in the Nineteenth and Twentieth Centuries: Europe and America in Comparative Perspective* (New York, 1986).

On white-collar development, see Susan Porter Benson, *Counter Cultures: Saleswomen, Managers, and Customers in American Department Stores, 1890–1940* (Urbana, IL, 1986); Jürgen Kocka, *Unternehmensverwaltung und Angestelltenschaft am Beispiel Siemens, 1849–1914* (Stuttgart, 1969), a pioneering empirical study, and his useful synthesis, *White-Collar Workers in America, 1890–1940: Social-Political History in International Perspective* (Beverly Hills, CA, 1980); Mario Konig, Hannes Siegrist, and Rudolf Vetterli, *Warten und Aufrucken: Die Angestellten in der Schweiz, 1870–1950* (Zurich, 1985); David Lockwood, *The Black-Coated Worker: A Study in Class Consciousness* (London, 1958; rev. 1990); and Michael Miller, *The Bon Marché: Bourgeois Culture and the Department Store* (Princeton, NJ, 1981).

On the impact on family, see Michael Anderson, *Family Structure in Nineteenth- Century Lancashire* (Cambridge, 1971); Hannah Barker, *The Family and Business during the Industrial Revolution* (Oxford, 2017); and Peter N. Stearns, *Be a Man! Males in Modern Society* (New York, 1990). For a good synthesis on family change, see Steven Mintz and Susan Kellogg, *Domestic Revolutions: A Social History of American Family Life* (New York, 1988), which has a useful bibliography.

For conventional coverage on children in industry, see Ivy Pinchbeck and Margaret Hewitt, *Children in English Society*, 2 vols. (London, 1969–1973). Distinctive approaches include Colin Heywood, *Childhood in Nineteenth-Century France: Work, Health, and Education among the "Classes Populaires"* (Cambridge, 1988); Katherine Lynch, *Family, Class, and Ideology in Early Industrial France: Social Policy and the Working-Class Family, 1815–1848* (Madison, WI, 1988); Peter N. Stearns, *Childhood in World History* (London, 2005); Robert McIntosh, *Boys in the Pits: Child Labour in Coal Mining* (Montreal, 2000); Kristoffel Georges Lieten, *Child Labour: Burning Questions: Inaugural Lecture* (Amsterdam, 2005); Carolyn Tuttle, *Hard at Work in Factories and Mines: The Economics of Child Labor during the British Industrial Revolution* (Boulder, CO, 1999); Sandy Hobbs, Jim McKechnie, and Michael Lavalette, *Child Labor: A World History Companion* (Santa Barbara, 1999); Hugh D. Hindeman, ed., *The World of Child Labor: An Historical and Regional Survey* (Armonk, NY, 2009); Peter Benes and Jane Montague Benes, eds., *The Worlds of Children, 1620–1920* (Boston, MA, 2004); and Jane Humphries, *Childhood and Child Labor in the British Industrial Revolution* (Cambridge, 2010).

On women and European industrialization, see Louise Tilly and Joan W. Scott, *Women, Work, and Family* (New York, 1978). A path-breaking study is Christine Stansell, *City of Women: Sex and Class in New York, 1789–1860* (New York, 1986). See also Mary Jo Maynes, Birgitte Soland, and Christina Benninghaus, *Secret Gardens, Satanic Mills: Placing Girls in European History, 1750–1960* (Bloomington and Indianapolis, IN, 2004); and Irene Padavic and Barbara Reskin, *Women and Men at Work* (Thousand Oaks, CA, 2002).

A fine introduction to the standard-of-living debate is A. J. P. Taylor, ed., *The Standard of Living in the Industrial Revolution* (London, 1975), in particular the articles by Eric Hobsbawm and R. M. Hartwell. See also Eric Hobsbawm and R. M. Hartwell, "The Standard of Living during the Industrial Revolution: A Discussion," *Economic History Review*, 2nd ser., 16 (1963–64), 119–146.

On factory workers and protest, see David Crew, *Town in the Ruhr: A Social History of Bochum, 1860–1914* (New York, 1979); and Patrick Joyce, *Work, Society, and Politics: The Culture of the Factory in Later Victorian England* (New Brunswick, NJ, 1980). Lenard R. Berlanstein, *The Working People of Paris, 1871–1914* (Baltimore, MD, 1984), is one of the most interesting monographs in opening new facets to the history of the working classes and their conditions. See also Standish Meacham, *A Life Apart: The English Working Class, 1890–1914* (Cambridge, MA, 1977); Peter N. Stearns, *Lives of Labor: Work in a Maturing Industrial Society* (New York, 1975); E. P. Thompson, *The Making of the English Working Class* (Harmondsworth, 1968); and Philip Dray, *There Is Power in a Union: The Epic Story of Labor in America* (New York,

2010). For developments in leisure, Hugh Cunningham, *Leisure in the Industrial Revolution* (London, 1980); and James Walvin, *Leisure and Society, 1830–1950* (London, 1978), are good introductions, the first with a fine bibliography. See also William J. Baker, *Sports in the Western World* (Totowa, NJ, 1982); Gareth Stedman Jones, *Languages of Class: Studies in English Working-Class History* (Cambridge, 1983); S. W. Pope and John Nauright, eds., *Routledge Companion to Sports History* (Abington, 2010); Benjamin G. Rader, *American Sports: From the Age of Folk Games to the Age of Spectators* (Englewood Cliffs, NJ, 1983); and Roy Rosenzweig, *Eight Hours for What We Will: Workers and Leisure in an Industrial City, 1870–1920* (Cambridge, 1983); and Randy McBee, *Dance Hall Days: Intimacy and Leisure among Working-Class Immigrants in the United States* (New York, 2000).

On the demographic transition, E. A. Wrigley, *Population and History* (New York, 1969), remains a useful introduction. See also Richard Easterlin, *Population, Labor Force, and Long Swings in Economic Growth: The American Experience* (New York, 1968); Charles Tilly, ed., *Historical Studies of Changing Fertility* (Princeton, NJ, 1978). See also Esther Boserup, *Population and Technological Change* (New York, 1981); Michael Drake, ed., *Population in Industrialization* (New York, 1969); the much-debated Thomas McKeown, *The Rise of Modern Population* (New York, 1976); and Robert Rotberg et al., eds., *Population and Economy* (Cambridge, 1986).

On migrations, see Stephen Castles, *Immigrant Workers and Class Structure in Western Europe*, 2nd ed. (Oxford, 1985); Patrick Manning, *Migration in World History* (New York, 2013); and Michael Piore, *Birds of Passage: Migrant Labor and Industrial Societies* (Cambridge, 1979).

There has been increased attention to certain other variables in relation to industrialization. Some important quantitative work focusing on literacy discusses whether measurable advances in literacy and schooling played a causal role in encouraging Western industrialization. A fine survey with good bibliography is Harvey J. Graff, *The Legacies of Literacy: Continuities and Contradictions in Western Culture and Society* (Bloomington, IN, 1987). See also Carlo Cipolla, *Literacy and Development in the West* (Harmondsworth, 1969).

Beyond Western Europe

On international impacts of Western industrialization, see Immanuel Wallerstein, *The Modern World-System*, 2 vols. (New York, 1980), and, as editor, with Terence Hopkins, *Processes of the World System* (Beverly Hills, CA, 1980). See also Albert Bergeson, ed., *Studies of the Modern World System* (New York, 1980); D. K. Field-house, *Economics and Empire, 1830–1914* (New York, 1970); and Tony Smith, *The Pattern of Imperialism* (Cambridge, 1981). An important study is Michael P. Adas,

Machines as the Measure of Men: Science, Technology, and Ideologies of Western Dominance (Ithaca, NY, 1989).

On the industrial revolution in the United States, see Jonathan Prude, *The Coming of Industrial Order: Town and Factory Life in Rural Massachusetts, 1810–1860* (Cambridge, MA, 1983); Charles Hirschman and Elizabeth Mogford, *Immigration and the American Industrial Revolution from 1880 to 1920* (New York, 2009); Alan Dawley, *Class and Community: The Industrial Revolution in Lynn* (Cambridge, MA, 1976); Michael H. Frisch and Daniel Walkowitz, eds., *Working-Class America* (Urbana, IL, 1983); Herbert Gutman, *Work, Culture, and Society in Industrializing America* (New York, 1976); Walter Licht, *Industrializing America* (Baltimore, MD, 1995); David Montgomery, *Workers' Control in America: Studies in the History of Work, Technology, and Labor Struggles* (Cambridge, 1979); Daniel Nelson, *Managers and Workers: Origins of the New Factory System in the United States, 1880–1920* (Madison, WI, 1975); Philip Scranton, *Endless Novelty: Specialty Production and American Industrialization, 1865–1925* (Princeton, NJ, 1988); Peter Temin, ed., *Industrialization in North America* (Cambridge, MA, 1994); Joe Trotter, *Black Milwaukee: The Making of an Urban Proletariat* (Urbana, IL, 1988); *Class and Color: Blacks in Southern West Virginia* (Urbana, IL, 1990); and Sean Wilentz, *Chants Democratic: New York City and the Rise of the American Working Class, 1788–1850* (New York, 1984). Recent works include Kevin Hillstrom and Laurie Collier Hillstrom, eds., *The Industrial Revolution in America* (Santa Barbara, CA, 2005); Andrew Atkeson and Patrick J. Kehoe, *The Transition to a New Economy after the Second Industrial Revolution* (Minneapolis, MN, 2003); Paul E. Rivard, *A New Order of Things: How the Textile Industry Transformed New England* (Hanover, NH, 2002); David R. Meyer, *The Roots of American Industrialization* (Baltimore, MD, 2003); Lawrence A. Peskin, *Manufacturing Revolution: The Intellectual Origins of Early American Industry* (Baltimore, MD, 2003); and Richard F. Teichgraeber, *Building Culture: Studies in the Intellectual History of Industrializing America, 1867–1910* (Columbia, SC, 2010).

On the industrialization of Russia and the Soviet Union, see William Blackwell, *The Beginnings of Russian Industrialization, 1800–1860* (Princeton, NJ, 1968); Boris Gorshkov, *Russia's Factory Children: State, Society and Law, 1800–1917* (Pittsburgh, PA, 2009); Victoria E. Bonnell, *Roots of Rebellion: Workers' Politics and Organizations in St. Petersburg and Moscow, 1900–1914* (Berkeley, CA, 1983); Robert W. Davies, Mark Harrison, and Stephen G. Wheatcroft, eds., *The Economic Transformation of the Soviet Union, 1913–1945* (Cambridge, 1994); William J. Chase, *Workers, Society, and the Soviet States: Labor and Life in Moscow, 1918–1929* (Urbana, IL, 1987); Robert C. Allen, *Farm to Factory: A Reinterpretation of the Soviet Industrial Revolution*

(Princeton, NJ, 2003); Rose L. Glickman, *Russian Factory Women: Workplace and Society, 1880–1914* (Berkeley, CA, 1984); Diane Koenker, *Moscow Workers and the 1917 Revolution* (Princeton, NJ, 1981); Hiroaki Kuromiya, *Stalin's Industrial Revolution: Politics and Workers, 1928–1932* (Cambridge, 1988); Moshe Lewin, *The Making of the Soviet System: Essays in the Social History of Interwar Russia* (New York, 1985); John McKay, *Pioneers for Profit: Foreign Entrepreneurship and Russian Industrialization* (Chicago, IL, 1970); William Rosenberg and L. Siegelbaum, eds., *Social Dimensions of Soviet Industrialization* (Bloomington, IN, 1993); John Scott, *Behind the Urals: An American Worker in Russia's City of Steel* (Bloomington, IN, 1989); David Shearer, *Industry, State, and Society in Stalin's Russia* (Ithaca, NY, 1997); and Reginald E. Zelnik, *Labor and Society in Tsarist Russia: The Factory Workers of St. Petersburg, 1855–1870* (Stanford, CA, 1971). On recent developments, see David Katz and Fred Weir, *Revolution from Above: The Demise of the Soviet System* (London, 1996); Robert C. Allen, *Farm to Factory: A Reinterpretation of the Soviet Industrial Revolution* (Princeton, NJ, 2003); Paul R. Gregory and Valery Lazarev, eds., *The Economics of Forced Labor: The Soviet Gulag* (Stanford, CA, 2003).

On Japan, see James W. Abegglen, *The Strategy of Japanese Business* (Cambridge, MA, 1984); William J. Macpherson, ed., *The Economic Development of Japan 1868–1941* (Cambridge, 1995); G. C. Allen, *A Short Economic History of Modern Japan* (New York, 1981); R. P. Dore, ed., *Aspects of Social Change in Modern Japan* (Princeton, NJ, 1968); Andrew Gordon, *The Evolution of Labor Relations in Japan: Heavy Industry* (Cambridge, MA, 1985); Johannes Hirschmeier and Tsunehiko Yui, *The Development of Japanese Business, 1900–1980*, 2nd ed. (London, 1981). See also W. Dean Kinzley, *Industrial Harmony in Modern Japan: The Invention of a Tradition* (London, 1991); Kaoru Sugihara, *Japan, China, and the Growth of the Asian International Economy, 1850–1949* (Oxford, 2005); Ian Inkster, *The Japanese Industrial Economy: Late Development and Cultural Causation* (New York, 2001); and Rudra Sil, *Managing "Modernity": Work, Community, and Authority in Late Industrializing Japan and Russia* (Ann Arbor, MI, 2002).

On fringe areas in Europe, see Alexander Gerschenkron, *Economic Backwardness in Historical Perspective: A Book of Essays* (Cambridge, MA, 1962), a classic study. See also K. J. Allen and G. Stevenson, *Introduction to the Italian Economy* (New Haven, CT, 1976); Charles W. Anderson, *The Political Economy of Modern Spain: Policy Making in an Authoritarian System* (Madison, WI, 1970); I. T. Berend and G. Ranki, *The European Periphery and Industrialization, 1780–1914* (Cambridge, 1982); Daniel Chirot, *Social Change in Peripheral Society: The Creation of a Balkan Colony* (New York, 1976); George H.

Hildebrand, *Growth and Structure in the Economy of Modern Italy* (Cambridge, MA, 1965); Jane Horowitz, *Economic Development in Sicily* (New York, 1978); and Charles Kindleberger, *Europe's Postwar Growth* (New York, 1973).

On the Pacific Rim, see Robert L. Downen and Bruce Dickson, *The Emerging Pacific Community: A Regional Perspective* (Boulder, CO, 1984); Stuart W. Sinclair, *Pacific Basin Economic Handbook* (New York, 1987); and Douglas Philips and Steven Lei, *Pacific Rim* (Los Angeles, CA, 1988). On the Pacific Rim concept and its implications in terms of the world economy, see David Aikman, *Pacific Rim: Area of Change, Area of Opportunity* (Boston, MA, 1986); Stephan Haggard and Chung-in Moon, *Pacific Dynamics: The International Politics of Industrial Change* (Boulder, CO, 1989); Staffan B. Linder, *The Pacific Century: Economic and Political Consequences of Asian Pacific Dynamism* (Stanford, CA, 1986); Ronald A. Morse et al., *Pacific Basin: Concept and Challenge* (Washington, DC, 1986); and Philip West et al., eds., *The Pacific Rim and the Western World: Strategic, Economic, and Cultural Perspectives* (Boulder, CO, 1987). On special topics, Dennis McNamara, *The Colonial Origins of Korean Enterprise 1910–1945* (Cambridge, 1990); and David Steinberg, *The Republic of Korea: Economic Transformation and Social Change* (Boulder, CO, 1989). See also Robert Wade, *Governing the Market: Economic Theory and the Role of the Government in East Asian Industrialization* (Princeton, NJ, 1990); and Edwin Winckler and Susan Greenhalgh, eds., *Contending Approaches to the Political Economy of Taiwan* (Armonk, NY, 1988).

On industrialization in Latin America, Leslie Bethell, ed., *The Cambridge History of Latin America*, vol. 6 (Cambridge, 1986), is the most useful general recent survey, in particular essays by William Glade, Rosemary Thorp, and Colin M. Lewis. There are also a number of excellent national studies, among them Wilson Suzigan and Anibal Villela, *Industrial Policy in Brazil* (São Paulo, 1977); Stephen Haver, *How Latin America Fell Behind: Essays on the Economic Histories of Brazil and Mexico, 1800–1914* (Stanford, CA, 1997); Sergio de Oliveria Birchal, *Entrepreneurship in Nineteenth-Century Brazil: The Formation of a Business Environment* (New York, 1999); Oliver J. Dinus, *Brazil's Steel City: Developmentalism, Strategic Power, and Industrial Relations in Volta Redonda, 1941–1962* (Stanford, CA, 2011); Marshall Eakin, *Tropical Capitalism: The Industrialization of Belo Horizonete, Brazil* (New York, 2001); and Alfonso Fleury and Maria Tereza Fleury, *Brazilian Multinationals: Competences for Internationalization* (New York, 2011). See also Charles Bergquist, *Labor in Latin America: Comparative Essays on Chile, Argentina, Venezuela, and Colombia* (Stanford, CA, 1986); John H. Coatsworth, *Growth against Development: The Economic Impact of Railroads in Porfirian Mexico* (De Kalb, IL, 1982); Warren Dean, *The Industrialization of São Paulo, 1880–1891*

(Austin, TX, 1969); and Barbara Weinstein, *The Brazilian Rubber Boom, 1850–1920* (Stanford, CA, 1983). On *maquiladora* industry in Mexico, see Maria Patricia Fernandez-Kelly, *For We Are Sold, I and My People: Women and Industry in Mexico's Frontier* (Albany, NY, 1984); Armando Razo, *Social Foundations of Limited Dictatorship: Networks and Private Protection during Mexico's Early Industrialization* (Stanford, CA, 2008); and Clark W. Raynolds, *The Mexican Economy: Twentieth-Century Structure and Growth* (New Haven, CT, 1970). On other major nations, see Peter Evans, *Dependent Development: The Alliance of Multinational, State, and Local Capital in Brazil* (Princeton, NJ, 1979); Laura Randall, *An Economic History of Argentina in the Twentieth Century* (New York, 1978). See also Juan Carlos Moreno and Jamie Ros, *Development and Growth in the Mexican Economy: A Historical Perspective* (New York, 2009); Armando Razo, *Social Foundations of Limited Dictatorship: Networks and Private Protection during Mexico's Early Industrialization* (Stanford, CA, 2008); Catherine M. Conaghan, *Restructuring Domination: Industrialists and the State in Ecuador* (Pittsburgh, PA, 1988); Miguel D. Ramirez, *Mexico's Economic Crisis: Its Origins and Consequences* (New York, 1989); Stephen Haber, *Industry and Development: The Industrialization of Mexico, 1890–1940* (Stanford, CA, 1995), and, as editor, *How Latin America Fell Behind: Essays on the Economic History of Mexico and Brazil* (Stanford, CA, 1997); Kenneth C. Shadlen, *Democratization Without Representation: The Politics of Small Industry in Mexico* (University Park, PA, 2004); and Fernando Rocchi, *Chimneys in the Desert: Industrialization in Argentina during the Export Boom Years, 1870–1930* (Stanford, CA, 2006).

On the Middle East, see Saniye Dedeoglu, *Women Workers in Turkey: Global Industrial Production in Istanbul* (London, 2008); and Charles Issawi, *Economic History of the Middle East and North Africa* (New York, 1982), and, as editor, *The Economic History of Turkey, 1800–1914* (Chicago, IL, 1980). See also Charles Issawi, ed., *Economic History of the Middle East, 1800–1914* (Chicago, IL, 1966); Ragaei El-Mallakh, *Saudi Arabia, Rush to Development* (Baltimore, MD, 1982), and *The Economic Development of the United Arab Emirates* (New York, 1981); Peter R. O'Dell, *Oil and World Power*, 5th ed. (London, 1981); and Roger Owen, *The Middle East in the World Economy, 1800–1914* (New York, 1987).

On India, see Lester Brown, *Seeds of Change: The Green Revolution and Development in the 1970s* (New York, 1970); Francine R. Frandel, *India's Political Economy, 1947–1977: The Gradual Revolution* (Princeton, NJ, 1978); B. L. C. Johnson, *Development in South Asia* (New York, 1983); Wilfred Malenbaum, *Prospects for Indian Development* (London, 1962); S. D. Mehta, *The Cotton Mills of India, 1854 to 1954* (Bombay, 1954); Thomas A. Tinberg, *The Marwaris: From*

Traders to Industrialists (New Delhi, 1978); A. Vasudevan, *The Strategy of Planning in India* (Meerut, 1970); Vivek Chibber, *Locked in Place: State-Building and Late Industrialization in India* (Princeton, NJ, 2003); Debdas Banerjee, *Globalization, Industrial Restructuring and Labor Standards: Where India Meets the Global* (New Delhi, 2005); Sharad Chari, *Fraternal Capital: Peasant- Workers, Self-Made Men, and Globalization in Provincial India* (Stanford, CA, 2004); Edward Luce, *In Spite of the Gods: The Rise of Modern India* (New York, 2008); and Nasir Tyabji, *Industrialization and Innovation: The Indian Experience* (New Delhi, India, 2000).

On Africa, see Frederick Cooper, *On the African Waterfront: Urban Disorder and the Transformation of Work in Colonial Mombasa* (New Haven, CT, 1987); *Struggle for the City: Migrant Labor, Capital, and the State in Urban Africa* (Beverly Hills, CA, 1983); and *Decolonization and African Society: The Labor Question in French and British Africa* (Cambridge, MA, 1997). See also E. A. Brett, *Colonialism and Underdevelopment in Kenya: The Political Economy of Neo-Colonialism* (Berkeley, CA, 1974); D. M. P. McCarthy, *Colonial Bureaucracy and Creating Underdevelopment: Tanganyika, 1919–1940* (Ames, IA, 1982); J. Forbes Munro, *Africa and the International Economy, 1800–1960* (London, 1976); Thomas A. Taku, *Framework for Industrialization in Africa* (Westport, CT, 1999); Peter Gibbon and Stefano Ponte, *Trading Down: Africa, Value Chains, and the Global Economy* (Philadelphia, PA, 2005); Banji Oyelaran-Oyeyinka and Dorothy McCormick, eds., *Industrial Clusters and Innovation Systems in Africa: Institutions, Markets and Policy* (New York, 2007); and James Ferguson, *Global Shadows: Africa in the Neoliberal World Order* (Durham, NC, 2006).

On China, see Jean Chesnaux, *The Chinese Labor Movement, 1919–1927* (Stanford, CA, 1968); Alexander Eckstein, *China's Economic Revolution* (Cambridge, 1977); Peer H. H. Vries, *Via Peking Back to Manchester: Britain, the Industrial Revolution, and China* (Leiden, 2003); Andre Gunder Frank, *ReOrient: Global Economy in the Asian Age* (Berkeley, CA, 1998); Michael Gasster, *China's Struggle to Modernize*, 2nd ed. (New York, 1983); Gail Hershatter, *The Wonders of Tianjin, 1900–1949* (Stanford, CA, 1986); Emily Hong, *Sisters and Strangers: Women in the Shanghai Cotton Mills, 1919–1949* (Stanford, CA, 1986); Victor Lippit, *The Economic Development of China* (Armonk, NY, 1987); Roderick Mac-Farquhar, *The Great Leap Forward, 1958–1960*, Vol. 2 of *The Origins of the Cultural Revolution* (New York, 1983); Thomas G. Rawski, *Economic Growth in Prewar China* (Berkeley, CA, 1989); Carl Riskin, *China: Political Economy—The Quest for Development Since 1949* (New York, 1987); Gilbert Rozman, ed., *The East Asian Region: Confucian Heritage and Its Modern Adaptation* (Princeton, NJ, 1991); Gilbert Rozman and Thomas P. Bernstein, *The Modernization of China* (New York, 1981); and Andrew Walder,

Communist Neo-Traditionalism: Work and Authority in Chinese Society (Berkeley, CA, 1986). On recent developments, see Vaclav Smil, *China's Environmental Crisis* (Armonk, NY, 1993); Gordon White, *Riding the Tiger: The Politics of Economic Reform in Post-Mao China* (Stanford, CA, 1993); and Chris Bramall, *Chinese Economic Development* (New York, 2009).

Recent Developments

On the postindustrial society concept, see Daniel Bell, *The Coming of the Post-Industrial Society* (New York, 1973). See also Alfred Chandler and Bruce Mazlish, *Leviathans: Multinational Corporations and the New Global History* (Cambridge, 2006). On the Great Recession, Adam Tooze, *Crashed: How a Decade of Financial Crisis Changed the World* (New York, 2008). On the Belt and Road initiative, L. Calabrese, *China and Global Development* (London, 2019); Harinder Kohli and others, eds., *China's Belt and Road Initiative* (Newbury Park, CA, 2019). On the decline of global poverty, Diana Beltekian and Esteban Ortiz-Ospina, "Extreme Poverty is Falling; how is poverty changing for the higher poverty lines," *Our World in Data,* March 5, 2018.

On environment and resource issues, a growing area of historical research, see D. H. Meadows and D. L. Meadows, *The Limits of Growth* (New York, 1974). Also worthwhile are B. W. Clapp, *An Environmental History of Britain since the Industrial Revolution* (New York, 1994); Richard H. Grove, *Green Imperialism: Colonial Expansion, Tropical Island Edens, and the Origins of Environmentalism, 1900–1960* (New York, 1995); Andrew Hurley, ed., *Common Fields: An Environmental History of St. Louis* (St. Louis, MO, 1997); Henrietta L. Moore and Megan Vaughan, *Cutting Down Trees: Gender, Nutrition, and Agricultural Change in the Northern Province of Zambia, 1890–1990* (Portsmouth, NH, 1994); Theodore Steinberg, *Industrialization and the Waters of New England* (Cambridge, MA, 1991); R. P. Tucker and J. F. Richards, eds., *Deforestations and the Nineteenth-Century World Economy* (Durham, NC, 1993); Richard White, *The Organic Machine: The Remaking of the Columbia River* (New York, 1995); Donald Worster, ed., *The Ends of the Earth: Perspectives on Modern Environmental History* (Cambridge, 1995); John R. McNeil, *Something New Under the Sun: An Environmental History of the Twentieth Century* (London, 2000); Gale Christianson, *Greenhouse: The 200-Year Story of Global Warming* (Harmondsworth, 1999); Mark Cioc, *The Rhine: An Eco-Biography, 1815–2000* (Seattle, WA, 2000); Tom Griffiths and Libby Robin, eds., *Ecology and Empire: Environmental History of Settler Societies* (Edinburgh, 1997); Andrew Hurley, *Environmental*

Inequalities: Class, Race and Industrial Pollution in Gary, Indiana, 1945–1980 (Chapel Hill, NC, 1995); Ramachandra Guha, *Environmentalism: A Global History* (Harlow, 2000); Richard Tucker, *Insatiable Appetite: The United States and the Ecological Degradation of the Tropical World* (Berkeley, CA, 2000); Stephen Mosely, *The Chimney of the World: A History of Smoke Pollution in Victorian and Edwardian Manchester* (Cambridge, 2001); and John McNeill, ed., *Environmental History: As If Nature Existed* (New York, 2010).

Index